AMERICAN MODERNS
From Rebellion to Conformity

Also by Maxwell Geismar

The Novel in America

Writers in Crisis: The American Novel, 1925–1940
(*Studies of Ring Lardner, Ernest Hemingway, John Dos Passos,
William Faulkner, Thomas Wolfe, John Steinbeck*)

The Last of the Provincials: The American Novel, 1915–1925
(*Studies of H. L. Mencken, Sinclair Lewis, Willa Cather,
Sherwood Anderson, F. Scott Fitzgerald*)

Rebels and Ancestors: The American Novel, 1890–1915
(*Studies of Frank Norris, Stephen Crane, Jack London,
Ellen Glasgow, Theodore Dreiser*)

American Moderns: From Rebellion to Conformity

Editor

The Ring Lardner Reader

Sherwood Anderson: Short Stories

Jack London: Short Stories

The Walt Whitman Reader

The Portable Thomas Wolfe

AMERICAN MODERNS

From Rebellion to Conformity

by MAXWELL GEISMAR

"Enchanted domain never awry
Persist beneath our native sky."

American Century Series

ⓦ HILL AND WANG · NEW YORK

ACKNOWLEDGMENTS

The author's thanks are due to the following newspapers, magazines, and publishing houses for permission to reprint material appearing in this book: The Chicago Sun-Times, The New York Post, The New York Times, College English, The English Journal, The Nation, The Saturday Review, Pocket Books Inc., and the Viking Press.

Certain articles in this book appeared first under different titles: The Hostile Necessity originally appeared in the *Saturday Review of Literature* as Prisoner of Letters; The "End" of Naturalism originally appeared in the *English Journal* as Naturalism Today and Yesterday; Time, Life, and Art originally appeared in *The Nation* as The Age of Wouk; The Nobel Prize originally appeared in the *Saturday Review of Literature* as Hemingway and the Nobel Prize.

AUTHOR'S NOTE

THE PRESENT volume began as a collection of articles and reviews written in the Nineteen-Forties and Fifties for a more or less popular audience. But in the course of revising the selections and bringing them up to date, a good deal of new material was added. Also, the essays on J. D. Salinger, Saul Bellow, James Jones, William Styron and John Howard Griffin, as typical new voices in our literature, are published here for the first time.

So this collection is in the nature of an informal daybook or journal of the times. Some of these articles are in the polemical vein which a critic uses with reluctance when his second nature, or his first, is to inquire, to balance, and to evaluate. The central focus of the volume is on the transitional decade from the Second World War to the middle of the twentieth century—from McCarthy to Sputnik. The historical setting is that of the uneasy "peace," the tensions of the Cold War, the return to "normalcy," and the epoch of conformity.

Or was it euphoria? In literature the period marked the decline of the classic modern American writers at the peak of their popular reputation. In criticism there was the movement towards higher and higher levels of aesthetic, or scholastic, absolutes. Some genuine good new writers emerged during this period, as recorded, in these pages; but there were no vital new intellectual or literary trends in general. It was not a fresh period; but then, how could it be? The social atmosphere was so heavy, dense, oppressive. The aesthetic air was so thin, pure and abstract.

There was indeed a state of general inertia in the arts, as the familiar sequel to an age of anxiety: of problems urgent and not resolved, while the surface of the globe, and outer space too, vibrated in the throes of change. The American literary scene of the Forties and Fifties must have presented to the rest of the world an odd and ironic spectacle at times; and perhaps the polemical note was indicated; and meanwhile I trust that this spectacle may also be instructive.

But here, as in my other books, the central concern is with the history of individual literary talents. I hope this collection will be useful as a study of these talents: the native writers, old and young, ancestors and innovators, who best represent us when they are most intensely themselves. Now that the "Revival of Normalcy" has produced only another cosmic fiasco, let us pay the proper respect to what is different, singular, personal, in the national temperament, but indispensable, enduring and creative.

MAXWELL GEISMAR

Harrison, New York.
January, 1958.

CONTENTS

Part Three: NEWCOMERS

AMERICAN MODERNS
From Rebellion to Conformity

Part One: IN GENERAL

PROLOGUE: THE HOSTILE NECESSITY

LITERARY CRITICISM is not a path to fame or fortune in the United States today. The practice of it involves something else— an interest in the field itself, a sense of necessity, or a personal commitment.

"Listen, my friend," Willa Cather once wrote, "no man can give himself heart and soul to one thing while in the back of his mind he cherishes a desire, a secret hope for something very different." But unfortunately that last sacrifice, that giving of oneself altogether and finally which Miss Cather described as the condition of any serious enterprise, implies a certain restriction of personal freedom. More recently, in the American edition of André Gide's *Journals,* there is an admirable account of an artist's struggle for discipline: the curiosity, the patience, the final passion which, as Henry James suggested, are implicit in the role of the critic when it is seriously undertaken. Oh, yes, very true, a solace, and a source of guidance—but what about the shock to the nervous system, the wear and tear on the physical organs which are also involved in the solitary struggle for perfection? Could one really issue a confidential memorandum on the price of immortality, or describe that odious routine of wounds and shrugs, of blows to one's vanity and one's pocketbook alike, which is the ordinary milieu of an appointment with destiny? The literary critic, like any other scholar or artist, attempts to preserve the past and to illuminate the future in a specific area of activity. But the present is usually devoted to maintaining a mere semblance of health or sanity in his own life and work.

Moreover, the somewhat superstitious reverence with which some people still regard this profession is largely dissipated when they learn that a literary critic is neither a museum piece nor a

journalist. The typical figures in the European tradition, such as
a Taine or Sainte-Beuve, were active cultural influences. Before
the great fortunes were established in our own society, the American scholar was still considered as deserving, if not honor, at
least a room and board; and even in the opening decades of this
century, the literary critic spoke as a reputable member of the
community. In our own time, the literary renascence of the
1920's was accompanied by a vigorous group of aesthetic historians and theoreticians. Such figures as Randolph Bourne, Waldo
Frank, Paul Rosenfeld, Carl Van Doren, and Lewis Mumford,
to mention only a few names, were active forces in the development of a new body of literature that, whatever its defects, as
H. L. Mencken said, would at least be "a faithful reflection of the
national life." Yet among the surviving members of this group,
there are only two or three, particularly Edmund Wilson in the
field of literary criticism proper and Van Wyck Brooks in the field
of literary history, who have consistently followed their earlier
interests. The others, talented and versatile as they were, turned
their energies into other areas—biography, political or cultural
history, scholarly research, or journalism—so that it almost
seemed that literary criticism in the United States was a spring-
board rather than a great tradition. Meanwhile the advocates of
"pure" literary criticism, that is to say, the semanticists, the
analysts of technique, the practitioners of a rigorous but self-
contained type of textual analysis, have come into power. The
interest in promoting a fresh and vital body of native literature
has been converted into a meticulous study of the classics.

However, I feel a note of self-righteousness in these general
remarks about the state of literary criticism today, and perhaps
an undertone of dismay and deception. The editors of the *Saturday
Review* have asked for a statement of my work habits and I don't
see why I should make a fool of myself in public. What I propose
to describe instead—since the essential thing about work habits
is to have them—is something that might be called methods of
work. It is possible that one device or another may be of interest
to readers or other writers.

The most difficult phase of my own work is reading the books
of the authors whom I write about, and I know that other members of my profession have the same trouble. Is there something
about the climate of a competitive society that makes reading—

during the daytime when ordinary people go to work—seem absolutely immoral, or worse yet, a waste of time? Perhaps that is one reason I make so many notes, in the hope that working with my hands will compensate for working with my mind. In the case of Henry James, who is my present subject, there are at least three hundred pages of notes, while the final essay should run from eighty to one hundred pages. These extra pages of notes are just so much extra bother; they represent examples of the novelist's work that can't be used, or repetitions of things that have been said before, or divergent themes in his books, or paradoxes and contradictions in his thinking. They are variations from the normal range of his writing.

But what is the norm? There is some value in taking notes, compulsive as their compilation may be, and painful as their exorcism is in the final draft. By their sheer weight and volume, as it were, and by the constant repetition of an author's favorite themes, phrases, personal predilections, and points of view, as well as certain instinctive gestures and attitudes that occur throughout a writer's work, they establish his central values, his temperamental responses, his technical equipment; the subject matter and the tone, in short, of his books. All that is left— provided that one has really read the works of an author completely and honestly and "innocently" enough, and has not merely paraphrased one's own convictions or the opinions of others—is to write the essay.

In my own case I have often noticed a curious moment of optimism and despair at this point. Everything is there for the essay, and it is always better than when it is expressed, simply because it is everything, and what one expresses is only *something*. One could often express the exact opposite with almost if not quite as much validity. It is the question of degree, of emphasis that is essential to catch in the work of any novelist; it is those very paradoxes, contradictions, and divergencies that make his work interesting; it is the extra pages of notes, the notes that one cannot use, that flutter around in the corners of my mind as I write. Write? Well, as I draw up an outline, just as they teach you in English 1, and set out, A, B, C, D, the themes and subordinate themes I intend to express, although any resemblance to the final essay may be purely coincidental.

For certain themes or central ideas "prove themselves" in the writing of the essay, while others don't. It may be that the idea is accurate enough but that the illustrations of it in the author's books are not convincing. Or that both the idea and the elaboration are right but not *as* right as an alternative idea; there is the question of emphasis again. Or it may be simply that the idea is wrong, after all. And after one has spent a week or longer in the attempt to clarify and develop it, with sharper and sharper phrases and an increasing sense of uneasiness and irritation, with the increasing conviction from somewhere in the middle area of the digestive system that the idea is wrong, one simply says to hell with it. Meanwhile, certain ideas or insights that have not appeared to advantage in the preliminary notes, begin to intrude themselves with more and more authority in the actual writing. They insist they belong there, that they be represented somehow, and then, with the same sinking feeling in the middle area, one goes back to the beginning of the essay to see if it can be changed. Those familiar romantic authors who used to insist that their novels really wrote themselves had a point, but they never explained what a disagreeable point it was—the cause of ulcers as well as art. I would frankly prefer to be a man who knew what he was writing about.

How I envy, too, those literary critics who can say just what they mean, immediately, and even verbally; who can render a considered judgment of any literary problem within the purlieus of parlor conversation, authoritatively and with a touch of hauteur as to the rather simple-minded and grubby American novelists with whom I happen to be dealing. After all, if one has been dealing with Kafka or Flaubert's technique . . . poor Sherwood Anderson, poor, poor Dreiser. I see them at their desks, these firm, decisive literary men of action, enunciating their polished phrases while they fold their gloves. And I think of the pages of verbal hysteria that comprise what I call a first draft of an essay.

There may be sense in not putting down a thought in final form, however, until you know that you really have a thought. It is hard to throw away a good phrase even when it is not quite accurate, and I have noticed that the best literary journalists or book reviewers allow their thinking to follow their writing. H. L. Mencken is perhaps the classic example of a man's style being the man; and this is still one secret of becoming a high-priced columnist or a literary editor. There is a point, also, during the

immediate process of writing, in letting the mind bring up everything it can in the way of implications and associations, even
though these come in the form of half-thoughts, verbal flashes,
incomplete or distorted images. Let it all come, as it comes. Get
it all out, and then go back and see what is there, and select—
and select.

All the same, it is difficult for me even now to look at those
first drafts, which I keep, I suppose, out of some obscure tendency
to masochism. A year or so ago a friend of mine in the South
asked for one of these drafts to help him in his own writing. He
returned the manuscript quickly but I have hardly heard from
him since. A little later I was forced to go through one of these
original drafts in order to verify the sources of quotations I had
used. The sources were listed there, but it was easier, or at least
lots more pleasant, to search through the pages of the published
books from which the quotations had been taken.

I hesitate to add that I have three or four drafts of each essay
or chapter that I have written, and that all of them run to about
twice the length of the finished piece. But it is impossible for me
really to cut and revise an essay, to see it from the *outside,* until
I have been away from it for half a year or so, and have done
something else meanwhile. And I have left out the final process
of revision, which is simply working over the final draft in terms
of lesser elements of style—usually such words as "in," "of,"
"but," "and," "nevertheless," "however," "too," "also," "about,"
"with," "among"—until the book has been published.

During the course of these remarks, I have been aware of the
critics who remarked that Thomas Wolfe's *Story of a Novel,* for
instance, was not a statement of how he wrote his books but a
confession of his inability to write them. Well, perhaps so; nevertheless they were written. I am sure that other writers can do
better than I have done, too, but the value of essays such as this
must be in their description of methods of writing as they operate
in each case, the way things really are. I remember Melville's
account, both in his letters and in *Pierre,* of feeling like a moose,
hamstrung, while writing *Moby Dick,* of those deadly feelings of
faintness, of writing blindly with his eyes turned away from the
paper, thus unconsciously symbolizing the "hostile necessity of"
being a states-prisoner of letters. Even H. L. Mencken himself,
in a weak moment, admitted the anguish of that point when the

brain, as it were, "stands to one side and watches itself pitching and tossing, full of agony but essentially helpless." And when the writer, sitting there in his lonely room, "gnawing the handle of his pen, racked by his infernal quest, horribly bedeviled by incessant flashes of itching, toothache, eye-strain and evil conscience," makes atonement for the crime of being intelligent, I wish somebody would show me how to write more easily, instead of pointing out what still remains to be done.

It would be pleasant to conclude with the statement that at least I can now read what I have already published without pain. I wish I could. I hope, however, when my series of books on the American novelist from 1860 to 1940 has been finished, to be able to return to each of the volumes and make them better. And perhaps this is the moment to mention that I am a literary critic of the historical school. As it happens, I am interested in our social patterns, and especially in what has happened to the national character during the last fifty years of industrial concentration and corporate capitalism. I am engaged in a project which is trying to evaluate the kind of life we have lived in the past through the work of major figures in our literature: a literary record which may well turn out to be either a tribute to our hopes or an epitaph of our decline.

Now I agree that a work of art is a separate identity, a particular and unique crystallization of experience achieved through a specific technique. But I see a supplementary, not a contradictory meaning in the fact that it is also the expression of a personality and the highest product of an environment. The real point of a work of art is indeed that it fuses and resolves all the forces around it, personal and general, into a unified experience. If a critic simply concerns himself with *how* this experience is transmuted into literature—the technical methods—he omits two-thirds of his proper subject matter, or of the work of art itself. Very likely, art is "aristocratic" in essence, that is to say, the record of special temperaments, or an aristocracy of talent. But it is ridiculous to confuse this with an aristocracy of social class. For the personality of the artist has always at its highest pitch represented a portion of the common elements of the human race at a specific time. It is just this mixture, this opposition of elements, that makes a literary work complex and interesting.

Unfortunately, too, very few writers turn out a succession of masterpieces, while even their poorest works can give us useful information about themselves, their period, and people, as well as their art. The body of literature by our leading novelists from the beginnings to the present time forms a personal and intimate diary of the American mind during this period that we can find almost nowhere else. Perhaps the native novelist is not the *only* expert who is qualified to examine the souls and life of a people. But at least, as Mark Twain said, he does not try to generalize the nation:

No, he lays plainly before you the ways and speech and life of a few people grouped in a certain place—his own place—and that is one book. In time he and his brethren will report to you the life and the people of the whole nation. . . . And when a thousand able novels have been written, there you will have the soul of the people, the life of the people, the speech of the people; and not anywhere else can these be had.

To get at the essence of a "thousand able novels," as well as the unusual novels, to preserve this material for common knowledge and illuminate it for the common good: that still seems to me a useful and appropriate function for one kind of literary critic today.

From the *Saturday Review*, January 29, 1949; reprinted in *Writing for Love or Money*, a symposium edited by Norman Cousins; Longmans, Green and Company, 1949.

Decline of the Classic Moderns

ON THE face of it, the famous names in American literature today are flourishing. Ernest Hemingway has just won the Nobel Prize, and William Faulkner won it in 1949. (Not to mention the American-born poet T. S. Eliot, who received the award a year earlier.) Hemingway also got the Pulitzer Prize in 1953, and Faulkner has been awarded two National Book Awards within recent years. Among the other surviving members of the celebrated younger generation of the 1920's and their immediate successors in the early 1930's, John Dos Passos has fallen somewhat from critical favor, and John Steinbeck has moved over to the edge of popular entertainment. But there is no question as to the commercial value of their work.

There is indeed only one question which has not been asked about these four major talents. Why has not one of them produced a fresh or important literary work in the last ten years? Why is the combined output of the group so repetitive of their best earlier work, so empty of any kind of growth or maturity—as though *their* world had stopped moving somewhere in the 1940's? In Hemingway's case one is grateful that *The Old Man and the Sea* is as good a tale as it is. But the theme which Hemingway still celebrates is that of solitary suffering in a black Darwinian universe—not too far removed from Jack London's—where one must kill the brothers whom one loves, even one's fish brothers, and where the sharks are the masterpieces of nature. The old man's luck was broken because he went "too far out." This verdict on the tragedy is typical of an artist who has always presented a world of painful consequences and no causes.

10

That Hemingway has always refused to understand the nature of his own private orbit of anguish is, I think, also clear. Signs of an absorbing narcissism, of childish heroics, of sadism and brutality within a sealed-off zone of torment, as it were, were found in his previous novel, *Across the River and into the Trees.* When we turn to the work of William Faulkner, we see greater possibilities of change and growth—and of the capacity to meditate about life, which after all has been the mark of the major world writers until this century. Faulkner has always had a wider frame of reference than Hemingway, including a sense of social organization and of the different kinds of human individuals who exist along with lovers, fighters, and animals. But in recent years he too has fallen below the level of his best early novels—*Light in August, The Sound and the Fury,* and *Absalom, Absalom!,* all written before 1936.

There are even more puzzling issues here. Certain elementary facts have been consistently ignored by the New Critics, who have descended like a swarm of locusts upon Faulkner's work. (Or, more accurately, like the mechanized corps of technicians which they are, armed with their laws of strategy and their canons of criticism, their depth-gauges, their tactile-meters, their handbooks of proper taste and codes of symbolism—all in a massive literary critique which should be called Operation Mississippi.) Directly after receiving the Nobel Prize, for example, how could Faulkner think of writing *Requiem for a Nun?* For this was not a serious work at all. It was a rather tedious sequel to *Sanctuary,* but with all the horrors gone stale and the sensationalism rationalized by a noble and moralistic "message." Was this to show that Faulkner, as the official spokesman for American letters, was repenting his past in public—or that he too, like John Steinbeck, was writing with one eye on the Muse and the other on Broadway?

What was distressing in this play was the author's lack of taste and self-criticism, as though, bewitched by a decade of homage, he could no longer make any distinction between the good and bad things in his work. The new novel, *A Fable,* although it received the National Book Award recently, is unique among Faulkner's books in being neither good nor bad but simply mediocre. The purpose of the novel is surely admirable. It is a plea for pacifism which suggests that people should simply refuse to fight any more. Yet as the story develops we realize it is giving a pseudoreligious interpretation, and a sort of Hollywood-miracle effect, to the false armistice at the end of World War I. It has succumbed to the present fashion of seeking supernatural causes for events that are purely natural, human, or, God forbid, social in their origins. And what really remains in our mind after reading *A Fable* is the familiar Faulknerian stance of horror and terror rather than the scenes of purified human nobility or religious piety. Yes, that, and the beautiful folkloristic tale of the three-legged horse, which has no connection whatsoever that I can determine with the central story.

This is an old habit of Faulkner's—throwing together completely extraneous stories, joining them with a great pretense of mystery, and letting the critics find the answer. Mark Twain did it too, without any pretense. But the serious question that is raised by Faulkner's much-quoted Nobel speech, by the moralistic sequel to *Sanctuary,* and by *A Fable* itself is of course that of his return to "faith." And it is also true that the code of moral precepts which the mature writer has apparently adopted is just as romantic and rhetorical as is, at base, his whole view of the Southern scene. I have always doubted whether Faulkner understands the deep South in the way that Tolstoi understood Russia, or Dreiser the American scene of his time, or even the way Ellen Glasgow understood the middle South. Faulkner has fashioned a more complex and modern myth of the old South, in which all the heroic virtues are in the decaying aristocratic families (Sartoris-Compsons); all the vices in the rising middle-class "modern" Snopes clan: a black and white society indeed, where all the "good" Negroes are peasants or primitives, like the Sam Fathers of "The Bear," if they are not servants.

Richard Wright presents another view of the Southern scene, one which Faulkner does not ever quite see. But Faulkner, too, belonged to that generation of the 1920's which grew up to scorn the society around them but which was forced, somewhere around middle life, to fall back upon it as a central source of moral support. The later books of Sinclair Lewis are false and flat precisely because of this dilemma. What Lewis had satirized without full comprehension he tried to apotheosize without conviction. Very similarly the last five or six books of John Dos Passos present a "conspiratorial" view of the United States in which those dangerous radicals of the early 1930's are still busily undermining the foundations of the free world. In *Most Likely to Succeed,* they control our society in a way they never really achieved in their prime. Or else these later novels of Dos Passos present the same standardized moralistic picture of the "good" American hero who has renounced his youthful radical "errors" and becomes, as in *Chosen Country,* a perfect Jeffersonian landlord, a husband and lover, a taxpayer, a patriot.

No middle course seems to be possible between the extremes of Marx and the extremes of Horatio Alger. And what one misses in this whole group of writers, what shows up most clearly in the failure of their mature work, is just that ingrown, inherent, and *biological* belief in life—rather than any sort of intellectual or rhetorical affirmation—which marked the earlier generation of American realists from the turn of the century to the First World War. I mean the generation which extended from Dreiser and Ellen Glasgow to such figures as Sherwood Anderson, Willa Cather, and in his own odd way even H. L. Mencken. The separation of the artist from the communal life had not occurred then. These earlier writers were whole figures, not experts in their own eyes; they were rebels, but not expatriates or outcasts. Sharply dissenting as they did from their immediate social or literary tradition, they still found enough in their general cultural heritage to support their life convictions, a far deeper thing than the matter of political labels or social ideas.

The new writers of the 1920's were specialized in this sense. They were technical innovators, strong individualists, gifted talents who discarded not only the past, of which they were often ignorant, but the commonplace present. Where is the density and texture of ordinary life in the literature of this period; or the complexity of natural and social character that we meet in the literature of the past; or the involved, tormented, resilient fabric of human relationships? (Steinbeck has often sought after and never quite achieved this; Faulkner has had it, at his best, and often dropped it for purely literary effects.)

Exactly as in the musical play about the 1920's, *The Boy Friend,* the typical figures in the literature of this period talk to the audience, not to each other. Or as in Scott Fitzgerald's work they are always perfecting their roles before their mirrors. In one sense, at least, the whole period now seems to be a miraculous fairy tale where nothing real could ever happen, and where the typical writers of the epoch, such as Fitzgerald, or Hemingway himself, or T. S. Eliot, were masters, not of life, but of a kind of romantic enchantment; wizards of illusion, who took us for a moment under the spell of their art.

Yet beneath the enchantment, where common life should be to sustain as well as to confine us, there was a void which no amount of café society or wild-game hunting, or even of political theorizing, could quite cover up. For in this process too the great attraction of communism in the 1930's was just as artificial as had been the flight from reality in the postwar period. The new social radicalism was in part at least a salvation from a personal emptiness which had slowly become apparent. Its purpose was to save the masses, the nameless faces whom these writers had never really known in the way that the older American writers had.

One perceives this attitude very clearly in Hemingway's social-protest play, *The Fifth Column,* and even in *For Whom the Bell Tolls.* A sudden convert to the Spanish crusade, Hemingway spoke about the American Depression in a ridiculous way. The great disenchantment of Dos Passos with the Communist cause also occurred during the Spanish Civil War; even while the radical artist of this period, from his leftist point of view, was dismissing the New Deal, just as the later Dos Passos did from the extreme right. Meanwhile Faulkner had been slowly swinging over to the only political stand which could emerge from his writing. The South could take care of its own, he said in *Intruder in the Dust.* Northern agitators should keep out.

So now in the middle 1950's, when conformity has settled down over the nation, perhaps it is not surprising that this group of writers cannot really function. None of them—not even Steinbeck, who *needs,* one might say, a social cause to ballast his fantasy—has been able to deal with his own society in his work, or to speak up on the fundamental issues of life and art today. Their writing shows this inertia, or worse. For if the history of the 1920's and 1930's was so largely an enchanted dream in their minds, then perhaps the present period is the true "reality."

How dreadful! How dull.

From the *Nation,* May 7, 1955.

Postscript to the Postwar Generation

The postwar novelists, the men under forty, are in a difficult spot. The majority of them have their spiritual roots in the literary efflorescence of the Twenties. But that period was not the start of a literary renascence, as everybody then thought, but rather the culmination of a movement that began with Stephen Crane and Jack London. By the 1920's the main force of this development in American fiction had already moved into the areas of technique and of individual sensibility: the high points of any aesthetic movement, and also the start of its decline. By now the literary power of the Twenties is becoming increasingly attenuated. The best new writers of today can hardly derive much real sustenance from it. But where does all this leave them? And in what directions can they go?

Among the writers whom John Aldridge grouped together in his provocative book *After the Lost Generation,* perhaps he was right in praising Vance Bourjaily as the only one who developed, rather than merely rehearsed, the typical themes of the 1920's. But what has happened to *all* these writers now? Surely a Truman Capote is only a Faulkner in fancy dress; his true métier, if I can guess at this, is probably closer to the innocent and lyrical scenes of William Saroyan. Frederick Buechner, who really did write a novel according to the best precepts of the New Criticism, came a cropper in his second book. A young writer needs more to keep him going than the amenities of an academic horizon. Incidentally, what is interesting today is that the level of college education is higher than in the previous generations of American novelists, many of whom were self-taught, rebellious, and isolated figures. But a formal education is not necessarily a good thing for a writer if it also means a lack of personal and lived experience during the formative years of his youth. The sheltering wings of learning and of reason which appealed to Ellen Glasgow, for example, were no substitute for the primary conflicts of life which she had missed.

In this first group of writers I myself prefer Jean Stafford, when her mature and sensitive talent succeeds in breaking through what almost appears to be a type of neurotic armor. And I omit Paul Bowles, who has shown to what extremes of cynicism (and commercialism) the novel of technique can fall. But directly opposed to these figures in the contemporary scene, there is a second group of realists and naturalists. Despite a series of critical obituaries which keep on proclaiming the death of realism in modern fiction, the best novels of the last few years have come from this area.

I mean such works as Norman Mailer's *The Naked and the Dead* and James Jones's *From Here to Eternity,* both of them solid and memorable books in a central line of American prose fiction. Out in Chicago, Nelson Algren, whose *The Man with the Golden Arm* won the National Book Award for fiction in 1950, has pursued the same vein. *Never Come Morning,* an earlier novel of his, was an excellent study of second-generation immigrants cheated and betrayed by the mores of a money society. *The Neon Wilderness* was a good collection of short stories on the same theme.

I have hesitated to call this loose school of writers by its true name of "social realism." Now that the Communists have debased the meaning of this literary trend, we shy away from it in fear and suspicion. Yet how essential this term still is (if we could only call it something else!) to define great works of the past, and how negligible any criticism is that avoids this area of our literature. Ira Wolfert's *Tucker's People,* a study of the numbers racket in the Depression, belongs here; and the same author's *An Act of Love* contains some of the most brilliant writing on World War II. Mr. Wolfert is a much-neglected author in general, who is solid and discerning, if sometimes rather heavy and diffuse, as in his least successful book, *Married Men.* Perhaps this novel needs condensation and revision; but like so many writers of the war generation, Wolfert is much more at home with male relationships than with men and women. Love is still our national literary failure.

This whole group of social realists, incidentally, was more or less ignored in Mr. Aldridge's survey of post-World War II fiction. He is too good a critic to let himself be beguiled, as Delmore Schwartz pointed out in the *Partisan Review,* by the snobbish cult of manners and social class, whatever that means in the real context of American culture. Does one really have to polarize these two phases of contemporary writing into a false dichotomy, or divide them off by such tags as Brutes and Aesthetes? In the contrast between the literary worlds of Henry James and of Dreiser the separation was already clear. But to set up these schools as irreconcilably opposed to each other—to choose one or the other as the standard—only weakens the value of both, and of the tradition which includes both. It only proves oneself to be an idiot. As in the world of political affairs today, the tendency to view history, along with literature, in these terms of polarized extremes can lead to disaster as well as to farce.

In point of fact the two historical schools at the turn of the century—the expatriates and the native realists—had as many resemblances as differences. A common culture had produced them. And among the younger writers today the most promising figures are likely to combine both points of view, even both techniques. The prose style of William Styron's *Lie Down in Darkness* was influenced quite as much by Thomas Wolfe as by William Faulkner: two writers who are also viewed as permanent opposites in some quarters. (And there was the young critic who once asked Maxwell Perkins how he could publish Hemingway *and* Wolfe.) Ralph Ellison's *Invisible Man,* another winner of a National Book Award, combines the extremes of poetic symbolism, in the vein of Kafka, with the bedrock actuality of Negro life in these emancipated states.

Probably the main trouble with John Hersey's *The Wall,* a novel which I admire but which has been accused of being "documentary," is simply that the writer's sensibility would not let him accept the facts of human horror and degradation which are described in the documentary records of Nazi behavior. It is curious, too, that perhaps the most original novel recently published, and one that deserves a wider circulation than it has had, John Griffin's *The Devil Rides Outside,* almost completely violates, as in a sense all original novels do, the critical canons which are usually set up for the convenience of literary historians more than for the sake of truth. Mr. Griffin is concerned with an odd theme these days: the necessity to renounce sexual, or more accurately carnal, pleasure in order to achieve spiritual truth and serenity.

It should be evident by this time that I am not one for arbitrary divisions in any area of human activity. But Mr. Griffin's touch is so fresh, and the dramatic action in his novel is so effective, as to stir in you the strangely persistent and no doubt highly neurotic yearning to achieve all by sacrificing all. His book is symptomatic of another trend among the new writers—the return to the security of a religious universe. But it is not fanatical, authoritarian, or the least bit fashionable in its values. It seeks a personal salvation which one respects.

Yes, the deeply religious, devoutly Catholic Mr. Griffin is a very different matter from the disciples of the New Criticism who are constantly tipping their literary hats in a sort of tedious homage to Mr. T. S. Eliot's universal religion. I suppose I am also thinking here of Mr. Alan Tate's slightly different brand of Deep-Southern, ultraconservative, clerical, royalist and neoreligious yearnings. This is the American branch of Mr. Eliot's institutionalized art, as Mr. Tate is something like Mr. Eliot's papal delegate to our universities and libraries. Isn't it odd that our English departments, which yielded themselves to the racist concept of the Anglo-Saxon "gentlemen" at the turn of the century, now flaunt the defiant banner of the Old South?

In this survey I have slighted the *New Yorker* school, best represented by James Thurber, E. B. White, J. D. Salinger, Irwin Shaw, and Edward Newhouse. And I should mention, on the opposite end of the literary spectrum, the experimental writing which is contained in the New Directions anthologies. From this source comes Tennessee Williams, a novelist and story writer, as well as dramatist, who has enriched the formulas of advance-guard writing. Jack Jones is another young writer who brings to the forms of surrealist fiction an unusual kind of humanity and humor. In this general area of experimental writing, too, there is Anais Nin, the mysterious queen of the Symbolist movement, and the gifted Maude Hutchins who writes of love with pagan laughter. Among the members of the "middle generation," and whatever one may say about their limitations, such figures as Robert Penn Warren or Mary McCarthy carry on the prestige and the authority of the professional writer in the United States today.

Yet both the older and younger members of the writing community today are now operating in the shadow of the literary revival of the 1920's. Their movement can no longer be a vain rehearsal of a vanished epoch. They also face a completely different historical period, and a far more difficult one for the arts, if not for civilization itself. It is ridiculous, as I say, to discredit the social novels of the 1930's simply because the Russian Revolution turned out to be a failure. The best of these novels were actually oriented to the native rather than the foreign scene. But in our own period the most generous visions of social idealism have turned into the horrid nightmares of tyranny and deep oppression.

Where can a writer turn who still wants to root his work in the reality of his own time?

The disenchantment of the literary left, which in many cases has become the extreme right, hangs heavy over him. He can't quite be reassured by the notion that when Frigidaires are distributed to every nook and cranny of darkest Africa (or Asia) the trials of a revolutionary century will be solved. He faces, as in George Orwell's *1984,* a world of continual warfare, of shifting politico-military alliances, and daily revision of the faiths, allegiances, and beliefs which depend on history's flux.

Pity the poor artist! The retreat either to the modes of personal sensibility or those of religious and social authoritarianism may be a refuge for him. But it is rarely a source of great art. The real drama and content of his period lie directly at the center of the chaos that surrounds him. It is there he must turn to come close to the spirit of the age, if he can only catch it. And surely no literary subject matter could offer him so many opportunities along with so many dangers. For our part we can only keep the boundaries of the middle way as wide as possible for him, preserve him from false orthodoxy, let him speak his mind without benefit of Congress—or even of captious critics.

This seems to me at least what some of the new voices of the mid-Fifties might begin to do, along with the things which they have always done, and which, as I hope, in their infinite variety and blessed perversity, they will continue to do.

From the *Saturday Review,* March 14, 1953.

THE "END" OF NATURALISM

THE HEIRS of the literary movement called "naturalism" are under attack from two sides today. The fashionable drift of literary criticism, as in the *Partisan Review,* has in effect pronounced the movement dead. As far back as the 1930's, Willa Cather, in "The Novel Démeublé," outlawed the mere novel of furnishings. The stress in this quarter has been for a return to the Jamesian novel of psychological tension and the Kafka novel of dream symbolism—both representing a withdrawal of the artist from the vulgar and disappointing currents of ordinary American life.

Yet even such a representative novelist of this school as Saul Bellow has suddenly changed to the old-fashioned native picaresque in *The Adventures of Augie March.* (The real influences on the book are those of Dreiser, in *Dawn,* and of Thomas Wolfe.) The naturalistic novels continue to come out, to exhibit unmistakable signs of life and vitality, and to capture the largest reading audience.

From this area have come what are really the most important works of fiction during the last few years—but here also is the second half of the attack on contemporary naturalism.

For it is undoubtedly true that ordinary readers, including many teachers and students of literature, have been confronted by a series of novels in which the language has been frank to the point of obscenity, in which the private lives of the characters—and often the private functions of the body—have been described with a candor amounting to zealotry. In their social environment these novels have often dwelt upon the sordid, the criminal, the brutal; their themes have hardly been suitable for the young American maiden we used to hear about. If, indeed, as the critic H. H. Boyesen described our literature at the turn of the century, this young maiden was "the Iron Madonna who strangles in her fond embrace the American novelist," a new generation of writers has taken its revenge upon her—over and over again.

No wonder that the average reader sometimes rises in protest or that Orville Prescott of the *New York Times,* for instance, was forced to defend his praise of James Jones's *From Here to Eternity* against a barrage of indignant epistles. Very often today, indeed, that "smiling side of life," which William Dean Howells believed to be typically American, has put on in contemporary fiction what appears to be only a permanent and frozen sneer. Yet, saying all this, I think it will be illuminating to return for a moment to such typical novels of the past as *To Have and To Hold, The Prisoner of Zenda,* or *When Knighthood Was in Flower.*

Compared with modern bestsellers, these earlier favorites now seem to have emerged from a different American world or another astral orbit. To read them again is to realize, in concrete form, the depth of the social and cultural change which has occurred in this nation during the last fifty years. In the typical Victorian romance a touch of the hand was a pledge of matrimony—and this in turn was a consummation barely to be hinted at after three hundred pages of baroque adventure. Now these books were written, of course, during a period of the utmost restriction about human relationships but of complete laxity about financial and political morals in our society. They were products of the "genteel tradition" which had imposed a timid and fearful literary orthodoxy upon what was on the whole, in the late nineteenth century, a freebooting, primitive, and empire-building society, spreading its arrogance and its achievements from Faneuil Hall to the Sierra Nevadas.

Thus, what we are now witnessing is a literary upheaval in a country only lately moralistic and provincial in the arts—a country before Kinsey, so to speak—in which the echoes of H. L. Mencken's attacks on the "Puritan Kultur" are still ringing in our ears. It is a literary upheaval in just those areas of expression which were only yesterday either completely taboo or the worst form of social and artistic heresy. And it is, historically, an extreme phase of the battle for freedom of artistic expression which ran its course in our literature from Stephen Crane's *Maggie* in 1893 to, let us say, Ernest Hemingway's *A Farewell to Arms* in 1929.

Some of the results may be a little hard to take, I admit, for
those of us who were raised on the popular romances of the
1900's or on the nineteenth-century classic English authors. (All
those great men, it has been said, agreed with each other not to
tell the truth about life.) The French writers of the same period,
and the classic Russians, had always felt far more at liberty to
describe the private side of both the body and the soul. And
part of our dismay at the spectacle of current fiction may be due
not so much to its boldness as to our own ingrained heritage of
polite literature.

But what is this naturalism? And how did it ally itself with the
first currents of modern American realism in the opening decade
of this century? Perhaps a brief look at the origins and development of what was, with all its faults, a great liberating movement
in our letters will help to clarify some of the modern novels that
dazzle and bewilder their readers.

Let me say directly that the definition of the naturalistic school
will vary somewhat in the case of each literary historian and,
perhaps more importantly, in the case of every novelist's use of
its ideas. It is likely that some of the present younger generation
of novelists in the United States are quite unaware that they are
naturalists at all.

Historically, the school came from the French novelist Zola,
the writer who formulated, in a grandiose but inspiring manner,
its principles and objectives. It has been called "realism plus
science." And it was, in fact, an attempt to relate the discoveries
of nineteenth-century European scientific thought—a system of
ideas which almost remade the modern world—to the literature
of the time. European naturalism attempted to dispel the superstitions and prejudices of its own period; to see human character
in a pragmatic light, and social environment as it actually existed.
But we have said that the American literary scene at the turn
of the century was even more repressive, circumscribed, and
artificial than Zola's France. In the words of Wilma Dykeman
Stokely, our writing was based on "a propriety so shallow it
excluded nature, a tradition so romanticized that it falsified history, a literature so literary that it overlooked whole areas of the
life around it."

The first group of twentieth-century American realists (as
opposed to the romance tradition) included Stephen Crane,

Frank Norris, Jack London, Ellen Glasgow, and Theodore Dreiser: those figures whom I have called "rebels and ancestors." In their struggle against the shallow and trivial literary climate of the 1900's, they were anxious to use all the intellectual resources of their period. They grasped at the support of naturalism's "science"—reassuring even when false—and they added to it, in a curious mélange, all the disturbing new ideas of European thought in the late nineteenth century. But it is important to stress again not only that these writers converted the European movement to particularly American purposes but that each artist —as every artist does—adapted a loose structure of prevailing ideas to the needs of his own temperament and the purposes of his own craft.

Thus Jack London first combined the opposite poles of Marx and Nietzsche in his literary philosophy, and in his later work described the worst extremes of a Darwinian cosmos of monsters and ghouls. Yet Theodore Dreiser, in his highest creative period around 1912, used roughly the same system of ideas to express not only the drama and beauty that could exist in a universe of blind natural forces but, as he believed then, the potential of American life to advance through such conflict to its own maturity as a civilization. It was this massive figure, Dreiser, whose first novel was suppressed (the tender *Sister Carrie*!), whose fourth novel, *The Titan,* was rejected by the publishers, whose fifth novel, *The "Genius,"* was banned in 1915, who became the master and innovator of his period. The success of his battle against the self-imposed custodians of the public morals—and then as now, I may add, they were usually the custodians of ignorance and prejudice—marked the final victory of the long struggle for literary expression in the United States.

This was the "coming of age," in Van Wyck Brooks's phrase, of the modern movement. For what has been called the "Sexual Revolution" in our native letters was actually, during this period, the freedom to discuss human character and human relationships in terms of those primary needs and drives which actually do determine our success or failure in life, which create our happiness and our follies. The next group of American writers to appear on the literary scene is more familiar today. It included Scott Fitzgerald, Sinclair Lewis, Ernest Hemingway, John Dos Passos, and William Faulkner. But to a certain degree the famous figures of the 1920's merely developed and consolidated the literary rights and privileges which had been earned for them during the grim struggle of their ancestors.

These writers, to be sure, carried the literary revival in the United States to its flowering and created the second great renascence in our letters. As at the peak of any such movement, they were specialized talents, master craftsmen who also, however, reflected in the aesthetic area the unbridled individualism of their social and economic environment. In a typically native fashion they often seemed as ignorant of their real heritage as they were indifferent to their future. With the advent of the Jazz Age, the flapper, the automobile, and Prohibition, the twentieth century arrived, in Sauk Center, Minnesota, as well as in Greenwich Village.

What happened to this glamorous and brilliant epoch we know all too well, if to our children it is only a casual passage in a textbook. In the following period of social disaster (which at the present moment, as though it were a national trauma, has been deleted from the record of the national consciousness) such later figures as Thomas Wolfe and John Steinbeck again turned the currents of American realism and naturalism back to the social principles and communal interests from which they had derived. Among the few major writers of the 1940's, Richard Wright and James T. Farrell carried the same literary convictions and values to other submerged and neglected sections of American life. Finally, an exotic, morbid, but undoubtedly powerful writer, Henry Miller, combined the earlier standards of native naturalism with the Parisian currents of symbolism and surrealism; and the circuit was closed.

In this brief space I have hardly been able to consider such technical issues of the naturalistic movement as its stress on "determinism," "materialism," and a mechanistic universe, or its method of using massive and sometimes overpowering detail to describe the social environment of a period. These issues are adequately discussed in the textbooks on American literature— although they are never so clearly established in the works of the writers as they are in the minds of the literary critics. Nevertheless, I hope this little survey of the modern movement in American fiction, simplified as it has to be, will contribute to our understanding of the strictly contemporary novel.

The victories have all apparently been won. The peak of the movement, and the works which established its place in world literature, occurred almost a quarter of a century ago. We are now in the sear after the flowering; the letdown after the climax. It is almost inevitable, as in the history of artistic movements, that we should have a period of technical virtuosity without serious purpose; of novelists who seem to have everything but values and convictions; of shock for the sake of shock. In their new-found freedom some of the modern realists have viewed the human passions themselves on a purely physical or even mechanical level. The excitations of the body have replaced the impulses of the heart. In another area these authors have succumbed to the illusion that the private and personal is *ipso facto* the universal and artistic; that the infantile modes of human behavior which are at the base of life are therefore its final goal; that whatever has *not* been described in the literature of the past has to be included in the literature of today.

But it is natural that inferior or purposeless talents—and sometimes real ones—should take momentary advantage of the whole new area of literary expression which has been opened up for them during the first half of the century. It is better, as always, to suffer the abuses of a few than to curtail the rights of the many; and, for myself, I believe there never can be too much freedom. Moreover, we have reached another turning point in the chronology of the modern novel. History is again filling the literary void with a new stimulus, a new challenge. For, while nineteenth-century fiction was sharply circumscribed in its evaluation of human character and human relationships, the artist's right to hold dissenting social or political ideas was almost unquestioned. To a large degree the early currents of realism and naturalism in the 1900's were tied to or actually embodied the western radicalism of the populist movements at the turn of the century.

The demand for social reform—for social justice—is very clear in a work like Frank Norris' *The Octopus,* a direct predecessor of John Steinbeck's *The Grapes of Wrath.* More surprisingly, it is just as clear in the early novels of the Virginia aristocrat, Ellen Glasgow. If Dreiser's Sister Carrie and the witless artist of *The "Genius"* were taboo, it was again typical of the period that the scathing indictment of our financial and political institutions in *The Financier* went almost unchallenged. Indeed, the main stream of our literature since 1900 is in large part a literature of dissent and criticism—which is also, as Robert Spiller has recently said, the fundamental condition of art in an open society, and the mark of its vitality. It is the fundamentally democratic condition.

But now in this new epoch of personal freedom for artistic expression, we have also moved into another period of social and political conformity—of timidity, fear, and suspicion. Ours is also an epoch of shifting social foundations in which the freedom, not only to dissent politically or socially, but even to criticize, has in turn become suspect. Those forces of self-appointed censorship in our past, those forces of ignorance and superstition, have gained a semiofficial status in our society and have gathered to themselves a semilegal sanction. This *is* a new and serious mode of spiritual repression which can lead easily from the social and political area to the religious, and so back again, in a vicious circle, to the most personal sort of opinions. It threatens the life atmosphere of American thought and American art.

For, if an artist has not yet felt the lash of official condemnation, he has already been sensitized to the less tangible but equally ponderous and oppressive forces of intellectual regularity in our present cultural atmosphere. Think for yourself—but think like everybody else.

Perhaps I can do no better to illustrate this point than to quote a passage from Ellen Glasgow's own work when, early in the modern movement for literary emancipation, she was describing the youthful heroine of *Virginia:*

Her education was founded upon the simple theory that the less a girl knew about life, the better prepared she would be to contend with it. Knowledge of any sort (except the rudiments of reading and writing, the geography of countries she would never visit, and the dates of battles she would not mention) was kept from her as rigorously as if it contained the germs of a contagious disease. . . . The chief object of her upbringing, which differed in no essential particular from that of every other well-born and well-bred Southern woman of her day, was to paralyze her reasoning faculties so completely that all danger of mental "unsettling" or even movement was eliminated from her future. To solidify the forces of mind into the inherited mould of fixed beliefs was, in the opinion of the age, to achieve the definite end of all education.

Written in 1913, it speaks for today; except that what was then Southern and feminine now promises to become general. So the battle has to be fought all over again—or, speaking more accurately, it is continuous, merely shifting from the realm of personal expression to that of social opinion, and back again to the personal. In this new period of crisis, too, it is interesting that the European novelists, who have faced up to the historical necessity more intimately than we have yet, have nevertheless managed to preserve a much larger area of intellectual freedom and speculation in their craft. I am thinking not only of French writers like Sartre and Camus, or Italians like Moravia and Silone, but of the Spanish author José Cela, whose recent book, *The Hive,* demonstrates a remarkable individuality in the very midst of an authoritarian regime.

Perhaps our young novelists today will have to seek support and precedent from their European colleagues in the task that faces them; just as did the rebellious ancestors of modern fiction more than half a century ago.

From the *English Journal,* January, 1954.

HIGHER AND HIGHER CRITICISM

WHAT IS happening to criticism in the Age of Criticism? A group of English writers in the pages of this magazine have already commented on the "Establishment" and the "Outsiders" in their country. But over here, where the dominant critical school is more solidly established, and even worse I think, the voices of protest have been muted or silent. To be sure, Van Wyck Brooks, the "grand old man" of our criticism, has been waging a kind of guerrilla warfare against the New Critics. The young firebrand, John Aldridge, has just delivered another blast at them, though from an exposed rampart. But Malcolm Cowley has expressed only some mild rebuke lately, while Edmund Wilson, who might have taken the leadership here, has wandered off to the Red Sea —no, the Dead Sea—and all the others are safely entrenched in the universities and academies.

For a literary movement that professes no interest in "economics," the New Criticism is surprisingly well organized, with its chains of communication running from the colleges to the dominant literary magazines (*Kenyon, Hudson, Partisan* reviews, etc.), to the foundations and fellowships. It could be called a literary monopoly. Starting originally as a reaction to the Marxist criticism of the 1930's, still under the shadow of Ezra Pound's disjointed fascism and T. S. Eliot's clerical royalism, it has been developed in this country mainly by romantic Southern conservatives like Allen Tate and Robert Penn Warren. Another branch of what is almost an interlocking directorate includes the literary ex-Communists seeking refuge in pure criticism; and such hesitant humanists as Lionel Trilling, who now represent the "Liberal Mind."

In the cross section of critical volumes now under consideration, there is an interesting debate in the little magazine called *Contemporary Issues* (London and New York) as to the amount of fascism in this general movement and the poetry it advocates. But the New Criticism also expresses an open abhorrence of "politics," except for its own advancement. Its central concern is the pure "work of art," interpreted by a textual criticism that has become increasingly elaborate and ingenious; bulwarked by a massive scholarship, medieval and scholastic in essence; and restricting its activities to a selected canon of "acceptable" authors upon whom the hosts of younger new critics descend en masse.

There is value in this close textual criticism, but there is also a point where it reaches an apex of intellectual virtuosity, of self-enclosed sterility. That is the impression one gets, at any rate, from Mr. Stanley Edgar Hyman's new anthology, *The Critical Performance,* prepared especially for the Vintage books, as a supplement to his earlier volume called *The Armed Vision*: an impression, in Mr. Hyman's case, of sublime complacency with everything contained in the volume. "We see the endless fertility of Aristotle in the Auden and Fergusson essays," he says, "and get some sense of the territories uncharted by Aristotle (we might name them 'Plato') in Buchanan and Richards." We also see the uncharted territories of Mr. Hyman's own thought which we might name as legion.

Now I confess that I am morbidly drawn to and fascinated by this vision of life and art in the middle of the twentieth century, and I only wish I could quote Mr. Hyman in greater detail as the best exponent of the Higher Criticism today. At the same time, he says, after having added Frazer to Aristotle and Plato, as the three central influences of "Modern Criticism"—God forbid—at the same time, the ultimate concern of all these critics is the text itself, the pure work of art; and here the critics "sing in splendid concert." And so they do, since there is no question of their intelligence, learning or dedication to their craft—but only of the purpose to which they are putting their talent.

This purpose, however, Mr. Hyman praises, with never an undertone of doubt or speculation, in a cantata of pious approval opening this splendid critical concert. The ten American critics represented in his anthology, hail from "such unlikely cultural founts as Idaho and New Mexico, Missouri and Kentucky," but

there may be some significance, he says, "in the fact that they all
went to school in the East, and at least four attended Oxford,
three as Rhodes scholars." There surely is significance in this
fact, or in the fact that Mr. Hyman makes it significant; but just
what significance, I leave to you. And the worst of it is that Mr.
Hyman, for all his devout allegiance to the critical cause, is not
even a perfectly pure new critic. He includes an essay by Constance Rourke on the American scene—though it is on our Indian
rituals. He includes psychoanalytical critics like Empson, and a
couple of outsiders like Herbert Read, and even the obsolete
Marxist, Christopher Caudwell, as a warning.

Messrs. René Wellek and Austin Warren, in their *Theory of
Literature,* an older work now reprinted in the paperbacks, would
surely not accept even such faint hints of subversion. If Mr.
Hyman's anthology is a perfect example of critics who match up
to the highest standards of the new criticism, Wellek and Warren
have put out what is surely the standard text of the formalist
group. And here, I should say, "psychology" is added to the list
of taboo subjects, along with history and biography. Out with
them all. The writer's temperament, assuming we could know
something about it, which Messrs. W. and W. purely doubt, has
no more to do with his writing than does the society or environment he inhabits. These factors, along with the history of ideas,
and the relationship of literature to the other arts, are all part of
the "extrinsic approach" in criticism, described here as hardly
to be condoned.

What is left for the critic to deal with? Since Wellek and
Warren use the first hundred pages of their treatise to dispose
of the things that must *not* be mentioned, let me add hastily that
they are not concerned with novelists either, or novels, but with
the *theory* of the novel; and not even with the emotions of literature, but "the feelings of emotions, the perceptions of emotions."
And what is most curious here is the tone of bland authoritarianism with which these aesthetic principles and laws are handed
down as the future methodology for all graduate schools of
English—which will not include human beings, I suppose, and
certainly not anybody who wants to write a creative work of
fiction, but only teachers, or the images of teachers.

How far has this influence already spread, with its formidable
scholarship, its yearning for absolutes in scientific aesthetics, its

passion for abtraction? *Society and Self in the Novel,* edited by
Mark Schorer, shows some typical symptoms of this whole configuration of the higher and higher criticism. There is, of course,
the familiar essay on Proust by Fred Dupee, who must be becoming almost as tired of his single subject as F. O. Matthiessen
became at the end of Henry James. Then there are two more
essays on James Joyce. Mr. Schorer himself uses the worst parts
of one of the worst novels by Sinclair Lewis to illustrate the
American novelists's "method of half-truths."

Yet Mr. Schorer in his own way is one of the few critics of this
school who seems to have a genuine interest in the conflict between society and the individual that has created the tension, and
the tragedy, for so many great novels of the past. For the rest of
these critics society, as a vital force, is so far beyond the horizon
of art—or at least of criticism—that it hardly seems to exist.
This is certainly the extreme point of the nineteenth-century revolt of the Symbolists—and the Dadaists, after them—who protested against the framework of a materialistic and scientific civilization which excluded human and artistic values. But here, in a
curious reversal of values, both society and humanity have disappeared from criticism, while "science" and "reason" conduct an
autopsy on the corpse of literature.

In the closed circuit of "proper" subjects for these critics (I
have forgotten to mention Yeats) even the name of Sinclair
Lewis appears as a surprise. He is one of the few living American
authors—well, I mean one not as long dead as Melville—who
has entered, though so unfavorably, the new critical arcana. The
New Criticism—which is in fact now old, established, and utterly
respectable—has no concern with any sort of truly creative new
literature. Like the academic scholarship of the 1900's, like the
neohumanists of the 1930's, it is both ignorant of and contemptu-
ous toward its own native literary tradition. And what strikes
one finally about this whole critical tendency is how completely
it reflects, in the spiritual area, the worst aspects of the American
society it has repudiated.

It *is* that society—with its emphasis on abstraction and techniques, rather than human values; with its conspicuous consumption of scholarship and learning; with its mass-minded and
"other-directed" stress on aesthetic concepts and laws; with its
yearning for refinement and "culture" in art, at the expense of

all vitality and life. One remembers that the robber barons also ransacked the treasures of medieval Europe to adorn their gothic mansions; turned Episcopal for the rites, like T. S. Eliot; collected Oriental miniatures, like Ezra Pound; and then showed the way for what their aesthetic grandchildren are now doing in the area of the literary trusts, combines and monopolies. Shades of Thorstein Veblen—and perhaps of Mamie Eisenhower! For there are disturbing echoes not merely of the past but of the present age in the prevailing distraction and euphoria of our fashionable school of criticism today. While the crucial and revolutionary issues of our time are being fought out in the dark, and the human race may be getting ready to be atomized, it almost seems that the real function of the New Criticism is to keep our best young intellectuals absorbed with their playthings, no matter what happens to the nation or the world.

So, at the opposite pole of the critical volumes under present survey, Walter Rideout's *The Radical Novel in the United States, 1900-1954* comes almost from the void. Was there a radical novel in this country, and what happened to it? Mr. Rideout himself presents his theme under the guise of sober scholarship. His method is that of the social historian rather than the literary critic proper. His rather narrow definition of "radical" as something apart from the main stream of the progressive reform movement in our society and literature during the last fifty years— Upton Sinclair and Jack London; but not Norris, Howells, or Dreiser at their best—minimizes the real scope of his survey.

Still, this is a solid, informative and interesting history of an area in our cultural history which is often ignored by conventional historians. I can do no better than to urge you to read it; and then take a look at Randolph Bourne's *History of a Literary Radical* to see some of the social influences which brought about the second great revival of our literature in the 1920's. Influences, I repeat, that the New Criticism has not the slightest knowledge of or concern with. Nor does it concern itself with a possible new revival of creative literature in the United States for which the first step must be to break through the formidable establishment of this critical school in our literary places of power.

Perhaps that is why the last three books in the present survey, all written from the middle ground of criticism, which is the human, the enduring ground of all good criticism, are so particularly welcome today. Frank O'Connor's *The Mirror in the Road-way* is a sometimes deliberately perverse defense of the respect-able nineteenth-century middle-class European novel against the onslaughts of twentieth-century decadence and neobarbarism. He uses no jargon, no carefully delimited standards of aesthetic value —excuse me, I mean "frames of reference." He even calls natu-ralism an extreme of realism, which it is, when you come down to it. And his portraits of the great nineteenth-century masters of fiction, English, Russian, and French, are acute, sympathetic, enlightening.

His object is simply to get into the minds and hearts of the writers whose work he describes, and I can think of nothing bet-ter, or more difficult, for a critic to do. The present reprint of E. M. Forster's *Aspects of the Novel,* a celebrated work now at a moderate price, certainly invokes the same literary "prin-ciple." "Perhaps we ought to define what a novel is before start-ing. This will not take a second," Forster says. And he para-phrases the French critic who declared that a novel is "a fiction in prose of a certain extent." Finally, I must confess that the last book on the list, *Our Literary Heritage,* is not even so scien-tific as O'Connor and Forster. It is in fact a picture book of American writers and their settings, taken from the famous Bettmann Archive of illustrations in New York, with a selected text from Van Wyck Brooks' five-volume history, *Makers and Finders.* But there is one picture of Henry James in a top hat, while every other reputable Englishman in sight wears a derby, that justifies the whole project.

Now I wonder if the New Critics have thought of using X rays.

From the *Nation,* November 10, 1956.

THE AMERICAN CONSCIENCE TODAY

MR. BURLINGAME'S *The American Conscience* comes at the right time. It is a survey of our moral behavior from the Plymouth Colony to the Great Depression; and one only wishes he had carried on this chronicle a little farther. What would he say now? Where is the American conscience today? The witch trials of the late seventeenth century in New England were the last desperate attempt of the Calvinist clergy to maintain the "covenant." These persecutions were followed by a wave of public remorse and spiritual reform.

We have had our modern parallels. But what covenant are we maintaining? is the question—while the specter of "atheistic communism" still looms as large, as unholy, and as hysterical in the national consciousness as did the histrionic epilepsy of Cotton Mather's adolescent maiden in the devil-haunted psyche of Boston and Salem. Our own purges of guilt by association—mainly with the bad, dead past of the New Deal epoch—have been followed not by remorse so much as apathy and inertia. If the nation does indeed face a crisis of survival, if the major areas of the world are in the throes of revolutionary social change, the American conscience today is paralyzed by its semblance of good fortune, outwardly, and by a consuming inner anxiety.

We must present—don't we?—an odd appearance to the disturbed continents of Asia, Africa, and Europe. What about a Secretary of State who parades the shell of Christian ethics to rationalize the mores of corporate capitalism—or of his own inscrutable whim? And a President who abandons all national initiative to the edicts of Divine Providence, and the good offices of Dag? In a society that boasts of its free press, its communication system of radio and television, its public schools, it is safe

34

to say the masses of our people have no idea of the realities of world history. I venture to speculate that in retrospect the period of the 1940's and 1950's will appear even more benighted and self-destructive than the giddy epoch of the 1920's that we are now celebrating as our golden period. Hoover, arise!

Such at least are the more somber reflections provoked by Mr. Burlingame's history of our moral triumphs and disasters in the past; and yet his chronicle also affords a vista of hope—or the consoling perspective of ancient follies. It is a popular history, plainly presented, lacking a certain level of depth analysis perhaps, or modern "sophistication" of historical interpretation. It takes no account, so we are told, of the fads and vogues that are continually passing through "the shadows of the academy." The central point of view is rational, sensible, sympathetic to human rights, "optimistic" in the old-fashioned democratic tradition. It is a relief and a pleasure to meet this again amidst all our current modes of neoreligious and neomystical thought.

The tone of the narrative lies about halfway between the professional debunkers of our history and the patriots. Mr. Burlingame has reservations, for example, about Tawney's thesis of the protestant ethics and the rise of capitalism; and yet he traces very clearly the influence of the first tobacco plantations on Southern religion. The Church of England had a hard time with the new Southern gentry. So, too, in the "Great Awakening" of the 1740's —and the campfire revivals of the Western frontier with their throbbing and shaking "converts"—Mr. Burlingame plays down the obvious sexual element; just as in general he prefers the nobility of the deist conception of man to the Calvinist stress on sin, and the Methodist path of redemption.

The great state documents of the young Republic *did* present a lofty vision of man's fate in the new world, and their influence elevates us today. But along the way, with a quiet irony, the narrative also stresses the seamy side of our noblest moral illusions; and perhaps this is the real flavor and spice of the book. The Bible State of New England grew rich on the rum trade and the slave trade even while it was debating whether "God casts the line of Election in the loins of godly parents." There is another fine section in the book which traces the true history of Old New York. From the start the Dutch and English merchants, whose greed operated under well-oiled official protection, and cared neither for religious nor civic values, created the Nineveh-on-the-Hudson.

"Throughout the American story when the public conscience has been confused, conscienceless men have had their most fruitful seasons." This is Mr. Burlingame's quiet verdict on the revolutionary epoch which set the stage for our subsequent moral battles. The Northwest Ordinance of 1787 evolved from another period of "greed, jealousy, political chicanery, and lawlessness." Hardly was the nation created when there came the first of the land-grant scandals which accompanied the growth of the young Republic. Some of our modern Washington lobbyists, staking their claims in what is left of the public domain, could learn a few tricks from the enterprising and precocious Connecticut minister, Manasseh Cutler, and his Ohio company. Private Enterprise did indeed create the new nation—plus large government subsidies.

The immense wealth of the American continent was the devil's trap for the American conscience. Despite Mr. Burlingame's faith, there are moments, sometimes years, in the national chronicle when we wonder if Calvin's low view of man wasn't the only true view. If to be human means only to be sinful, then perhaps our extraordinary cultural proscriptions on sexual pleasure can be viewed as a sort of national penance for the manifold delights of avarice. Yet the present narrative also stresses the story of Roger Williams, of the Quaker martyr Anne Hutchinson, of Washington, Franklin, and Jefferson, of the Dutch and German pietists who followed William Penn, of the crucial and agonizing antislavery struggle.

In the Mexican War and the conquest of Texas, the New England writers articulated the true voice of the national conscience. (Although it was the enraged and apopleptic "mercantile conscience" of New England which advocated secession from the union during the Jeffersonian Embargo Acts.) And in the grand sell-out of the Robber Baron period, which marked the close of the Bible State in our history, and the origins of a new American empire, pagan and materialistic rather than religious and ethical, there were still the "wild men," the fanatics and visionaries of the populist and agrarian causes. Indeed it was the "atheists," the radicals, the immigrant dreamers of social justice in the late nineteenth century, who mainly inherited and preserved our true cultural heritage.

The old ancestral line of the Republic—a Henry Adams, a Henry James, an Edith Wharton—retreated from the vulgar and violent spectacle of American life near the turn of the century. But such an old-fashioned native American writer as William Dean Howells (to add a literary superstructure to Mr. Burlingame's social chronicle) joined the radical currents of social protest, where Walt Whitman had preceded him, and where a Theodore Dreiser would follow him. Through such figures as these, the Progressive Movement of the 1900's can be traced back to the Transcendentalists and forward to the New Deal itself. And it is just this central tradition of American conscience and belief that has been almost blacked out of the national consciousness today.

It is another odd historical situation where our intellectuals have somehow combined with the advertising sloganeers and the chambers of commerce to disparage or deny the peculiarly American social, moral and artistic achievements of the twentieth century. But as *The American Conscience* also shows, much the same reversionary trend occurred in our country during the crisis of the French Revolution. The ill-starred course of the Russian Revolution in our own day, the specter of the police state with all its cruelty, tyranny, and barbarism, accounts for the present paralysis of American thought. The virtue of Mr. Burlingame's book is that it affords us this perspective, among many others; while this latest historian of our moral fiber also reminds us of our deepest native heritage.

Perhaps, as was said during the Depression years, things aren't as bad as they seem today—they couldn't be.

From the *Nation*, April 27, 1957.

THE AGE OF WOUK

Marjorie Morningstar *

THE NOVELS of Herman Wouk lie in a curious realm between art and entertainment. We have had a tradition of similar works from William Dean Howells to John P. Marquand, but few of these writers have been able to break through the formulas which have brought them popular success. It is more than a matter of money or prestige; it is a question of the writer's whole approach to experience, which wavers uneasily between his own convictions and the opinions which will soothe or delight his audience. These writers always seem to know more than they say, to feel more than they can express, and their typical literary form is irony.

Mr. Wouk takes pleasure in setting up a series of illusions that demonstrate his talent and perplex our minds. The central masculine figure in this new novel † by the Pulitzer Prize-winning author of *The Caine Mutiny* is a frustrated artist who espouses a philosophy of "hits," or of extroverted egotism, as the driving force of life. Though Mr. Wouk is sardonic about his hero, there is a certain ambiguity of focus about the novel as a whole and we are never sure whether it is a romance or a satire.

* There has been some comment on the "friendly tone" of the *New York Times* review of the novel, and the polemical spirit of the *Nation* article which follows it. There is a change of tone, of course, but just how "friendly" is the review—except to those who did not bother to read it? The real point is that the second article was written in response to the *Time-Life* version of our literature at the mid-century, which used and perhaps abused even Mr. Wouk's yearning for authority and conformity, as is made clear in the article.

† *Marjorie Morningstar.*

38

The heroine is a young New York Jewish girl, Marjorie Morgenstern, who decides to be an actress, and picks an appropriate
American name. Marjorie's talents are small, she never pursues
her career very seriously, and the point of the novel is something
else altogether.

What the story conveys, and often quite brilliantly, is the tragicomic meeting of traditional Jewish culture and the American
success myth. The children of the immigrants abandon the best
part of their heritage in order to take on the worst aspects of
their new environment, and Mr. Wouk has a sharp eye in describing their antics. There is a bar mitzvah scene very early in the
novel, where Marjorie's poor Bronx relatives meet the prosperous
West Side Jewish families whose ranks she aspires to join.
"What's burning in that copper pot, I wonder," says one of these
figures. "Money," says another. The miracles of Lowenstein the
caterer have replaced the presence of God.

The larger problem is of course the denigration of all immigrant culture by a society that marks its children only with the
stamp of material success, and that, historically, gave up its
own religious orientation somewhere around 1870. Marjorie is
ashamed of her grasping, ambitious mother, her hardworking but
uneducated father. To a certain degree she breaks away from
the milieu of her youth where the size of the engagement ring
determines the caliber of the bridegroom. She spends a period of
her theatrical apprenticeship at a typical summer camp called
South Wind and there she meets Noel Airman, another displaced
Jewish conscience, who wants to be a Broadway playwright.

He is a shining apparition of the artistic life to a sheltered
young girl, and he becomes Marjorie's great romance. (He is
actually a volatile and disorganized Bohemian who ends up quite
correctly as a television writer.) Their anguished and tormented
and rather adolescent love affair occupies a large part of this
large novel, but during the course of this adventure Marjorie
meets various other flamboyant and shady characters in the
motion-picture and theatrical world.

Some of these minor portraits in the novel, like the disreputable
Broadway producer, Guy Flamm, or the cynical Sam Rothmore
of Paramount, or the witless and wolfish actor, Voen, are very
well done, too. But the entertainment industry is both worse and
better than this; and what Mr. Wouk is trying to establish, I

think, is that his heroine's sentimental education is both typical of her culture and wrong. Marjorie finally marries a prosperous lawyer, settles down, and has children in a little Westchester town and becomes a pillar of the community.

The young writer in the tale, Wally Wronken, who has always adored Marjorie from afar, finds her at last serene, matronly, and dull. "You couldn't write a play about her that would run a week, or a novel that would sell a thousand copies. There's no angle." I would guess that Mr. Wouk's novel will sell much more than a thousand copies; and what it lacks is not an angle but a center.

In the juxtaposition of old and new forms of Jewish culture, one misses the real warmth, wisdom, and humor of an ancient folk tradition whose transient resting place was the Bronx or Brooklyn. Mr. Wouk's Old World figures are stagy and contrived; he is more at home with their American descendants. And why should that narrow, complacent, comfort-loving world of commercial success, which Mr. Wouk satirizes so brilliantly at the start of the novel, become at the end the only possible horizon for his heroine?

If this is the story of a false emancipation, it is also that of a sterile compliance; and one has the impression that the author refuses to see the alternatives. The world of art or of intellect, for example—or even the profession of acting, which Marjorie abandons without a qualm—is not inhabited completely by the disorganized talents and aesthetic frauds that the novel describes. And even in Westchester, is there no other course for Mr. Wouk's heroine except a total social conformity?

The problem of revolt and authority has preoccupied Mr. Wouk in the past. But here as in *The Caine Mutiny* it is settled by a final bow to the red tape of a bureaucracy or to the proprieties of a social class, under the impression that these are among the eternal verities. *Marjorie Morningstar* is very good reading indeed. But to this reviewer at least, the values of true culture are as remote from its polished orbit as are, at base, the impulses of real life.

From the *New York Times*, September 4, 1955.

Time, Life, and Art

Time magazine featured "novelist Herman Wouk" on its September 5 cover. The book column carried a large and laudatory article on the author of *The Caine Mutiny* and the current bestseller, *Marjorie Morningstar*. A week later *Life* magazine featured both Herman Wouk and Sloan Wilson, author of another bestseller, *The Man in the Gray Flannel Suit*. The September 12 *Life* editorial was devoted to the subject of the American novel. Such cultural enthusiasm is unusual in the Luce publications, it is even somewhat alarming, as when a banker endows a college; so let us try to see what it means.

The *Time* article was an incredible affair even for a magazine whose policy has always been to denigrate serious books and to elevate the mediocre. Mr. Wouk's new novel was a mutiny against "three decades of U. S. fiction dominated by skeptical criticism, sexual emancipation, social protest, and psychoanalytic sermonizing." I am not sure what the last item means, but if *Time* was referring to the tradition of social protest in American fiction, it dates back at least to 1880, or about seven decades. It includes Walt Whitman, who was for sex, and William Dean Howells, who was against sex, and practically every major American novelist since then. If Mr. Wouk is really leading a mutiny against this tradition, he is going to have his hands full.

Yet there is a curious and vital connection between sexual inhibition and social conformity that the editors of *Time* have found out, and Mr. Wouk is a perfect example of their thesis. He becomes indeed in their glowing eulogy the House Author of the American Way at the middle of the twentieth century. First of all, he is rich; no more starving artists with ragged clothes and irresponsible thoughts. No more Emerson or Melville or Hawthorne, even, who was fired from his customhouse post, and had subversive ideas about the Puritans. The modern American novelist can look the American industrialist straight in the eye; in fact, if he is like Wouk, he is an industry by himself. Even lesser authors like Hemingway and Faulkner have not done so badly in a financial way lately, though *Time* does not list the current value of their enterprises as it does for Mr. Wouk.

And he also, as we discover, has spiritual or hidden assets. He comes from Russian immigrant stock and is a devout Orthodox Jew "who has achieved worldly success in worldlywise Manhattan while adhering to dietary prohibitions and traditional rituals which many of his fellow Jews find embarrassing." *Time* is more at home in this murky element, which carries the latent threat under the guise of paternal blessing. As a descendant of the same tradition myself, and with great respect for its true achievements, I find this passage not only embarrassing but vulgar. After all, Moses did not offer his people the choice between eating the Golden Calf or worshiping it. And now the *Time* article comes to the point. Although Mr. Wouk is a highly sensitive member of a religious minority, "he is one of the few living U. S. writers who carries no chip on his shoulder and who gives the U. S. straight A's in his fictional report cards."

Thus the Luce organization has redefined the meaning of the Jewish tradition in the New World (to make money) and the meaning of American literature itself (to write good report cards). *The Caine Mutiny* did just this, we are told, by affirming Mr. Wouk's belief "in 1) decency—in language as well as deeds, 2) honor, 3) discipline, 4) authority, 5) hallowed institutions like the U. S. Navy." Remember that I am quoting, and there is even more: "In *Marjorie Morningstar,* Wouk will set more teeth on edge by advocating chastity before marriage, suggesting that real happiness for a woman is found in a home and children, cheering loud and long for the American middle classes, and blasting Bohemia and Bohemians. Wouk is a Sinclair Lewis in reverse." And indeed, then, he is, for even Lewis never quite reached this unhappy ebb in his later novels.

Yet Mr. Wouk too must have shuddered and recoiled a little when he read this blunt summary of his aims; and I am treating him here as a symbolic figure. As a human being, as fellow-artist, he is being victimized as much by *Time*'s praise as other writers have been by *Time*'s malice. For even the Luce editorialist must have had his tongue in cheek when penning this *gemütlich* version of God, fatherland, family, and our leaders right or wrong. What about other hallowed institutions like the United States Army —or the Marines? What a howl must have gone up in the publicity offices of the Pentagon! More seriously, I submit that most serious writers do have an inherent belief in decency and honor. But it is just this belief that so often has made them rebel against empty discipline and blind, dangerous, or evil authority. Even Thomas Mann's *Felix Krull* thought it was a great triumph when he cheated the Prussian army out of his rogue's body.

Incidentally, while *Marjorie Morningstar* does advocate an odd kind of semichastity, it also describes the most prolonged necking bout in recent literary history. By the time of marriage there is probably no need for sexual activity. As for the American middle class which, for example, William Dean Howells believed to have been corrupted by the plutocratic spirit in the 1900's, and which *Time* is now inculcating with such alien ideas, I still think it has that last atavistic democratic trait—a sense of humor. At least the *Life* editorial on the American novel was on a higher plane, and took a more generalized line. It did quote the man behind *The Man in the Gray Flannel Suit*. "The world's treated me awfully well," said Sloan Wilson, "and I guess it's crept into my work." Yes, that, and a brilliant advertising campaign that also pushed the book, and created what we may call a "well-packaged novel."

Shades of Henry James, and of Theodore Dreiser—both of whom the world treated rather badly. But *Life* is still not quite satisfied with either Wilson or Wouk or even Lionel Shapiro's *The Sixth of June* which, though it revolves about a triangle, "is not resolved by adultery." This is only a beginning, apparently; what is the real trouble? "Ours is the most powerful nation in the world. It has had a decade of unparalleled prosperity. It has gone further than any other society toward creating a classless society." Yet after all this, says *Life,* our literature still sounds "as if it were written by an unemployed homosexual living in a packing-box shanty on the city dump." Our writers can't forget the depression, or they are "obscenity-obsessed," as in the recent parade of war novels, or they lack spiritual purpose—"the unquenchable reaching of man's soul for a truth higher than reality."

Logically, I don't know what can be made of this hodgepodge
of half-truths. There is also the little matter of the atomic bomb;
but when, asks *Life,* was life ever secure? "Atomic fear or not,
the incredible accomplishments of our day are surely the raw
stuff of saga." Yes, they are, and one would welcome a new
generation of novelists who would look into such things as
McCarthyism, or the white-collar equivalent of Nixonism, or the
loyalty oaths and security dismissals, or the large-size looting of
our natural resources, or the marriages of the corporations, and
the rise of the stock market while small business and farming de-
clines; or the hostility of Asia and the alienation of Europe while
our public mind is both intimidated and dazzled by a series of
shifting advertising slogans. "Who speaks for America today?"
Life asks, and I am afraid that the United States of America
speaks for itself.

Our writers do indeed lack a spiritual purpose, which in former
generations was accompanied by a broad social base; and the
present stress of our most gifted talents on private studies of
pathology is also symptomatic of the larger, the national disease.

What is clear, however, is that both *Time* and *Life* are laying
down a program for a new slap-happy optimism mingled with a
proper respect for whatever exists and a species of domestic
drama that will avoid all bad language and all serious human
issues. We are back again to that "smiling side of life" which the
Victorians believed to be the true American side, though we have
been through a sewer of corruption since then, and are now sitting on top of a volcano. This new literature will be based on the
principle of "Woukism." The object will be to persuade millions
of people that they are completely different from all the other
people whom they are exactly like. "Peace, Prosperity, and
Propaganda" will be the grand theme of the new literature, and
all deviants from the norm, whether biological or aesthetic or
ethnic, will be tolerated so long as they do what they are told.

In the Age of Wouk, the new writing will certainly have the
impulse of revolt, but not the act; just as Marjorie Morgenstern
—the "American Everygirl," as we are told—must first rebel
against her environment in order properly to conform to it.
There will be a little, or quite a lot of sex, so long as it is never
fulfilled and has no meaning. There will be the usual periods of

doubt, heart-searching, and despair in the lives of these new folk figures of the American Way—in order to have a happy ending. Marjorie will always marry the man in the gray flannel suit in the typical configuration of the classless—and mindless—society. Well, what does it all really mean? I suspect that the final impact of the atomic age has had the effect of a lobotomy upon the national spirit. Don't look now, but we're all dead.

From the *Nation*, November 5, 1955.

Part Two: AMERICANS AND MODERNS

THEODORE DREISER

THEODORE DREISER'S first novel, *Sister Carrie,* is a landmark in modern literature. It has had a dramatic career as a novel, and the story is still worth telling.

According to Dreiser's own account, the book was submitted to Harper and Brothers in 1900, and was refused. It was then accepted by Doubleday Page, to whom the novelist Frank Norris had recommended it with great enthusiasm. It is generally believed, however, that Mrs. Frank Doubleday, the wife of the publisher, subsequently read the manuscript and was horrified at its frankness. *Sister Carrie* was published, but no copies of the first edition were ever sold. Surely this contributed to the collapse of Dreiser's health at this period; he gave up his literary ambitions for ten years and turned to editorial work. His second novel, *Jennie Gerhardt,* was published in 1911, and it was only then that *Sister Carrie,* too, was accepted on its merits.

A decade of silence on the part of a great artist is an eloquent testimonial to the moral taboos which ruled over and constricted our literary taste at the turn of the century. Yet the hardship of Dreiser's career at the very start only served to temper and confirm his convictions about his own work. His fourth novel, *The Titan,* was again blocked from circulation by the publishers who had originally contracted to take it; one year later, in 1915, *The "Genius"* was banned and became the center of another literary storm. Moreover, some of Dreiser's close friends were alienated by his pioneer study of sexual pathology in a play called *The Hand of the Potter,* while at the height of Dreiser's popular success, in 1925, *An American Tragedy* was banned in Boston. This record, admirable to the point of being suicidal, is typical of a temperament that responded instinctively against every attempt at suppression or censorship by a still more ruthless innovation in the area of the arts.

There is little question that Theodore Dreiser is the most distinguished member of the whole group of modern American novelists. One test of a writer's value lies in the series of illusions and superstitions which surround his work like a halo or a smoke screen, and, perhaps more than most, Dreiser's novels have been obscured by a fog of errors and misconceptions. He is a fascinating and complex personality. Yet in the essay that established his literary position, the critic H. L. Mencken also declared that the Hoosier master was "elephantine, doltish, coarse, dismal, flatulent." These are practically the same words that are used to describe him today by the New Critics, while even some of Dreiser's literary disciples tend to reduce him to a solemn pioneer of realism.

He was a realist. He was opposed to the Victorian ideals of refinement and gentility, since they distorted the truth about human nature, and he wanted to cut through the dirt of our own Gilded Age, perhaps the most immoral epoch in the national history, and the most hypocritical. The great tycoons of Dreiser's youth—Jay Gould, Rockefeller, Morgan, Harriman, Yerkes—might do as they pleased with the railroads, the banks, the utilities of the nation. Sister Carrie's crime was that she was poor, innocent, and pleasure-loving.

Yes, he, partly through his own innocence, perhaps, and early origins, told the truth about life when he could discover it. Probably nobody else in our literature has had such a direct and intimate feeling for the common forms of experience, pleasant or disgraceful. But he was also, like Balzac, who is the closest European counterpart, one of the high romantics of literature.

What gave his work its remarkable texture, its glamour, really, was simply his sense of the variety and mystery of life on all its levels. From the mansions of the titans on Fifth Avenue to the vile Chicago slums, it was all a drama for him, and he makes it a drama always. It is odd, too, that such a solemn author should have been able to create the bright gallery of women in the course of his novels—from Carrie and Jennie Gerhardt and the Aileen Cowperwood of *The Financier,* who is one of Dreiser's most fascinating figures, to the Roberta Alden of *An American*

Tragedy and, in the same novel, Sondra with her dreadful baby talk.

I have mentioned the best novels during the course of this introduction. But *Dawn* and *Newspaper Days,* the first two sections of his unfinished autobiography, are remarkable volumes and should be placed along with the Cowperwood trilogy as a major work. Here are the Indiana towns of the 1880's, with their ignorant, violent, and dubious western-country types—since the Dreisers had a habit of living in questionable neighborhoods: that is, the habit of poverty. Here, too, are the series of "boarders" who often had their eye on the attractive Dreiser girls (or vice versa). Then there are the Dreiser boys, stealing, gambling, drinking, rebellious, in jail; there is brother Paul Dreiser, successful composer of "The Banks of the Wabash," far removed from this family scene.

The chronicle of Dreiser's youth contains not the slightest note of self-pity, however; what attracts and entertains us is the sparkle of his narrative. The father of this sprawling brood was a failure and a religious fanatic. The family's longest period of happiness was due to the generosity of Paul's mistress, the heroine of his song, "My Gal, Sal," and, in Dreiser's own words, "the reigning courtesan of the area." This was actually the young writer's first meeting with luxury and pleasure, and the autobiography rises to a kind of lyrical climax here.

In the second volume, *Newspaper Days,* the budding author, fresh from the corruption of municipal affairs in Chicago, the rackets of political journalism, the industrial warfare of Pittsburgh in the 1890's, surveys the field of polite American fiction (William Dean Howells, Thomas Nelson Page, Constance Fenimore Woolson) in an ironic passage:

These writers seemed far above the world of which I was a part. Indeed I began to picture them as creatures of the greatest luxury and culture, gentlemen and ladies all, possessing estates or at least bachelor quarters, having horses and carriages, and received here, there and everywhere with nods of recognition and smiles of approval.

Compared with this realm of sweetness and beauty and goodness, Dreiser concluded, he had no tales to tell. In fact, he was already brooding over the chronicle of *Sister Carrie.*

The central theme of the novel is, of course, the struggle of a young country girl, half aware of her powers, to protect herself against the "cunning wiles of the city." The time is around the Nineties, the scene is Chicago. Carrie forms an alliance with Charles Drouet, a traveling salesman, and then with George Hurstwood, a prosperous saloon keeper, who leaves his family and business in order to take Carrie to New York. The story is simple in outline, tight in structure, intense and dramatic in action. It is very different in tone from the novels by the French realists or, say, from Stephen Crane's *Maggie: A Girl of the Streets.*

Indeed, on a first reading of Dreiser's novel, which is so full of tenderness and of that brooding sense of pity which suffuses all his stories, it is difficult to understand why the book caused such a furor at the turn of the century, and was driven from publishing house to publishing house for almost ten years. Isn't it curious, too, that the readers who complained most vehemently that Carrie not only lived in sin but prospered through it, should have ignored the collapse of Hurstwood, one of the most famous episodes in the novel?

But *Sister Carrie* is not merely a literary landmark; it is a work of art, as fresh and interesting today as when it was first written. And if Dreiser cut through the moral hypocrisy of his time, he had all too firm a grasp of natural law. This poignant fable of stock characters and familiar American types is based on the oldest human passions—and such passions are in one sense always illegitimate, since to the degree that they elevate and transform a person, they may consume and destroy him. Or at least they destroy that part of him which was formerly accustomed to live without delight, and they make him unsuited for trivial things. Hurstwood, through love, becomes a thief and a beggar—

Remind not Eros of his Wings.

Perhaps that is the true "moral" of *Sister Carrie,* and it may also explain the latent taboo, even now, on Dreiser's work, or the unconscious resentment by those who wish to avoid their emotions.

For, Theodore Dreiser was above all a writer who concerned himself with the instinctual bases of life. A "varietist," as he called himself in private life, a worshiper of Ishtar and Aphrodite in his early years, he believed in accepting the human affections and impulses, good or bad, in all their power, their uncertainty, their essential tragedy. He was for the "fools of love," as against the fools of wealth or of worldly success. The ordinary people of the world will understand this, and *Sister Carrie* belongs to them. It is a memorable statement of the human condition under the most banal circumstances, and a source of the shared life which every great artist offers to his audience.

Introduction to Pocket Books edition of *Sister Carrie*, 1949.

ERNEST HEMINGWAY

At the Crossroads

THE LITERARY event of the season—whatever coming season it is—should be Ernest Hemingway's new novel. It will be published about ten years after *For Whom the Bell Tolls*. During this period, Hemingway has consolidated his position as a literary spokesman for the United States and a sort of roving Ambassador of Letters—perhaps the first native novelist to fill this role so well since the death of Mark Twain. The contrast between the rigorous discipline of Hemingway's art and the extravagance of his personality has already been pointed out; it is useful to remind ourselves that he is still considered to be the greatest living American writer.

Hemingway's entertaining and elusive accent of provincial innocence stems back to the dead-pan humor of the frontier; the description of writing in terms of professional athletics is a familiar pose of this muscular aesthete, who has, however, always searched for extreme emotional states in acts of physical tension.*

This is a good time to evaluate Hemingway's position in terms of his own period and literary tradition. He has influenced his generation more deeply perhaps than any other American artist, and he has already established, despite certain obvious limitations, a durable and celebrated body of work.

* The *New York Times* submitted this article to Hemingway for his comments. The Old Master, returning home on a freighter in a rough sea, delivered a bit of prose which disclaimed any knowledge of criticism or critics. More recently his answer to adverse criticism has been an offer to take on the offending critic in a duel, a boxing match, or any other bout of physical prowess. Which doesn't really settle the issue.

A doctor's son, born in Oak Park, Illinois, in 1898, a young newspaper reporter for the *Kansas City Star,* he very early announced his verdict on the commercial revolution in the United States which had already, in the 1920's, begun to transform a society of independent farmers and businessmen into a nation of salesmen. He chose instead the Indians and the Michigan woods —the idyllic scenes of his first book of stories, *In Our Time* (1925), that are contrasted so sharply with scenes from the First World War.

In a sense Hemingway's milieu is war; he was fortunate to have lived in an epoch whose stages of destruction correspond so closely to his inner needs. In a variety of later stories and novels he made the theme his own, and became the chronicler of a civilization that was tearing itself apart.

For even his early sketches of adolescence, so light in texture and lyrical in tone, are haunted and secretive in emotion. The love story in *A Farewell to Arms,* which established Hemingway's popular reputation, is set against a background of social disintegration, of human suffering which led to the Italian defeat at Caporetto. Pleasure and pain are even more constantly related in *The Sun Also Rises,* and as intimately joined. And just as in Freud's poetic thesis, the will to suffer seems more firmly rooted in the biological processes of the main characters than the impulse of delight.

Yet the story of Jake and Lady Brett Ashley, these modern lovers who continuously nourish the passion that is denied to them, became a prototypical alliance of the postwar period—the model for an entire group of gifted and despairing souls who revealed their disenchantment in the vain hope that perhaps they, too, would sound like Hemingway's people. But vainly, for it was only in a novel that a Lost Generation could feel its plight with such intensity and live it out with such magnificence.

The postwar generation in Hemingway's work was frustrated with an intense and cunning purpose, with an almost diabolical sense of disillusionment that was very different, say, from the Jazz Age characters of Scott Fitzgerald's stories. Some of the later writers, particularly Thomas Wolfe, began to question whether there ever had been a Lost Generation in fact, and turned the phrase in a new direction—toward the industrialists of the 1930's. Actually, *The Sun Also Rises* did reveal the processes of a tormented and intricate imagination whose central purpose became clearer in the years that followed.

This was the period—between 1927 and 1937—of *Death in the Afternoon* and *The Green Hills of Africa,* both of them valuable and illuminating books, though marred by an uneven and sometimes callow tone. It was the period of that "separate peace" first announced by Nick of *In Our Time,* of Hemingway's refusal to serve time "for society, democracy and the other things." It was the occasion for his farewell to the States. It was no use to pretend that a country that was finished was still good, he said; and he had renounced the smells of peace as well as the "comforting stench" of comrades in war.

Yet, as it turned out, this was also the period of his great dark stories—his best stories of dissolution and destruction. By 1933 he had published four volumes of tales; the best of them, now collected in *The Fifth Column and the First Forty-nine Stories,* are surely a permanent contribution to literature.

Almost all of them, the good ones, are tales of suffering without catharsis, of the opiate that fails, of the drugged consciousness that remains sensitive only to pain. In "The Gambler, the Nun, and the Radio," the Hemingway hero avoids thinking "except when he was writing." Here, too, is the statement that bread is the opium of the people. In "A Clean, Well-Lighted Place," the waiter in the Spanish café understands all those who do not want to go to bed, who need a light for the night. "What did he fear? It was not fear or dread. It was a nothing that he knew too well. It was all a nothing and a man was nothing too. It was only that and light was all it needed and a certain cleanness and order." "The Short Happy Life of Francis Macomber" is perhaps the best aesthetic development of this theme, while "The Snows of Kilimanjaro" is a remarkable reverie of guilt and punishment.

It is here that Hemingway emerges most clearly as the artist of disaster, the poet of catastrophe, the natural historian of the organism that seeks only to die in its own way. Earlier, in "A Pursuit Race," the manager of the burlesque troupe has told the central figure of the story that they had a cure for dope addicts. " 'No,' William Campbell said, 'they haven't got a cure for anything.' "

In this connection we might also remember Freud's statement,

written when the mass neurosis of fascism was beginning to
sweep over the European world, that life as it is imposed on us
"is too hard for us, too full of pain, disillusionments and impossible tasks. In order to bear it, we cannot do without palliatives."
The cultural background of Hemingway's work between the wars
is obvious, and Edmund Wilson has pointed out the sensitivity of
this artist as a gauge of social morale. At the utmost point of his
isolation, indeed, Hemingway seemed closest to the temper of the
times. It was only when he "came back home," in the novel called
To Have and Have Not, in 1937, that certain limitations of his
work became apparent.

For surely a central theme in Herman Melville's work—the
"horrible vulturism of earth"—is a dominant subject of Hemingway's, while Theodore Dreiser, again, was concerned very deeply
with primitive impulses and affections. Yet both of the older
writers include a broad basis of "realism" in their work, and
sometimes even deal with the raw materials of social and economic processes. What attracts us in Hemingway's writing is the
intensity and complexity of emotional experience; what we miss
is a sense of that "ordinary" life, in all its variety and mystery,
that had always been the core of the great novels, at least.

The central dramatic situation in Hemingway's work is usually
that of "grace under pressure"—and the trap is usually closing.
One sometimes has the notion that Hemingway would hardly be
interested in his characters if they were not in a trap, and when,
as in *To Have and Have Not,* the pressure has been removed
from their lives, even temporarily, they lose much of their vitality.

To a certain degree, however, this mood was characteristic of
that entire, famous Younger Generation of World War I, including Scott Fitzgerald, William Faulkner, and sometimes even such
older and transitional figures as Sinclair Lewis. Perhaps Hemingway's early satire, *The Torrents of Spring,* takes on more significance in this respect. For it marked the separation of the
postwar generation of writers not merely from their literary
ancestors, such as Dreiser and Sherwood Anderson, but from the
dominant social forces and cultural patterns of American life as
a whole. And probably the real price that the Younger Generation paid for a sense of absolute freedom was revealed in their
delayed search for values which the older writers had taken for
granted and had assimilated in both their lives and their craft.

The pattern is familiar in Fitzgerald's work and we may see it in Sinclair Lewis' attempt to idealize the chronicle of Babbitt, or in the collapse of John Dos Passos' literary achievement with the collapse of his belief in the Marxist revolution, or in William Faulkner's reversion to a sentimental, not to say chauvinistic, Southern romanticism. In Hemingway's case we may notice the facile enthusiasm of his political play, *The Fifth Column,* in 1938, and the more theatrical sections of *For Whom the Bell Tolls*— another social "crusade," incidentally, that takes on trappings of self-immolation.

Yet there are superb sections of writing in his story of the Spanish Civil War, and many of the battle scenes are the best things that Hemingway has done. It was clear almost from the start that he was essentially not a realist at all, but a "nocturnal" artist, as Malcolm Cowley has described him, and the danger of the narrow framework of Hemingway's art is simply that it may not sustain his narrative of the darker elements in human nature.

His work as a whole has been a sort of literary catalyst which has affected the entire course of American writing, and like a catalyst it has remained untouched by and superior to all the imitations of it. Such writers as Dashiell Hammett, James Cain, and the entire hard-boiled school of American novelists stem from Hemingway's work. Among the new writers there are talents as varied as Ira Wolfert, and Norman Mailer who show his influence.

Yet there is no young writer who as yet measures up to his standards; and indeed the young writers should not try. Hemingway's prose line—that simple, flat declarative sentence to which he has imparted so many enigmatic and disturbing overtones— is the perfection of a tradition that originated in Thoreau and Mark Twain. And there is no member of that now all too sedate Younger Generation of World War I whose work we can, at the present time, look forward to with the same measure of anxiety and hope.

From the *New York Times,* July 31, 1949.

A Year Later

Across the River and into the Trees is an unfortunate novel and unpleasant to review for anyone who respects Hemingway's talent and achievement. It is not only Hemingway's worst novel; it is a synthesis of everything that is bad in his previous work and it throws a doubtful light on the future.

It is so dreadful, in fact, that it begins to have its own morbid fascination and is almost impossible, as they say, to put down. The story concerns an American officer, a professional soldier, in Italy. He has a bad heart and is about to die. He is in love with an Italian countess whom he calls Daughter. But Colonel Richard Cantwell is a caricature of such figures as the Lieutenant Henry of *A Farewell to Arms* or the Jake of *The Sun Also Rises*. The love story is a "romance" and written mainly in what I can only describe as Indian prose: "They stood there and kissed each other true."

The sex is oral and anatomical mainly; the passion, so far as I can see, is purely verbal. There is not one scene of genuine feeling; what is even more curious on the part of the artist who could understand Lady Brett or Catherine Barkley is the heroine's complete lack of sensuousness or feminine perception. She is a fantasy of the completely docile, pliant child-bride and is useful in the novel merely as interlocutor for the Colonel's overwhelming narcissism. Petting her, the Colonel reflects that he is assisting "at the only mystery that he believed in except the occasional bravery of man." But the true mystery of *Across the River and into the Trees* is Hemingway's concept of love.

Although the dialogue has become so stylized that it is impossible to carry on a serious conversation, the Colonel also offers us (usually in bed) a set of opinions about modern life which may be summarized as follows. The GI's are all "sad Americans," while their commanding officers are politicians and frauds. The only professional soldiers were the Germans. The United States is now "governed in some way, by the dregs," including an amateur pianist and unsuccessful haberdasher. But the French are even worse, mainly jerks. Everybody who has written about the last war to date is either a journalist or a jerk. Etc. In a moment of insight the Colonel does describe himself as "the unjust bitter criticizer who speaks badly of everyone," and this is indeed a disappointed and distasteful point of view.

What is even more distressing than the articulation of this morbid and infantile egotism (the Colonel has a habit of referring to himself as a good boy or a bad boy) is the implicit set of values in the novel. "The hell with anything American except me," the Colonel says, but could anything be more American than his notion of "fun" and his rigid code of behavior? The ideological background of the novel is a mixture of *True Romances,* Superman, and the Last Frontier. And the setting of the novel is a perfect instance of Veblen's conspicuous consumption. The Colonel drinks to Leclerc's death with a magnum of Perrier-Jouet Brut 1942 and knows the feeding habits of lobsters from the Dalmatian coast. His companion, the young countess, speaks casually of her butler and maid while she impulsively slips her lover the family jewels. But the Colonel moves warily from duck shoot to duck shoot and even at his favorite café, after the tourists and diplomats have gone, he is alert for plots, intrigues, sudden death, and makes sure he has both his flanks covered.

As in the case of Sinclair Lewis, the late phase of Hemingway's work—this vulgar and snobbish vision of social superiority and luxury—is essentially middle class. And yet what marks this psychological universe is precisely the lack of any sort of middle ground. Just as the Colonel's friends range from waiters to the Italian nobility, but exclude an average citizen, the only alternative to "fun" is desperation. He is himself either barbarous or kind, a good boy or a bad boy; everything is either wonderful or dreadful, and the love affair oscillates between these precarious poles of emotion. The Colonel indeed lives in fear that the "spell," such as it is, will be broken.

"Do not let anything spoil it. . . . Let's not think about anything at all." Don't speak. Don't think. This is, of course, a familiar refrain in Hemingway's work from *In Our Time* to *For Whom the Bell Tolls.* It is the motif of the great dark stories of the 1930's, and one remembers the author in "The Gambler, the Nun, and the Radio"—the writer who never permitted himself to think except when he was writing. It is in one sense the secret of

Hemingway's art because at his best he expressed so well the intuitive values of life, and because the "wound" in his work—the sense of hidden suffering and of shared anguish—was actually what gave it the complex, ambiguous, rich tone.

But all that is left here is the scab and the pus, as it were, of the true insights. The suffering and anguish are a mark of superiority, not of human communion; the double identification in Hemingway's best work with both the hunter and the hunted has been resolved into the code of the snob and the killer. This is a cosmos of jerks, this is Winner Take Everything, this is to Have and to Have and to Have. There are still good things in *Across the River and into the Trees,* and it is possible that the novel will serve as an emotional release for an intricate and tormented talent, very much as *The Torrents of Spring* did in the earliest phase of Hemingway's career.

But surely this, to use his new lingo, is not the work of the man who was there. Nor did Walt Whitman's original phrase of compassion—"I was the man. I was there"—mean what Hemingway now means.

From the *Saturday Review,* September 9, 1950.

The Nobel Prize

Ernest Hemingway is the fifth American writer to win the Nobel Prize. The list has included Sinclair Lewis, Eugene O'Neill, Pearl Buck, and William Faulkner in previous awards. The rebels of yesterday have become the ancestors of today; and what this imposing roster of native artists really commemorates is the coming of age of American literature in the 1920's, and its status as a world literature by the end of the 1930's.

It is surely right and fitting that Ernest Hemingway, who contributed so much to his movement, should share in the honor now accorded to it. We should celebrate; yet at a moment when the recent work of the surviving members of this gifted generation has been so disappointing, perhaps we should also meditate. I imagine that Hemingway, too, has received his prize for the wrong book, and for the wrong period of his work. It is problematical today whether he will produce anything to match the best work of his past. *The Old Man and the Sea* is supposed to represent a "new development" in his craft. But I doubt if his writing can be extended beyond that area where it has been so original, so inimitable—as his present disciples in the Scandinavian countries will find out—and also, in certain respects, so unfortunately restricted.

As in the "style-making mastership" of the Nobel Prize novel, the image of the solitary individual drifting on some unfathomed Gulf Stream of time is a central one in Hemingway's work. He is essentially a poet, and a high romantic individualist, alienated from the world, and charting a dangerous course between glamour and despair. He is a poet of youth, unable to face the complexities, or even the advent, of maturity. The drab circumstances of common existence are, so to speak, suburban; what he has always sought has been the exotic. Beneath a somewhat tenuous realism that extends only from climax to climax, never from day to day, he is the chronicler of intense emotional states that are deeply felt, beautifully projected, and never quite understood.

He is an unparalleled craftsman, in short, whose work has always moved along a narrow ledge between art and absurdity. And the point is that the primary conditions of his writing have made it difficult either to sustain the mood of his best stories, or to develop from them. Even in his first book of stories, *In Our Time* (1925), the contrast between an idyllic youth in the Michigan woods and the accumulated horrors of the First World War already showed the future extremes of Hemingway's art.

These extremes were actually the center and core of his work, where all the middle ranges of experience were denied. In his first novel, *The Sun Also Rises* (1926), the gaiety of Hemingway's desperate little group of expatriates was even more extravagant, the despair was symbolized in the physical impotence of the hero. Yet Hemingway *was* gay—a quality of art that seems almost unknown to our generation of depressive novelists and solemn critics. In *A Farewell to Arms,* his first popular novel, he was warm and touching in the love affair of the deserter-hero. "You and me," Nick says to Rinaldi, "we've made a separate peace." And this separate peace actually embodied Hemingway's renunciation of both Europe and America for almost a decade; and his refusal, described in the short stories of the time, to participate even in the responsibilities of ordinary human relationships.

Can one reach the bottom of this chasm of withdrawal from life and still return to the surface unchanged? In the 1930's Hemingway drifted uneasily from his big-game hunting in Africa to the bullfights of Madrid, wherever death could be seen and felt at close quarters: wherever life was quick and doomed. Like Stephen Crane, whose influence he showed, along with that of Thoreau and Mark Twain in his prose style, he was obsessed by destruction. When it did not exist before him, in a death-ridden social epoch, he sought it out. And, like Crane, he did not want to understand either the social forces that were moving his period to these mass festivals of slaughter or the psychological sources of the morbid fascination within himself. Reason and intellect, as pursued by the social realists of war such as Tolstoi—this is something that Hemingway has always scorned, and perhaps feared.

But he was in full control of his own talent during these years. The great short stories of his "dark period" which are collected in *The Fifth Column and the First Forty-nine Stories* are the core of Hemingway's lasting work, his bid for immortality, and the true basis of the Nobel Prize award. When he returned to the American scene again, briefly, in *To Have and Have Not* (1937) his talent already showed signs of deterioration. And when he moved onto the best-seller list with his big novel of the Spanish Civil War, *For Whom the Bell Tolls,* he paid the price for his complete indifference to social and political affairs.

The Spanish War was suddenly a "crusade" for Hemingway— that odd American word which substitutes moral fervor for intelligence. But the best portraits in the novel were still those of punchdrunk anarchists and rebels; the hero was another solitary and self-destructive romantic individualist; the central love affair was impossible, except for Hollywood. I think we will do well to forget Hemingway's press interviews and magazine articles during the last ten years, and his public role as an American sage. One might point to Walt Whitman's late years as a better example for our young writers; but history forgives much of an artist who has already changed the course of history. *Across the River and into the Trees* recorded the worst side of the late Hemingway. *The Old Man and the Sea* was in part, at least, a return to the heroism of the solitary individual, set against a hostile universe, which Hemingway has always celebrated.

That this universe is also blind, or that Hemingway is blind to it, is the defect of this writer's singular virtues. Like Scott Fitzgerald, like T. S. Eliot, and so many other typical figures of the American Twenties, Hemingway is also a Prospero of the mood story. When the magician's wand is broken, when we have escaped from the spell of the poetry itself, perhaps the area of Hemingway's fiction does seem more like an enchanted island than a complete world. If we set him against the perspective of the generation of social realists who preceded him and opened up his way, from Jack London to Theodore Dreiser, his work shows what has gone out of modern American prose, as well as what he has distinctively brought to it. Perhaps he has omitted too much in order to gain that crystal clarity, that ambiguous simplicity, that permanent luster of his best short stories. But what is there nobody can deny; and literature will preserve it.

From the *Saturday Review*, November 13, 1954.

JOHN DOS PASSOS

The *U.S.A.* Trilogy

IN THE 1920's, a galaxy of new stars appeared in the firmament of American letters. Foremost among the writers of the period, John Dos Passos carried on the traditions of social criticism which had marked the origins of our modern realism in the 1900's, and almost alone he felt the perspectives of history and of culture.

For that reason his work seems better today than that of some of his contemporaries when the great figures of the postwar epoch have run their fiery and narrow course, and when the glow of a brilliant period has turned to embers.

But the *U.S.A.* trilogy does hold up. *The 42nd Parallel. 1919. The Big Money.* These three books are still the most striking example of the panoramic novel that we have. Their purpose is the study of American society—the whole nation—during the first quarter of the twentieth century. First the Newsreels establish the climate of opinion; they are an entertaining record of political and historical events, popular songs, scandals, crimes—the jumbled chronicle of humanity at work. As the new century dawns in the age of empire, a certain General Miles falls off his horse, the city officials know nothing of vice, President McKinley is in his office, the Gaiety Girls are mobbed in New Jersey and

There's been many a good man murdered in the Philippines
Lies sleeping in some lonesome grave.

Thus the opening of *The 42nd Parallel.* The second of the technical innovations which marked these novels—the Camera

65

Eye—is the subjective study of a literary figure usually identified
with the author himself and presenting his views in the reveries
of a poetic prose. Between the complete objectivity of the newspaper headlines and this broken, submerged, interior monologue
are, then, the Biographies. These brief portraits of outstanding
figures in our society run from Eugene Debs—

While there is a lower class I am of it, while there is a criminal
class I am of it, while there is a soul in prison I am not free

—to Fighting Bob La Follette in *The 42nd Parallel:*

This was the tenyears war that left Wisconsin the model state where
the voters, orderloving Germans and Finns, Scandinavians fond of
their own opinion, learned to use the new leverage, direct primaries,
referendum and recall.

And they are among the best achievements in the book.

Lastly, in the whole complex of "separate features"—which
are combined and brought together with an admirable virtuosity
so that the separate strands in the narrative continually cross and
recross each other, meet and part—are the Novels. They are
fictional studies, five of them in the first book of the trilogy, of
typical American lives which Dos Passos viewed as the product,
rather more than the cause, of the cultural framework which he
described around them.

One notices that these fictional lives work up from the lower
orders of society in the story of Fainy McCreary ("Mac") to
the brilliant portrait of J. Ward Moorehouse as the embodiment
of the highest form of success in the United States. He is a Public
Relations Counsel. In the story of Eleanor Stoddard, who becomes Moorehouse's friend and feminine consort, Dos Passos
showed his early gift, too, as a satirist of the upper classes, while
the portraits of working-class people—the ostensible protagonists
—are usually weaker. But all the fictional characters are perhaps
a little more convincing as appearance rather than reality—or as
documentaries rather than true human destinies. And one realizes
that their human relationships are, as it were, only the accidental
contact of drifting and isolated atoms.

That is typical of Dos Passos's work both before and after the
U.S.A. trilogy, and perhaps it was an indication of the personal

responses in the writer which contributed to his acrid and despairing view of life in America. Yet in the whole trilogy, *The 42nd Parallel* is the opening book: the book of youth, the book of beginnings. It describes both the start of the American century and the opening phases of the fictional characters who will continue to move throughout the entire story.

In this sense, it is the freshest and least desperate of the three books. Moreover, Dos Passos is always at his most sensitive and lyrical point in episodes of childhood—possibly his characters are betrayed by maturity quite as much as by a corrupt social system.

It is a genuine tribute to *The 42nd Parallel* to say that it is still "good" almost twenty years after it was written, in a decade very different from the one in which it first appeared. For we live in the revolutionary age which Jack London, before Dos Passos himself, had prophesied in *The Iron Heel:* an age of terrorism, disguise, shifting personalities, and anonymous men. In this period of cataclysmic social change, the allies of yesterday have become our mortal enemies of today, and brutal enemies our new friends, while the horrors and atrocities of the 1930's and 1940's are forgotten before the prospect of worse things lying before us.

Quite similarly with values and beliefs, we see the spectacle of writers and artists, as well as statesmen, repudiating ideas which they've cherished most dearly to this point. And they may be judged fortunate perhaps when they achieve a reversal of opinion through inner conviction rather than through pressure of those inquisitional bodies in all societies today which try to enforce conformity and rigidity of thought in an epoch of flux.

It is an unhappy time, too, for those who need absolutes or seek them desperately through the realization of a universal instability. In my view John Dos Passos has also carried to an extreme degree the rejection of his former principles. The fear of the Communist tyranny has cast its shadow over even the slightest trace of the social reforms which in the *U.S.A.* trilogy were the only vista of salvation.

But there is a little irony in the durability of art which confronts the eternal—and perhaps grateful—temporality of history. The writer could not, even though he wanted to, obliterate the

work that remains the best achievement of his career, and a
cornerstone in modern American fiction.

Introduction to Pocket Books edition
of The 42nd Parallel, 1952.

Although history doesn't watch the calendar, the year 1919 was
a breaking point in American life. It marked the end of an epoch
of social reform which had sprung from the populist and progressive movement at the turn of the century. It opened a decade of
social anarchy under the mask of "normalcy"—of pleasure seeking and private gain, of material success and trivial moral values.

I mean the period which has been glorified as the Jazz Age.
And I know of no other modern American novel which has
summarized the ending of the earlier epoch and the beginning of
the new one better than *1919*. Though complete in itself, this is
the second volume of a major trilogy by John Dos Passos. The
first volume described the years from 1900 to the opening of the
First World War. The third volume concluded the story of a
modern nation, and the three books were given the general title
of *U.S.A.*

The underlying structure of the present book (or its organic
rhythm) is that of a universal disaster during the war years; a
brief and desperate hope, a grinding disenchantment. Thus the
first of the new technical devices which Dos Passos used, the
Newsreel, stressed the increase in economic wealth during a
period of mass suffering. *"Capitalization grown 104% while
business expands 520%."* The fertilizer industry was stimulated
by the war, we are told again. The financial world welcomed a
rebirth of the railroads while the first shells from Big Bertha were
landing in Paris; during this quaint and now archaic battle, in
which nevertheless men still died or were mutilated by the millions.

The newspaper headlines are the running historical record of
the period in which the central action of *1919* takes place. In
addition to the ironical confrontation of real values and real
estate values, one notices the increasing emphasis on crime,

strikes, and riots. GANG LEADER SLAIN IN STREET and
WELCOME HOME TO OUR HEROES and MACHINEGUNS
MOW DOWN MOBS IN KNOXVILLE. Then there is another
satiric excerpt from the popular songs of the period: "America,
I love you."

At the other end of these new techniques employed in the
novel, the sketches called the Camera Eye describe the completely subjective responses of a solitary observer, presumably
the novelist himself, during the development of the story. The
opening note is that of death on the personal level of experience.
("When the telegram came that she was dying . . . when the
cable came that He was dead.") Bereft, alone in the world, an
orphan in the drama of international conflict, the young spectator
in Dos Passos' novel faces the prospect of his own annihilation—

the winey thought of death stings in the spring blood that throbs
in the sunburned neck up and down the belly under the tight belt
hurries like cognac into the tips of my toes and the lobes of my ears
and my fingers stroking the fuzzy closecropped skull

shyly tingling fingers feel out the limits of the hard immortal skull
under the flesh. . . .

And he searches for some desperate alternative to the universal
tragedy. *"No—there must be some way. . . . If you hit the
words Democracy will understand."*
Following his adventures in the war we see also the birth of a
short-lived revolutionary idealism. "We'll make everything new
today is the Year I Today is the sunny morning of the first day
of spring." And the final bitter comment in the last words of the
last Camera Eye on the casuals of the war. "KEEP OUR BOYS
FIT for whatthehell the war's over scrap."
Similarly, the Biographies in *1919*—probably the best of the
technical innovations which Dos Passos used to extend the range
of the novel form—record an antiphony of hope and despair in
this drama of historical tensions. They open with the portraits of
Jack Reed and Randolph Bourne, typical intellectuals of the
epoch, who are set against the famous profile of the House of
Morgan, the caustic if inadequate satire of "Meester Veelson."
The key to these studies, and to the central perspective of the
book, is in the biography of the less-known journalist Paxton

Hibben, the Hoosier Quixote. "Thinking men were worried in
the middle west in the years Hibben was growing up there, something was wrong with the American Republic." After the war,
when Captain Paxton Hibben's classmates at a Princeton reunion
pretended to lynch him for being a radical (a college-boy prank
twenty years too late), the novelist added: "No more place in
America for change, no more place for the old gags: social justice, progressivism, revolt against oppression, democracy; put the
reds on the skids."

Prophetic words which reach us now from a book written
twenty years ago! Perhaps foremost among the whole cluster of
famous poets, critics, fiction writers of Dos Passos' own period,
he knew the historical background of the change of social temper
in the 1920's—even if he also assumed that what was transient
was permanent, and saw only one pole in the alternating forces
of American energy.

In the book, however, the mutilation of the lumberjack leader
Wesley Everest ("Paul Bunyan") by a group of local patriots
confirmed the novelist's darkest fears. The Biography of the
unknown soldier who was buried at Arlington ("The Body of An
American") sounded taps for the hope and eloquence of the
democratic dream. And it is in terms of the multidimensional
structure of *1919,* and of this acrid historical perspective, that
we should read the Novels. They are the fictional lives that were
at the center of the old-fashioned novel and are now viewed as
only one facet of what is really the life of a nation.

The Johnny Moorehouse of *The 42nd Parallel*—an ambitious
and slippery publicity man in the first volume of the trilogy—has
become Major Moorehouse, the "key to the key men" who were
drafting the Versailles treaty. Joe Williams, the unhappy sailor,
has gone steadily downhill, while his sister Janey has inched her
way upward to become Moorehouse's secretary. (I mention these
figures to clarify the action in the present novel.) Eleanor
Stoddard is now Moorehouse's social mentor and "platonic"
friend. The contrast between the misery of the European scene
at the close of the war and the slick, velvety upper world of power
politics is at the center of the fictional portraits.

In the panoramic novel there is no longer a single hero or
heroine. But two new figures, Dick Savage and Eveline Hutchins,

come to dominate the scene in *1919.* Their aspiration is to reach the arcanum of political and financial affairs. To Eveline, Major Moorehouse is "sincere and appealing"; she is stirred in spite of herself by his patriotic salesmanship. The whole mediocrity of her character and her struggle is illuminated by this observation, and by her own moment of revelation. "Oh, I lead such a silly life." As in so many of Dos Passos' portraits, the cozy idyl of childhood draws into a maturity that is ignoble and tedious.

But the most serious weakness of the Novels is in this area. Both Dick Savage and Eveline Hutchins are studies of a prim, tight, timid middle-class American temperament. They, like the figures whom they emulate in the "upper" circle of J. Ward Moorehouse—and by inference in the upper circles of American society—lack all the vital drives. The victims of a slow disintegration, they are hardly worthy of anything else; very much like the typical figures of Ernest Hemingway, they are people to whom things happen. There are no portraits of animal power in Dos Passos' work, as there are in Dreiser's work, for example: no studies of the passions, vices, and lusts which, if they make human character fallible, also make it memorable.

The range of temperaments in this fictional survey of our national types only extends from the mediocre to the meretricious. One notices how few elements of satisfaction there are in the lives of Dos Passos' people, how often their sexual experiences are inadequate. The brief affair between Eveline Hutchins and Moorehouse is a debacle. When Dick Savage meets "Daughter" and has what amounts to the only valid love experience in his life, he still finds himself "sweating and straining in her arms." In turn she reflects that "It was all right, but . . . they didn't have a very good time."

Nobody does. You may remember that the auctorial observer in the Camera Eye was also described as a solitary, introspective figure. The account of his early years hardly mentions friends or acquaintances, not to speak of lovers and the personal relationships that are so distressing and consoling and essential. The narrow range of emotions and experience in Dos Passos' fictional narratives is probably not so much a description of the national character as a reflection of his own temperament. The novelist seems to have been as incapable of recording the moments of plain human gratification and pleasure as his characters were of enjoying them.

But the whole group of American writers after the First World War felt disinherited in their maturity, by a society of boom and bust, if they had not already felt that way in their youth. Any historical work reveals the historian as well as his subject; and his social environment along with his own nature. If, on the whole, *1919* is still a brilliant picture of the scene it describes, it also speaks for the subsequent period in which it was written. It represents the judgment of the 1930's upon the dawning epoch of the 1920's. And it carries as an undertone many of the typical beliefs of the depression years.

So this novel has a particular importance today. For we are the witnesses of a new intellectual trend not merely to return to the 1920's, in effect, but to delete the entire decade of the 1930's from the national consciousness as though it were a national trauma—something to be exorcized rather than to be understood. That period of American life, which had its own triumphs of native fortitude and native ingenuity, has been systematically falsified and distorted. Bewildered by what has happened to us since then, we are engaged in the process of finding scapegoats rather than solutions: of taking a hopeless revenge upon the irrevocable past. We are punishing individuals, on a scale whose magnitude is novel and morbid, for the movement of historical forces which they, no more than we, could hardly have foreseen.

To read *1919* at the present time is to become acutely aware of our own position as well as our uneasy heritage. It brings us closer to the durable truth of things which all serious literature attempts to discover and preserve in the midst of the crimes and follies that surround it.

Introduction to Pocket Books edition
of *1919*, 1954.

The Big Money was published in 1936, in the middle of the big depression. The central theme was the study of the boom and bust period of the 1920's. But the John Dos Passos of that period really knew what had happened to his society while most of the famous postwar generation of writers only felt and reacted against it. The glittering spires of New York, the shining hotels where Scott Fitzgerald's flappers had danced till dawn, or the brilliant salons of the "enfabled rock" in Thomas Wolfe's work, meant something quite different here. "Well, Charley, that's where they keep all the money."

Through a deliberately flat tone, *The Big Money* is also the most acerbic novel in twentieth-century American prose fiction. It is the third, final, and best volume of a major trilogy. In a few rather spectral scenes some of the earlier figures in the trilogy appear in the background of the present narrative. The Johnny Moorehouse of *The 42nd Parallel* has become a magic name in the new industrial art of public relations. A lonely, sick, and unbearable old man, he is a pretentious bore.

His chief assistant is the Dick Savage of *1919,* now a complete hypocrite, whose career ends with a brutal and alcoholic binge in the underworld of Harlem. Eveline Hutchins, the leading feminine figure of the trilogy, commits suicide after the last of a series of inadequate lovers has deserted her. Her friend Eleanor Stoddard marries a little Russian prince; and we see her surrounded by the chirping sounds of cultivated sycophants.

These are really ghosts and shadows in the present novel, ruins of another epoch before the First World War. The real weight of *The Big Money* lies somewhere else: in the investment and banking firms of Wall Street, the factories of Detroit, the grotto-shrines of Hollywood. The present hero, Charley Anderson, this "dumb mechanic," as he calls himself, is carried along by the golden wings of the aviation industry in the 1920's. He sells his machine shop, double-crosses his first partner and early friends, makes a quick fortune as the "Boy Wizard" of Detroit financial society. But he is in reality a front-man and stooge for the promoters and bankers, the puppet of his period. His personality reflects the aspirations of a new American culture based on the production line.

Men and machines, and machine-men. Easy money and mass entertainment; paper fortunes and celluloid gaiety. That is the real focus, the unifying structure, the life movement of *The Big Money.* Thus the Biographies in this caustic and edifying panoramic novel open with the story of Frederick Winslow Taylor, founder of "scientific management" and industrial efficiency; the speed-up. Then there are the profiles of such other historical figures as Henry Ford, the Wright Brothers at Kitty Hawk, and Veblen, sardonic philosopher of the epoch, whose books established "a new diagram of a society dominated by monopoly capital." The spirit of this heavy, obstinate Norwegian country sage broods over the narrative. His message is summarized as "the sabotage of production by business, the sabotage of life by blind need for money profits."

But these studies are balanced by that of Rudolph Valentino, in the field of popular entertainment, and by the beautiful sketch of Isadora Duncan, Bohemian rebel, bankrupt artist, and lover of life. As in the previous volumes of the trilogy, the Newsreels are used to establish what might be called the official climate of the period. They alternate from the headlines of new mechanical inventions—lubricating systems, gears, clutches—to the stories of Peaches Browning, Peggy Joyce, and the Pig Woman. And meanwhile the auctorial observer in the Camera Eye—the last of the technical innovations Dos Passos used to expand and enrich the conventional form of the novel—continues an incessant monologue of incertitude. In the novel's famous passages on the Sacco-Vanzetti trial, he thinks back to the original immigrants at Plymouth, the roundheads, the sackers of castles, the kingkillers, haters of oppression who had landed "on the beach that belonged to no one   between the ocean that belonged to no one and the enormous forest that belonged to no one." He reads the epigrams of Martial; ponders the course of history to discover "what leverage might pry the owners loose from power and bring back (I too Walt Whitman) our storybook democracy."

Eloquent and acrid phrase! But was it only a "storybook democracy" that had existed from the empyreal chants of Whitman to the quicksand of doubt on which Dos Passos had actually based his trilogy of modern life in the United States? In any case *The Big Money* records finally the failure of all social idealism in the nightmare world of technology and finance. If Charley Anderson is the tragic hero of the novel, and a good one, Mary French, the radical heroine, is probably the dreariest figure in the whole trilogy. She is the most admirable morally of all Dos

Passos' dubious ladies, and the least fulfilled. Confronted by her saga of frustration, we might well prefer the novel's cinematic queen, Margo Dowling, who becomes America's Sweetheart just because she lacks any human affection.

While the upper world of "success" in the trilogy ends only in alcoholic dissolution, what can be said of the fictional protagonists who have represented the side of the underdog? The careers of such minor figures as Charles Edward Holden, George Barrow, Ben Compton, Don Stevens (whose crisscrossing lives give *U.S.A.* its narrative density) are all equally disastrous. If the liberals in these novels turn into "labor-fakers" and cowards, the radicals are either fanatics of punchdrunk nomads; and the dismal conclusion of Dos Passos' social-working heroine is intended to sum this up. When we turn back to *The Big Money,* twenty years later, we realize that it marks the start of the central disenchantment in this writer's career which has continued, with lowered hope and failing nerve, to his more recent books.

There are obvious personal elements here, which I have mentioned in the earlier introductions to this series. Just as Dos Passos' people are secure only in the transient warmth of childhood, and as maturity always represents disappointment, the novelist himself has returned to the Jeffersonianism which prevailed in the childhood of the Republic. The central stress of Dos Passos' work is on becoming, never being, yes; but one must choose somewhere between infantile yearning and evolutionary maturing. Must the enchantment with the ideal be matched by an iron hostility to the possible, with all its flaws? As in the case of the European writer Arthur Koestler, Dos Passos' recent career illustrates the plight of an intellectual in a period when all ideas are reversible, when history is only what the newest historians say—and when the novelist must fall back upon the central human values which have, so far at least, survived all sorts of social catastrophes.

People must live, and get pleasure from the worst of all possible worlds. In Dos Passos' chronicles they suffer most in what should be their high moments. In *The Big Money* itself, while the psychobiological impulses of the human organism are stressed more openly, they are rewarded—or punished—even more bitterly. This artist, too, in the whole generation of writers and thinkers who came under the sway of the Marxist and Hegelian approach to history, was curiously insensitive to the guiding principle of polarity: to the conflict of opposite forces in societies as well as in individuals. There is no question about his central picture of the boom period in American life. It is all too true; yet what is here viewed as a permanent inferno was only, after all, an augury of the abyss.

Now indeed when we appear to stand on the brink of the same prospect once more, and the big money is back with us again in all its blind arrogance—when we have moved a little farther along on the enigmatic parabola of time, but know the future is shrouded even more heavily in darkness and in mystery—we might wish, for Dos Passos' sake as well as ours, that this eloquent spokesman of lost causes, this urban Achilles who has been sulking in his agrarian tent, would return to the arena again.

He would be welcome back to the roster of very different American writers, from Melville and Whitman to Howells and Dreiser and Thomas Wolfe, who have united in a common defense of the individual in the New World; whose methods have been different as times and perils have differed, but whose underlying values are similar. Meanwhile I think we should close our eyes to what Dos Passos has written since *U.S.A.* But we should return to the trilogy itself with all our grateful senses refreshed by the vision of an artist at the summit of his craft.

Introduction to Pocket Books edition
of *The Big Money*, 1955.

The Failure of Nerve*

Among contemporary novelists the role of John Dos Passos has been that of the rational social historian, and his value has been

* It is curious that the early Dos Passos was so much concerned with this theme, and this phrase, which appears in his essays and travel books. The boldness and brass of the *U.S.A.* trilogy was almost a deliberate attempt to escape from the shell of the rather morbid, brooding, introspective young artist's self-image—to which, after the collapse of Marxist values, the later books have returned.

great. The three novels that are now collected under the title of *U.S.A.* are surely a central literary achievement in our period; nobody can afford to ignore them. In turn *The Grand Design* is the final volume of a new trilogy which opened with *Adventures of a Young Man,* published in 1939, and continued with *Number One,* published in 1943. In terms of craft *The Grand Design* is probably the best novel of the new trilogy.

Here is the story of the New Deal years in American life—of newspaper sheets that told

> *of panic at the locked doors of banks*
> *of stalled factories*
> *and foreclosures and sheriff's sales and dispossess notices*

—and I do not know where the events of these years have been made more dramatic or interesting as fiction. Dos Passos has smoothed out and integrated the experimental techniques of his earlier work; he has developed a remarkable technique of narrative suspense, he is undoubtedly one of our best contemporary prose stylists. Unfortunately I must add that *The Grand Design* also seems an entirely superficial novel—and that it represents what may be called a modern collapse of values.

The Spotswood family is the connecting link between the three novels of the trilogy. Now, as it ends, we see the point of the connection more clearly. In *Adventures of a Young Man,* Glenn Spotswood, the radical son, ended in disillusionment and death. In *Number One,* Tyler, his older brother, became a disciple of a reactionary Southern demagogue. In *The Grand Design,* Herbert Spotswood, the father, is a pathetic "liberal" radio commentator; all three members of the family arrive at exactly the same frustrated and empty philosophical position. In addition, the main characters of *The Grand Design* include Millard Carroll, a small industrialist who gives up his business to join the "do-gooders" of the New Deal, Georgia Washburn, who becomes a secretary, and Paul Graves, an agronomist and farm boy who is the actual hero of the novel. The villain of the piece is Walker Watson, who is apparently a composite of Henry Wallace and Harry Hopkins, and a thoroughly disagreeable fellow.

There is quite a list of minor characters, including Judge Oppenheim (an intimate of "the Boss") and the Gulicks, the Dillings, and various other Washington officials, socialites, VIP's.

The "illusion" of the New Deal—all its hopes and plans in terms of the common people—is brought to us in the free verse sections of *The Grand Design* which correspond to the Camera Eye in *U.S.A.* The reality of the New Deal—the politics, the personal feuds, the bureaucratic struggle for power—are developed in the straight prose sections.

Indeed the great narrative gift of Dos Passos is simply the perpetual balancing of illusion and reality in his novels: the anticipation of something wonderful that is about to happen, conveyed to us time and time again in the verse chronicles—

> *To make America over from Portland, Oregon, to Brownsville
> on the Rio Grande, from the southwest deserts to the forests of
> spruce and fireweed and fir round the lakes the glaciers left,*
> *in cities and suburbs and county courthouses,*
> *we stand in line, we sit at deal tables to fill our forms, we answer
> the questions of social workers, we tell our tales, spell out our
> histories. . . .*

And then the slow, dragging realization (as we read the prose chronicles) that the illusion is bound to end in scandal and gossip and dirt. But did it, quite? For all of its talent, *The Grand Design* seems to this reviewer both distorted as history and lacking in essential literary and human values.

Naturally I don't mean to say that a novelist can be judged primarily by his social or political views; that is too naïve. The most gifted artists have not always held the most progressive views about life; rather, if anything, from Shakespeare to Dostoevski, the reverse. The point is that Dos Passos, as the historian of American society among the novelists, ought to have a specific responsibility to history, while his picture of the New Deal is at the same time distorted to the point of being obsessed.

One notices, for instance, the almost complete emphasis on agrarian reform at the expense of the "obsolete gangrenous cities." One notes the curiously petty, trivial, and malicious portraits of the leading New Deal figures. If the Woodrow Wilson of Dos Passos' *1919* was a warped and bitter President, the F. D. R. of *The Grand Design* is merely a voice on the telephone, a tilted chin, a smile. In this sense the novel is actually not a picture of the New Deal but of New Deal Washington at its worst. It shows us all the dreadful machinery of official power but never the results. It is morality play without a moral.

And yet the agrarian hero of the book, Paul Graves, who seems to embody all of Dos Passos' present solutions for the problems of industrialism, monopoly, and labor unions, is a particularly stuffy individual. He has indeed something of the enthusiasm of a gentleman farmer doing his best for a sharecropper. As the reader goes deeper in this novel, he becomes more sharply aware of the author's essential remoteness from all the forms of common life that lie outside the realm of theory. In a sense, Dos Passos has never been a realist at all—in the sense of Dreiser, say. He has been a sort of romantic visionary, and he has always to some degree lacked the real base of a novelist's craft: an interest in people as such, a knowledge of possible experience, a curiosity about life simply as life.

But the "real" world of the *U.S.A.* trilogy—that is to say, the fictional world of Dos Passos' own characters—was sustained by the brilliance of its creator's historical and philosophical world— by precisely that eloquent, hopeful, if always skeptical belief in the Marxian dialectic against which he has now turned so remorselessly and completely. If the *U.S.A.* trilogy was probably too much Marx and not enough Jefferson, it is still true that the world of illusion—the Marxian dream—gave its poignance to the world of actuality. There was a real adversary in those days —the dragon of capitalism. There is no comparable dragon, or conflict, in the Spotswood trilogy.

Even the verse chronicles in *The Grand Design* become increasingly pointless as the novel records what is in Dos Passos' view the failure of the New Deal, the developing tyranny of the central government, the farce and catastrophe of the Second World War. Only in the story of Georgia Washburn, a terrified and hysterical woman, who moves from disaster to disaster, does the present work approach the best of Dos Passos' writing. Thus it seems inevitable that he will have to secure either a better human basis for his work or a more generous rationale of history to sustain it. Meanwhile one can only regret that an accomplished literary technique is accompanied by such a narrow view of life, and that this bright star in the great literary constellation of the 1920's should now sparkle so dimly.

From the *New York Times*, January 2, 1949.

The Theme Is Fear

Dos Passos' new book *The Theme Is Freedom* is a collection of his political prose written from 1927 to 1955, together with a running commentary which tells us what he now thinks of what he thought then. A diary of his political development, it is also a dialogue of conflicting beliefs, an uneasy altercation with the past. It is of particular interest as it throws light not only on Dos Passos' own career, but on the whole movement of the Twenties, and on the present literary scene. To be blunt, what has gone wrong with him, and with us?

Though Dos Passos is primarily a historical novelist, this question is not purely a matter of political opinion. Even critics who are sympathetic with his present beliefs, such as Granville Hicks, have felt the decline in his fiction. In retrospect, the work of Dos Passos falls into three periods. There is first the expression of the lonely dissident, the aesthetic recluse, in *One Man's Initiation* (1920) and *Three Soldiers* (1921). The recent revival of William March's *Company K* should remind us of the eloquent but essentially isolated quality of Dos Passos, E. E. Cummings, and even Hemingway as chroniclers of World War I. But almost alone among the high individualists of the 1920's, those gifted expatriates and exiles, Dos Passos had, by the end of the decade, found a cultural base for his literary work.

This base was a theoretical rather than strictly political Marxism. The product of the second period included *Manhattan Transfer* in 1925, and the major trilogy, *U.S.A.,* published from 1930 to 1936. These are still the core of Dos Passos' fiction; they are persuasive and penetrating novels; and their description of American civilization, which hardly applied in the 1930's, may seem all too prophetic in the 1950's. But the crux of the Dos Passos problem is right here, too. The collapse of his belief in the Russian Revolution, the disillusionment with the methods of the Communist Party, led not only to a major revision of his thinking, but, apparently, to a complete cessation of his creative energy and his human emotions. There was a psychic wound that has never stopped bleeding.

It is a familiar wound—the stigma of contemporary literature. It has marked and afflicted the careers of Richard Wright, of Malraux in France, of Koestler from middle Europe, and a host of others. It is a central factor in the paralysis of the American intellectuals during the last decade. Bitter ex-radicals like Sidney Hook, or constrained liberals like Lionel Trilling, or romantic reactionaries like Allen Tate and Robert Penn Warren, have set the tone; which is, I think, no tone at all.

And yet a writer who is concerned primarily with his art should be able to traverse this ideological abyss and keep some sort of perspective. Although a "social critic" myself, or anyhow having been labeled as one, I have never believed that the political area of a writer's thought contains the secret of his creative urge; very often it makes no sense at all. Among the group of Marxist refugees in the literary world, certain figures like Silone in Italy, the late George Orwell in England, or Edmund Wilson and Malcolm Cowley in this country, have still managed to keep their human values intact. Among the others, one may wonder what deeper strain of emotional dependence makes them nurse and cherish their social disappointment to the point of trauma.

One remembers the central emotional configuration in Hemingway's early work: the hunter, the hunted, and death. Beneath the factional feuds which have torn apart the intellectuals of the Left, isn't there some still deeper inner attraction which may draw together the fanatical Communists and the fanatical ex-Communists in an embrace of mutual destruction? In the case of Dos Passos himself, who never yielded to the extremes of this psychopolitical movement, whose great merit was that he used the Marxist critique always with an edge of skepticism and irony in his best work, is there no other recourse from the curious malady of his maturity? One reads *The Theme Is Freedom* with these questions in mind; one feels that what this artist is seeking is both social *and* emotional freedom; and in the end, I think, this book provides us with neither. He, too, is rewriting history—the occupational disease of our age—but his inner speculations travel in circles of fear and frustration, while the Communist cage puts bars between him and the world.

There is the familiar material on the Sacco-Vanzetti case and
the Harlan miners, where Dos Passos received his first practical
lessons in social injustice. There is the account of the Spanish
Civil War, where Dos Passos met the harsh and terrifying reality
of Russian power-politics; and left the movement. There is the
description of the New Deal which he now rather grudgingly
concedes was a legitimate and peaceful social revolution. There
is, finally, his own spiritual return to Jeffersonian democracy, and
to the political heritage of the "English-speaking peoples," which
he first announced in *The Ground We Stand On* (1941). All of
these facts seem to me true and legitimate. But there are such
odd undertones, innuendos, omissions, distortions in this narrative that what should be an informal history of an epoch, witnessed by a sensitive and gifted observer, becomes a nightmare.

One notices the underlying scorn for the "social do-gooders"
and "Greenwich Village radicals" to whom Dos Passos himself
belonged. (He equates Bohemia and Revolution in these pages
as though there had never been a radical and progressive movement in the United States before 1920.) The failure to send arms
to the Spanish Loyalists was Franklin Roosevelt's fatal error;
he is described with the same malice that Dos Passos showered
on the "Meester Veelson" of *1919*. Because of this, no doubt,
Dos Passos manages to work up some enthusiasm for the Pacific
war (and Navy Secretary Forrestal, and for the "deep, traditional
patriotism" of regular army officers), while the European theater
comes under the heading of "Mr. Roosevelt's Crusade." In "the
year of our defeat," at the Nuremberg trials, after the fighting had
stopped, Dos Passos realized "the full horror of what had been
going on."

Not on the Nazi but on the American side! The war against
fascism loses all focus in Dos Passos' mind because Russia was
our ally, and American liberals were "too busy hating Hitler" to
listen to the real truth. The climax of this phase of Dos Passos'
thought (he resents being called reactionary) comes in the *Life*
magazine article on the failure of Marxism. The New Deal is evil
because it leads to English socialism, and English socialism is evil
because it leads to Russian communism. That is the real catch—
the bugaboo that haunts Dos Passos' mind and corrodes his
thinking, just as the House of Morgan was the perfect villain of
the First World War. He is a writer obsessed by demons, in the

shape of ideas, and these demons take the form of savage and destructive symbols of omnipotent power, which terrify him.

One might add, very likely, symbols of *paternal* power. I am not trying to reduce the realities of political conflict to a matter of psychological complexes; but neither, I think, can Communist paranoia be fought by democratic schizophrenia, unless we are all mad. "The nightmare went along with us, back to Paris, back to the States," Dos Passos said after the Spanish War. "It's a nightmare you have to learn to live with all day and every day." This may be true, but such a man is obviously in no condition to think very clearly. And the point is that this emotional syndrome of fear, terror, obsessional hatred, and perhaps underground attraction, of which Dos Passos is the clearest example, has colored and conditioned our whole intellectual climate during the last decade.

It accounts for our strange concentration of anxiety on the one ritualistic theme of anticommunism, by which every other issue has come to be measured. Thus our crucial domestic battles have been fought out on the popular level, while our intellectual journals have hardly dared to mention them. Our best literary work has come from writers who are outside this intellectual orbit, where panic has slowly subsided into inertia. One notices that Dos Passos himself, settled in the shadow of Monticello, has lost just those attributes of the old republic which made a whole line of country squires—from Jefferson to Franklin Roosevelt—such a potent force in our social evolution.

Dos Passos, indeed, has become a frightened landlord, guarding his ancestral estate. And as I write these lines, another old-fashioned Southern agrarian, William Faulkner, has just declared that in the final crisis he will have to stand by Mississippi, and shoot down the Negroes in the streets. Well, good-by to all that.

From the *Nation,* April 14, 1956.

Finale

That familiar figure of the early Dos Passos, "Vag," the homeless young man, rebel and outcast, taking to the road, leaving
the urban and industrial centers of the nation behind him in the
search for new life: has he really turned out to be the disgruntled
proprietor of Monticello, the anxious and worried landlord of
our literature, who is the present custodian of the Republic's
true heritage?

The decline of Dos Passos' work is another tragedy in contemporary letters. But if the trouble with the later Hemingway or the
later Faulkner is that they are not really serious any more, perhaps the trouble with Dos Passos is that he has become much
too serious. There is a strain of monomania in the books of his
later period. Only he knows the truth of the historical processes
today, the nightmare omens of disaster, and even if he were
quite correct, the literary projection of this catastrophic vision
lacks dignity, power, and feeling. What one objects to, in the
end, is that Dos Passos' view of life has become so petty. If we
are all really going down, as he preaches, in a universal debacle,
let us go down with some grandeur.

And with a little humor. When the air-raid sirens wail and
howl so fatefully over New York City—the urban center that Dos
Passos views with scorn—the average man in the street behaves
more gracefully than this artist's "heroes." As I said in the 1940's
about the human narratives in the *U.S.A.* trilogy, it was sometimes questionable whether Dos Passos' people really were worth
saving. Both the Marxist "salvation" of the early writer and the
Marxist doom of the later one are in a sense irrelevant. What is
at stake here is the writer's narrow and desperate view of human
beings and human relationships, which was at some earlier points
tragic in part, and which has become merely sordid.

Why? What is the matter; what is the missing key to this
affectional flaw in so gifted and intelligent a writer; and what

could change it? One reads every new book by Dos Passos with a kind of hope against hope that the writer has discovered and resolved this issue; that some new emotional spring of belief, of human concern, of human charity even, has been released in him—and each new chronicle drags out the same bitter, halting course. In Dos Passos particularly, as the "historian" of his period, the novelist who came closest to knowing what his world was really all about, and who faced this world most directly, one has the sense, that the whole famous literary generation of the Twenties is not only "lost," but debased.

Perhaps the fortunate ones like Scott Fitzgerald, who was so slowly and painfully coming to realize his own inadequacies as an artist, died early; fortunately for their reputations, at least. Few of the others among this group of bright, sparkling, literary prodigies, gifted and rebellious children of the arts, have been able to convince us of their maturity. It almost seems that some essential human component—the capacity to live and learn, as it were—the component of growth and development—was omitted from their literary apprenticeship. If the American novel has indeed moved from rebellion to conformity in the first half of the twentieth century, that does not quite mean that rebellion is the only road to artistic achievement, or that conformity means only failure. It is likely that the major writers combine both elements within themselves in a kind of polar tension. It may be that the generation of the Twenties cut all their ties too drastically, including the conservative ones of a fixed human and social environment, consoling and soothing, if so often tedious or irritating; while the generation of the Fifties have cut no ties.

And what, in the luminous and glittering aesthetic Twenties, or the dense, oppressive, ominous, and calcified Fifties, what in the American air itself creates such improbable extremes, unfruitful both for life and for art? But returning to Dos Passos again, whose literary career is symptomatic and fateful, the scene of *The Great Days,* the most recent of his novels, in 1958, is neither luminous nor truly ominous, but surely dense, oppressive and in the deepest sense degrading. It is perhaps the final step in the process of a literary or fictional decline; it would be hard to go further. It seems also to be the most personal of the later novels, where the author is speaking more directly about himself, and to his reluctant readers, and in this sense, it is of interest. One reads it rather as one did the Hemingway braggadocio of *Across the River into the Trees,* with a certain morbid fascination.

The hero is a former "celebrity," a noted journalist who has come upon bad days and is trying to make a comeback. His first marriage has ended in disaster and the death of the wife he loved. His journalism, imbued as he has been with the moral fervor of telling the truth, has gradually deteriorated. He finds himself without a family (his children have also betrayed him), without a job, and at the end of his financial resources. In the old days, he thinks, whenever things got too difficult, a trip would solve them; a familiar refrain in Dos Passos' work. And so he takes another trip, to Cuba and the islands, with a new girl whom he plans to marry, to change his luck.

He is almost a Fitzgerald or a Hemingway protagonist, one man alone, his saga that of talent, dissipation, and ruin. His drunken reveries of "the great days" may remind us also of the Dick Savage of *1919.* But the causes for the present predicament of Roland Lancaster are not in the mores of a savage, competitive finance-capitalism. They lie, rather, in the bureaucracy and tyranny of the New Deal epoch, which has in effect lost the Second World War, ruined the nation, and surrendered the world, and the future, to Russia. This is a standard lament in the later work of Dos Passos—isn't it?—and given this thesis, which is both familiar and ridiculous, one might expect at least a fresh development of a trite but now almost macabre theme.

The form of the novel is that of the flash-back. The hero's reveries occupy more than half of the novel's action; and this narrative of the past, told in the first person singular, is little more than a recapitulation of Dos Passos' own volumes of journalistic reporting in the Forties. The war in the Pacific had its moments, so this sermon runs, particularly with the executive officers of the navy whom Dos Passos met. The European war was a mess, and the Nuremberg Trials a fiasco. The Germans "were guilty as hell" all right, but if Franklin D. Roosevelt and his cabinet had been in the chairs of the Nazi criminals, would their record have looked so very different?

This last suggestion is an imaginative spurt which occurs for the first time in *The Great Days,* so far as I remember, and for my part the answer is yes, their record would have looked very different. (In one year of occupation, Dos Passos says, the "honorable German burghers" were turned into criminals, though perhaps this process happened all by itself, before the trials, under the Nazi regime; while German authors like Thomas Mann or Erich Remarque take a different view of these "honorable burghers.") But Moscow dominated the Nuremberg Trials, of course, just as it stole the fruits of our victory, and perverted our gullible humanitarian principles—though Dos Passos does not quite follow out this standard line of reactionary logic, and add that F.D.R. should be dug up and impeached. Roosevelt was dead anyway "from the neck up" long before his stroke, the present hero does say; and the Washington scene of the novel is peopled by the familiar personages of the reversionary Dos Passos.

There are the Prime Minister's cigar and the President's wheel chair. (The jaunty cigarette holder seems to arouse Dos Passos' special ire.) There is the friendly fireside voice; and yet "when the time came to run up a butcher's bill our Hudson River gentleman would sit there drinking blood with the best of them." The novel takes place, if by indirection, in the highest circles of official Washington; and there are also the cantankerous Herman Boggs (Harold Ickes?); the ailing Walker Watson (Harry Hopkins), carried over from the dismal Spotswood trilogy; and Navy Secretary Roger Thurloe, obviously patterned after the brilliant and neurotic James Forrestal. If indeed the Dos Passos journalistic narrator is divided into the present ruin of a man and his memories of the "great days" which have ruined him, then Thurloe himself, the man of action, the counter-New Deal theorist, the only cabinet member who understands the true meaning of the war, the Russian menace, the grim future, is the real hero of the narrative.

Thurloe is almost the other half of Roland Lancaster. It is the Navy Secretary who keeps the journalist out of official uniform, and sends him out to learn the real truth about the Pacific war and the European peace. Their ideas agree perfectly; they are the people who understand the "real truth" of what is going on— the true nature of the nightmare and the disaster—and they form an underground government of two, as it were, which is the only real resistance to the ignorant and corrupt (and conspiratorial?)

New Deal bureaucracy. True, Thurloe gradually takes over Roland's wife, and may or may not be having an affair with her; but what is this small domestic sacrifice compared with the blood brotherhood of similar ideologies? When Thurloe finally jumps out of the high hospital window, "Ro" has lost his last true friend. His collapse is inevitable.

The process of this disintegration (which forms the present action of the narrative) is hardly more credible, however, than the so-called historical background of *The Great Days*. The girl whom Roland has brought to Cuba, whom he intends to marry, and on whom he has pinned all his hope of a comeback, turns out very poorly. She is in fact frigid, a complete narcissist, who has no contact with the outer world beyond "fun" and "kicks." She outdrinks Roland steadily and persistently; she rebuffs him sexually, and worst of all, she will not listen to the compulsive and repetitious chronicle of his failure. During most of the Cuban interlude, which completes his ruin, Roland is really out of action: a drunken spectator of his mistress's perverted antics—but hardly a figure to rouse our sympathy.

If, indeed, his political judgment is no better than his human judgment, the novelist has sealed his protagonist's doom, and his own. There is a curious vein of self-pity which runs through the latest fiction of John Dos Passos. The entire relationship of Roland and Elsa is based on a plea for "sympathy" and "understanding," which is never given to him, and perhaps rightly so. His career has moved only from the terrible "unhappiness of adolescence" to the frustration of defeat "when you are a man grown and aged." He has spent the best years of his life, so he claims, trying to evolve an "American democratic theory" which will match the Marxist theory. (This is the joint project of Thurloe and Lancaster in the novel, their unique discovery, just as though there had been no Jefferson, Lincoln, Emerson, Melville, and Whitman before them; but we begin to realize that the older American figures are too radical for the later Dos Passos.) And yet he has only succeeded in being called an appeaser, an isolationist, an "American Firster" or even a Fascist. How very odd! And how true, perhaps. For if Roland Lancaster is the spokesman of this new brand of American democracy, it is a sorry affair. If great poets need great audiences, as Whitman said, then great beliefs

also need great prophets. As in almost all of Dos Passos' fiction,
the human core of his philosophical concepts is absent. Perhaps
the central deficiency in his political thought rests after all, upon
a psychobiological failure.

Moreover, the frustrated and defeated Dos Passos spokesman
confesses that he has been called a witch-hunter, an alarmist who
sees nightmares under every bed. All his liberal friends have deserted him, and Dos Passos, like David Lawrence, puts liberals
in quotes. "How is it that nobody has any friends any more?"
But as Emerson said, in formulating the democratic credo which
Roland Lancaster is searching for: "The best way to have a
friend is to be one."

And to put the question bluntly, is the later Dos Passos really
a friend of the human race any more? That is the issue which his
work from this point on will have to resolve; and meanwhile
we are conscious that the best portraits in the novel are those of
malice or frustration or jealousy. There is the unpleasant Cuban
painter Pinillo who despises everything American and glorifies his
"proletarian humility." (Dos Passos is suspicious of modern
art too; while the revolutionary group in the story is treated with
contempt.) "He points to the hollow place under a turn in the
stairs where a skinny little girl in a torn pinafore with great blue
circles under her eyes is encouraging a naked yellow baby to
deposit a small turd." This, we are told, is the people's state of
nature, their Garden of Eden. This, says Dos Passos by implica-
tion, is the People! But what it really is, one imagines, is the key
to Dos Passos' present picture of life.

No wonder that the "democratic" hero of the novel is sexually
impotent. Or that the heroine's obsessive search, in *The Great
Days,* is for those secret charms of "Ñañigo" which will teach a
frigid girl how to love. How to love! This is, or should be, the
true theme of the novel, as Dos Passos almost knows—or the
future theme of his writing—while the last half of the present
story is concerned only with the artificial devices of sexual stimu-
lation. For Ñañigo, as we learn, is the voodoo cult of Cuba, the
secrets of the Devil and the dark continent, which linger on just
below the surface of civilization. In another context, from Faust
to Hawthorne, it is also the hidden lore of the forest, the witches,
and the Life Goddess herself. As in all the great mysteries which

surround our existence, the pact with the Devil can be a source of
power for the artist; or at least it is essential for him to know this
area of being. Perhaps this is just what has been missing in the
psychic repressions which have characterized the present writer's
sense of human character. But Dos Passos has made the wrong
contract.

WILLIAM FAULKNER: BEFORE AND AFTER
THE NOBEL PRIZE

Intruder in the Dust

AT THE present time William Faulkner is among the three or four leading American novelists. If you count Ernest Hemingway primarily as a short-story writer, and John Dos Passos as a fictional historian of our society, Faulkner almost stands alone in the classic tradition of the novel. And his literary reputation is particularly high at the moment.

But Faulkner's career has been compounded of neglect and sensationalism. He has been harmed by the worship of literary cults and cliques almost as much as by popular ignorance of his work, while his own literary methods have not helped this situation. The best books of his early period, *Light in August* or *The Sound and the Fury,* were experimental in form, elaborate or often deliberately obscure in expression. His general reputation was founded on *Sanctuary,* a harsh, violent, and essentially superficial flowering of a rich talent. Even today those who admire him most seem largely indifferent to his true quality—or how often he has sacrificed that quality through impatience or rhetoric.

Intruder in the Dust is a typical Faulkner novel in this respect. It will probably be attacked by reviewers who are put off, and not without reason, by the obscurity of its language or the intricacy of the novel's structure. At least two men are murdered during the course of the narrative, and another commits suicide. An old Negro named Lucas Beauchamp is held for the first murder and is about to be lynched. But Lucas is the friend and blood relative of some of the old Southern families around Jefferson, Mississippi. The narrator of the story, a young Southern white boy, is particularly involved with Lucas, whom he sets out to save with the assistance of his uncle, Lawyer Gavin Stevens, and a foolhardly Southern spinster called Miss Habersham.

But this is only the beginning of the story, and to those who don't know Faulkner I can hardly suggest its ramifications both in terms of personal relationships or the general social scene of the South. The unfolding of the plot merely provides a framework for the larger symbolism of the novel, and again we see that peculiarly Faulknerian panorama in which Negro and white are bound together by the irony of history, and involved in an inextricable web of shame, guilt, and evil. Lucas's real crime is not the shooting of Vinson Gowrie—of which he is actually innocent, although he refuses to admit his innocence—but the fact that he refuses to admit his inferiority as a Negro. Or rather, being a Negro, he refuses to admit that he is not also a man and, incidentally, of better stock than the Scotch-Irish hill people, who are not McCaslins, not even Edmonds, but just "these new folks."

Unfortunately Vinson Gowrie is one of the Scotch-Irish hill people, and the young narrator of the story is also involved with them. By threatening to lynch an innocent man simply because of the pigmentation of his skin, they threaten his, Chick's, security and honor as a Southerner. As I understand it, and it is not always easy to understand Faulkner's work on a first or second reading, the central theme of *Intruder in the Dust* is actually the emotional education of another young Southern ex-aristocrat through the processes of murder, mob violence, and race hate.

The trouble is that this central theme is all too familiar in Faulkner's work, and it is now presented in a diluted and popularized form. The boy Chick, his worried mother, philosophical uncle, and shadowy father are reflections of earlier and better Faulkner characters. Lucas Beauchamp is a far more interesting and memorable personage than the white folks of the novel, but one notices also that his main role is apparently to endure and to survive, while some Southern Negroes may want to do a little more than this, and some have to be content with less.

Intruder in the Dust is really a Gothic romance in the best Southern style with stage props and literary puppets instead of people and events, and the language, which conceals so much else, fails to conceal this. It is still superior to the average novel but it is far inferior to the work of Faulkner at his best. One might say that even Jefferson, Mississippi, the center of Faulkner's Deep Southern cosmos, has come under the influence of Hollywood, while the more explicit philosophy of the novel also reflects a sentimental and romanticized expression of a familiar Southern chauvinism.

It would be a curious climax to Faulkner's career if the great Southern literary rebel and realist of the early 1930's should become, in his own polar and tortuous fashion, the Thomas Nelson Page of the 1940's. But a serious writer is entitled to his own license and luxury, and we can still afford to wait for the best of Faulkner.

From the *Saturday Review,* September 25, 1948.

Requiem for a Nun

"What do you want? What in God's name do you want?" cries the heroine of Faulkner's new play-novel. "I told you. Truth," says the hero. So let us accept Faulkner's thesis and admit at once that this new work by a serious and gifted artist is absolutely worthless.

It is not only trite and sophomoric in its values, but it is pretentious and, I happen to think, badly written. I'm not sure whether it is worse to conclude that Faulkner wrote it as a potboiler for the Broadway and Hollywood stage, or that he honestly believes in it.

And I say this not as a detractor of Faulkner's work but as an admirer of whatever has been good in it. This story is a sequel to *Sanctuary,* and you might ask why he picked the most sensational and least serious of his early works to make over into a cheap thriller and a puerile morality play.

Temple Drake is married to the Southern boy whose drunken driving got her into the Memphis sporting house. She has two children and is a respectable member of the Mississippi country club set. All is forgiven apparently—only her colored nurse has murdered her youngest child and has been condemned to death, quite rightly, one would think.

However, Gavin Stephens (who is Faulkner's prototype of a true Southern gentleman, and has defended the Negro girl in court) is not satisfied. During the rest of the book he attempts to get the truth out of Temple, and while this takes some time since all the characters revert into the postures of Greek tragedy at the crucial points, it all—ultimately, which is too late for my taste—comes out.

Temple Drake has been blackmailed by the brother of the man she fell in love with during her imprisonment in the sporting house. She has also fallen in love with her blackmailer. (It seems that all three of them, the two brothers and her husband, Gowan Stephens, look somewhat alike.)

The fact is that Nancy Mannigoe, the colored nurse, has committed the crime in order to prevent Temple from ruining her life again by deserting her husband and children for the sake of another impure love. And Temple must confess her sin publicly not indeed to save the Negro nurse (who is also a former dope-fiend and prostitute) but to save her own soul.

Does it seem a little farfetched? It is; and perhaps the ornate, mysterious, and bombastic language that Faulkner uses here is designed to prevent us from ever understanding the real plot of his play.

Anyhow Temple has one child left, and at last atones for her sin, while the Negro girl is happy, presumably, to die for the sake of the white folks' salvation. The problem of the Negro has always bothered Faulkner (that is to say, the problem of denying the true Negro problem in the South today), and what a convenient solution this is!

But even in Heaven, as we are told, Nancy Mannigoe will be destined to play a menial role—and do work that has to be done —while "the harp, the raiment, the singing" are not for her, not now.

So *Requiem for a Nun* is still a requiem for a second-class nun, and "Sanctuary Revisited," might be a better title for the play.

Faulkner has also surrounded the play proper with a longish

prose narrative dealing with the early history of Jefferson, Mississippi, which is a better piece of writing, but which has very little to do with the main action. If it isn't presumptuous, I'd like to add that Faulkner doesn't seem to understand the South.

From the New York *Post,* September 23, 1951.

Two Studies of Faulkner

I must confess that I read the advance sheets of Edith Hamilton's essay on Faulkner in this magazine with some astonishment. What is the author of *The Greek Way* doing in the Deep South of Faulkner's tales—this region of shadows and swamps and attic secrets, of ancestral halls in which echo only the sobs and shrieks of the decaying and the demented.

It is a long step from Athens to the Compsons and the Snopes clan of Jefferson, Mississippi, and Yoknapatawhpha County. Yet Miss Hamilton puts her finger on just those weaknesses in Faulkner's work which Irving Howe tends to minimize or deny in his *William Faulkner: A Critical Study.* Mr. Howe himself can do excellent work, as in his recent review of *Witness* for the *Nation.* He can do good work as in his studies of Sherwood Anderson and Walter Reuther. I have never seen him quite so prosaic as in his new interpretation of a writer who is, after all, with all his faults, an interesting and colorful artist.

What is the matter? My guess is that Mr. Howe, when trying to take a middle position between the present group of Faulkner idolators and a group of almost fanatical Faulkner haters, somehow found himself nowhere. Perhaps it is impossible to take a rational position about Faulkner anyhow—for the best things in his work proceed from an altogether different level of feeling and superstitution. Take the items Miss Hamilton has listed: the "curse" on the South in Faulkner's work; the fear and hatred of women; the perverted Puritanism; the lack of true individuality in many (though not all) of his characters, who are indeed viewed as "volitionless servants of fatality." One could add to this list a fear and hatred of the Negro which is expressed in Faulkner's literary fantasies even while he denies it on the conscious level. As a Southerner, of course, he likes the old-fashioned Negroes—servants and small farmers who know their place, or ex-slaves or old men, like the Lucas Beauchamp of *Intruder in the Dust,* who are in no danger of upsetting the cultural institutions of the South.

Mr. Howe takes the other line and stresses the "positive" elements of Faulkner's work—as Robert Penn Warren recently did, and as Faulkner himself did in his Nobel Prize speech. There is only one trouble with this argument—it doesn't work.

For why was it that directly after the Prize, Faulkner produced *Requiem for a Nun,* which is undoubtedly one of the most contrived and adolescent works he has done, and which displays all his old prejudices and superstitions even more strongly under the guise of a lofty new moralism? No, Faulkner is good and at times even superb just when he expresses, not any sort of democratic or progressive credo—but the typical phobias and deep, haunting fears and obsessions of the cultural background whose supreme literary voice he really is. The decaying, incestuous Southern planter aristocracy in *The Sound and the Fury;* the tortured mulatto hero of *Light in August* who—touching the center of the buried fear and terror in the Southern mind itself—is the lover and then the murderer of the white woman who has urged him to become a rapist in her sexual fantasies: these are Faulkner's great and permanent achievements.

They may not be attractive, I admit, to Miss Hamilton's sense of classic harmony; they seem to escape Mr. Howe's analysis altogether—but there they are. One might add a third book, *Absalom, Absalom!,* where Faulkner described both the origins and the fall of his haunted Southern dynasty in the chronicle of Sutpen, a prototypal figure of the Southern planter. And perhaps a fourth—*The Hamlet,* which describes the antics of Faulkner's new Southern ruling class, the Snopeses, who personify everything that is small, cunning, avaricious, corrupt, and comic. I should say that Mr. Howe's study is often acute and penetrating on this area of Faulkner's work—closer to social-economic patterns in the South—if it is weak on psychological and deeper cultural issues. For Faulkner is also an artist who is completely bound in by the class and caste concepts of his ancestry and origins. Every attempt he has made to break through these bonds of the spirit has only been further evidence of that "slavery" indeed to which the white masters as well as the black workers and servants of the Old South subjected themselves and their children, even to the latest generation.

Lillian Smith's *Killers of the Dream* had some very pertinent things to say about this aspect of modern Southern culture. I wonder what Faulkner would think of them. Richard Wright has also written about the Southern Negroes of Faulkner's own state who may not be content, as the white artist has recently suggested, to wait one hundred or a thousand years more for their salvation. Because Faulkner has not been able to break through the taboos of his own social class—as for instance the Russian novelists of the nineteenth century did break through them—his work is often limited or, as in *As I Lay Dying,* grandiose and rhetorical. But when he is back on his own ground—those shadows, swamps, morasses, and psychic quicksands of the still-haunted mind of the South which he knows so surely and so intuitively—he is still, as in his big books, a major writer: and one whose peculiar limitations are almost as illuminating to the cultural historian as are his grand flashes of genius.

From the *Saturday Review,* July 12, 1952.

A *Fable*

William Faulkner's new novel, entitled *A Fable,* is in part a religious allegory based on the events of the false French armistice near the end of the First World War. His last two novels *Intruder in the Dust* and *Requiem for a Nun,* had to my mind the mark of Hollywood and of Broadway on them. Only, as if to atone for his earlier use of shock and sensationalism, Faulkner imposed a high-flown morality upon very dubious narratives. In *A Fable* he has again tried to reconcile his rhetoric and his instincts.

The false armistice of 1918, in Faulkner's version of it, was based upon the mutiny of a French regiment which simply failed to move when it was ordered to attack. A form of passive resistance to any further fighting, the mutiny spreads to other French regiments along the battle line, and to their German counterparts. The first memorable portrait in *A Fable* is that of General Gragnon, the division commander, who orders an artillery barrage to be thrown down on his rebellious troops, and then requests authority to shoot the entire regiment.

Some of these episodes of war are excellent. One of Faulkner's gifts has always been that of narrative power. Even when his stories are difficult to follow, they are interesting to read, and the new novel uses his familiar techniques. There is the long cutback (sometimes within a long cutback) where we follow the adventures of "the runner," a mysterious soldier who apparently has been clubbed to death at the beginning of the story—we are never quite sure. There is the silence of the "aghast and suspended city" —in these typical Faulknerian phrases—when the Parisian women learn that their husbands, brothers, and lovers are to be executed for the mutiny. The narrative itself moves by a series of brilliant, if sometimes momentarily inscrutable, detours to the inmost center of the Allied high command. Only here do we begin to realize that the novel in turn has been shifting from the level of realism to that of religious symbolism and mysticism—that it is, in effect, a modern version of the Christ story.

It is on this last level that the novel fails. And it also throws a significant light not only on Faulkner's earlier career but on that whole famous "lost generation" of American writers to which his youth and apprenticeship belonged. In the foreword to *The Faulkner Reader,* a collection of representative selections from the whole body of his work, this gifted and eloquent novelist stresses again, as he did in his Nobel Prize speech, and as he does once more in *A Fable,* that the function of literature is "to uplift men's hearts." Nobody can quarrel with this; all great writers have done it; the only question is how? I think that Faulkner's great error during the last decade of his writing has been to substitute an empty moralism, however sincere, for the true uses of his own genius.

He *did* uplift our hearts in *The Sound and the Fury,* in 1929. This novel, which is quite correctly included in *The Faulkner*

Reader, still remains his primary work and, despite a highly experimental technique, it is a great and touching book. The underlying emotions of the story are those of infancy: the love of brother and sister in a dreadful and decaying Southern family, with a drunken and rhetorical father, an ailing and nagging mother. These intricate family relationships were also at the base of Faulkner's *tour de force* during this early period. *As I Lay Dying,* published the following year, was almost a "poorwhite" parallel of *The Sound and the Fury.*

But a quarter of a century ago Faulkner was not concerned with upholding the "old verities" he lauded in his Nobel Prize address. His purpose then was to show the life around him, and indeed to dispel the mist of that prevailing Southern legend whose whole significance, as Ellen Glasgow had realized before Faulkner, was to keep the truth from the South.

When, in 1932, he came to face the real issues of his environment and culture even more directly in *Light in August,* his second important novel, the accent of horror was dominant in the tortured love relationship of the hero with Negro blood and the Southern spinster. The hero was named Joe Christmas; even then Faulkner was obsessed, perhaps, by the Christian symbolism. But the real issue was that of a society which was devoutly, almost rigidly, religious in name, and had in truth renounced the inner spirit of all religions. More recently Lillian Smith has been describing this central paradox of Southern society, where the race question has made a mockery of the Christian code.

It was logical, perhaps inevitable, that in Faulkner's third major novel, *Absalom, Absalom!* (1936), he came to view the South and its people as forever "cursed" and "doomed." These are among his favorite and recurrent adjectives together with all the forms of the word "outrage" which have marked his style more recently. *Absalom,* the story of the two half brothers, one of them part Negro, who are the last descendants of the plantation aristocracy in the Old South, was also Faulkner's last real try at authentic tragedy in fiction. Since then the Snopes clan, scheming, conniving traders, merchants, and politicians, without dignity or honor, have taken over the New South in Faulkner's work. The emotional tone has changed to that of folk comedy, very often brutal, sadistic, or "clever."

It seems clear that Faulkner, like Ernest Hemingway, has

never really been able to accept the conditions of modern life
in his own country. In one fine story, "The Bear," included in the
"Reader," Faulkner, rather like Hemingway in Africa, has returned directly to the virtues of the primitive wilderness. In the
work of both these writers—the two great stars of that brilliant
literary constellation which first appeared over our horizon in the
Twenties—the glowing dreams of adolescence and youth have
also been stressed over the sober, constrictive, and perhaps dis-
heartening demands of maturity.

Wasn't this the dominant trait of that whole generation, including such figures as Sinclair Lewis and John Dos Passos, who
were raised and nourished on the acids of skepticism and revolt
in the Jazz Age? In my own view, that is why the older generation of Dreiser, Sherwood Anderson, and Ellen Glasgow sometimes seem, if less gifted craftsmen, more enduring as artists or
as literary figures.

That is why, when the new age of the Thirties and Forties
called for other values than those of ridicule, such a writer as
H. L. Mencken went so sour. And that is the primary problem
which Faulkner has been trying to come to terms with in his own
work during the last decade.

In *A Fable,* too, one notices the vestigial suspicion of city life
and city people—the symbols of the twentieth century—on the
part of this deep-country novelist. There is the "open reliant in-
corrigibly bucolic face" of the Iowa farm boy in uniform, who is
compared with the killer Buchwald, grandson of a Polish rabbi,
and on the way to becoming an American gangster. Another
of these soldiers, Polchek, with a "knowing, almost handsome
metropolitan face," is the modern Judas among the twelve military disciples who have conspired with a French corporal to
instigate and direct the mutiny.

In the novel's climax, when we discover that this "corporal"
is the illegitimate son of the French Marshal who sentences him
to death, "with God and with love," we realize also that Faulkner
has intended these two figures to illustrate the two poles of man's
mundane power and his eternal spiritual aspirations. But these
"aspirations" are never really embodied in the novel itself; they
are still sermons. They represent Faulkner's own "need to believe" in the maturity of his art. But they also represent a kind
of abstract belief which has never been rooted in the life around

him, the life of his own country, and of his own time. This remains his central problem as a writer, just as it remains the problem which so far has not been grappled with successfully by the other gifted literary figures of his generation.

From the *Saturday Review*, July 31, 1954.

The Meaning of Faulkner's Humor

Faulkner had humor, often ironic and bitter, in the series of dramas and tragedies he wrote about the Old South. But the meaning of his humor about the New South, personified in the Snopes clan of *The Hamlet* (1940) is a very different matter.

Those who are surprised at the recent statements on integration which have come from the Nobel Prize Moralist—America's literary spokesman before the world—might do well to look at Faulkner's novels. Not at the rational and moral statements in them, either, but at their prevailing imagery and true dramatic action. The critics who have been celebrating this artist as the foremost symbol of the progressive, modern, "civilized" South have not understood the real psychological forces in his work. Faulkner is, or was, a major artist simply because he revealed the darkest recesses of the Southern psyche: the folds and flaps of fear, ignorance, and prejudice.

But he is a writer who is more than half infatuated with, or strangled by, the psychic demons he has conjured up. Never mind his rhetoric on state occasions. He too belongs with the class of Southern men whom Ellen Glasgow described as having learned to talk and to preach before they learned to think. What is the real picture of William Faulkner's South? The Compsons and Sartorises are the aristocratic families, to which were later added the McCaslins and De Spains. (The Sartoris line was originally a romantic SatEvePost projection of the Old South, and only later became respectable.) But at the end of *Absalom, Absalom!* —as early as 1936—the grandiose visions of Thomas Sutpen, another royal Southern planter, were destroyed by the "bloody aberration" of the Civil War. The true heirs of southern destiny, we were told then, were figures like the poor-white Wash Jones (or the Bundrens of *As I Lay Dying*), or even worse.

Meanwhile the Snopes clan, another branch of poor-whites, appeared as the real descendants of these earlier figures. Tragedy or compassion were no longer possible in Faulkner's view of the modern South. A hard, brutal, sadistic kind of "folk humor" was the only possible response to this cunning, avaricious, amoral tribe of dollar-chasing, power-hungry Southerners. *The Hamlet* describes the rise to power of Flem Snopes, who sells off his worthless land to the people of Jefferson, Mississippi, by persuading them that there is treasure buried on it. The novel is filled with the antics of horse-thieves, arsonists, blackmailers, idiots, and state senators. Poor-white trash which has been elevated by cleverness and corruption into wealth and power. But is that famous Snopes' love affair with a cow really so funny? I found it less than hysterical; though Faulkner himself seemed to accept, and to enjoy, the perverse antics of his new reigning line of termites.

The point is that many great artists of the tragic vision, from Shakespeare on, have turned in their later phases to the comic muse. What else indeed is possible for a person who sees how impossible life really is? But the tone of Faulkner's late humor is very different from this. Based on malice, cruelty, perversions, tricks, it is essentially a medium of showing the artist's distaste for the prevailing forms of Southern society. It is not the comedy of submission to life which Faulkner is showing us here. It is closer to the anal-sadistic humor of contempt and defiance—of scorn and superiority. It is really not, to this critic at least, very funny; it is a hatred of life.

One must also ask to what degree Faulkner's view of the legendary Old South (all moral grandeur) and of the despicable New South (all moral corruption)—of this eloquent scene of high tragedy, and this low area of cheap comedy—is really accurate? There are plenty of Snopeses in the contemporary Southern scene, we know for sure, in the high places of business, politics, education, and culture. We see them all around us at the moment, as far up as the governors' mansions. Perhaps Faulkner's unconscious, phobic visions of the South have really produced the final parable of the Snopes clan. But was the Old

South really so pure and guiltless, as we are told; is the New South composed of Wash Joneses, Bundrens, and Snopeses only? And if that is so, why should Faulkner himself, the aristocratic dissenter, the visionary of the glorious past, the central literary spokesman of the South, add his own voice, as he recently has, to this prevailing chorus of ignorance, bigotry, and corruption? His own grounds for action may be different; the net result is the same.

It is all rather confusing, and Faulkner himself hardly clarifies the issue. In his latest statement on the segregation issue to the *New York Times,* he argued that "white people and Negroes do not like and trust each other, and perhaps never can." (That is, the "new Negroes." Faulkner's best Negro portraits in fiction, usually quoted to show his "emancipation," are always those of the old-fashioned type.) But, added the Sage of Mississippi, there is something more important than this fact—if anything could be more important, one may think, than that Negroes and whites *do* learn to like and trust each other. What is now necessary and urgent, Faulkner says, is that we federate together, show a "common, unified front not for dull peace and amity, but for survival as a people and a nation." (Dull peace and amity indeed, and we begin to see why Faulkner's novel of peace, *The Fable,* became hollow at the end.) Our nation, he continues, will have to stand firm, unified for liberty "in an inimical world which already outnumbers us." And the Negroes, he concludes, will have to do their part in forming this united front of hostile blacks and whites against that "inimical world" which does indeed outnumber us, and which is composed so largely of the darker-skinned races who are the Negroes' brothers.

Very odd, this Faulknerian logic. And one remembers that in Faulkner's earlier statements on the same subject, where he admitted he would have to stand with his own people, in the final pinch, even if it meant shooting down these same Negroes in the streets, he was confident that his own black "boys" would assist him in this project. Would they really? Those "boys" of his might set the artist straight, if he really cared what they thought, and had not read, perhaps, so many romantic Southern Civil War novels of gallant officers and loyal black retainers. (It almost sounds, too, as if Faulkner had been reading Hemingway's Superman novel, *Across the River into the Trees.*)

But *The Town,* in 1957, as Faulkner's latest literary work, and a sequel to *The Hamlet,* is the final link in this over-all pattern of tragedy, comedy—and shall we say, farce? Here indeed the Snopes clan are even more grotesque, rapacious, villainous, distorted, and inhuman. They are further along on their rise to power, the destruction of the Old South, the final corruption of the New South. The central figure is again Flem Snopes, and like the protagonist in *Sanctuary,* where lurid melodrama and brutal comedy were also joined, we are told that he is impotent. But here the dollar sign, rather than the corncob, is the true wand of power. Typically, too, Flem's wife is the mistress of Mayor De Spain, another decadent modern "aristocrat." In Mrs. Snopes herself, we confront Faulkner's familiar and fascinated horror at devouring feminine sexuality. And the still deeper fear, perhaps, as I have mentioned elsewhere, both cultural and personal, that the Negro and the Female will finally unite to devour the South itself.

As in a whole line of southern novelists, sexuality is assigned to the lower classes, and ultimately to the Negro race. (This was also a common theme in our Darwinian and racist novelists of the 1900's, who may have influenced Faulkner's early thinking.) Tradition, culture, and white "aristocracy" seem to lead to sexlessness—if also, as in Flem Snopes's case, does the pursuit of money. Meanwhile, in the novel itself, he struggles to gain control of the old Sartoris bank—though one wonders, after all, just how the Sartorises made *their* money.

There is the "good" Southern lawyer, Gavin Stevens, a latecomer in Faulkner's upper hierarchy, but one who represented conscience and morality in such novels as *Intruder in the Dust* and *Requiem for a Nun.* But nobody can keep up with the Snopeses, not even Faulkner. The book is really a series of tall tales, weird and grotesque, forced and strained, the waste product, so to speak, of what was a fine imagination. The comparison with some of Steinbeck's "humorous" books is also obvious. This is hasty and careless and trick art, in which everything is sacrificed to the "comic" effect, if you are among those who think it is comic. Faulkner is hoping to get by on what is still, at times, the sheer power and brilliance of his prose style or by the magic of his name for the popular audience.

If the Snopeses are indeed related to the tribe of Southern politicos presently in power (and a promised third volume in this "comic" trilogy will presumably carry them there), and to the new race of Southern merchants, industrialists, and bankers who support these politicians, then what a legitimate theme for satire they really are. The Southern scene does offer great dramatic possibilities for a writer today, and Faulkner is in a unique position to render a true service to his culture, his tradition, and his art. But this writer is not serious any more. The "humor" of the Snopes chronicle is a hasty gag rather than genuine social satire. It almost seems that the artist's contempt for all phases of modern life, which was clear as early as *The Sound and the Fury,* has prevented him from learning the truth about the modern South.

Why else should two out of three books produced after the Nobel Prize (with its much-publicized nobility of artistic aspiration) strike us as not only poor, but trivial or cheap? (While the third book, *The Fable,* is at best mediocre.) This is the real tragedy for Faulkner, for the South, for American letters; and the mass of undiscriminating adulation given to this author recently has been no real help. Yet in fact the direction of Faulkner's later career was evident in even the best of the early novels, as I said before. And the meaning of Faulkner's "poor-white" humor should be clear now. This artist can indeed entertain himself at the expense of the New South and the Snopes clan, for in his own mind, also, this whole new ruling class is to be only the temporary, if loutish, custodians of his ancient ancestral home land. In *Absalom, Absalom!,* we are told that the poor-white descendants of Wash Jones himself will be conquered in turn by the illegitimate Sutpen line: by the brutish Negro, Jim Bond. "I think that in time the Jim Bonds are going to conquer the western hemisphere," says the suicidal Quentin Compson. "Of course it won't quite be in our time and of course as they spread toward the poles they will bleach out again like the rabbits and the birds do, so they won't show up so sharp against the snow. But it will still be Jim Bond; and so in a few thousand years, I who regard you will also have sprung from the loins of African kings."

So be it; and perhaps it is this dark and recessive fear, rooted in the phobic depths of Faulkner's own fancy, which has led him to his present position on the racial question. Is this really Faulkner talking today, or is it, say, the estranged minister Hightower in *Light in August,* who is lost in the dusty memories of the Civil War, "caught by the dead who had conceived him," and growing to manhood "among phantoms." Is Faulkner himself now living among the phantoms that his own dark and fertile imagination has, in the past, conjured up so magnificently? But in the plain light of day, what nonsense it all is!

SINCLAIR LEWIS

Diarist of the Middle-Class Mind

SINCLAIR LEWIS has been called the Bad Boy of the national letters. In a way the celebrated critic of the national manners who established the new realism of the 1920's in the American mind and established the American mind in contemporary literature deserves his title. His literary career, lasting over a quarter of a century, has been marked by controversy, dispute, and perpetual ferment.

Main Street sold over a million copies and was translated into a dozen languages. During those big years of his own career and of that whole new literary revolt of the Twenties which Lewis, along with Henry Mencken, seemed in many ways to represent most fully, there was little doubt as to both Lewis' value and his sparkle. His journalistic sorties against the "classical" critics, who then as now represented for the most part the alliance of little minds and great books, were bold and entertaining. His rejection of the Pulitzer Prize was based on the ground that it was an attempt to make writers "safe, polite, obedient, and sterile." His later acceptance of the first Nobel Prize to be given to an American writer contained an admirable statement of the new literature's intentions and achievements. "The American writer ought to perceive," Lewis said, "that he has . . . the most exciting country in the world; the greatest diversity of races, from Icelanders to Japanese and Negroes; the widest sweep of climate." In practice, too, Lewis seemed to be fulfilling Henry Mencken's vision of a national literature, no longer imitative and timorous, which would present a firsthand examination of the native scene in wholly native terms. As early as 1922, in *Babbitt,* Lewis not

107

only added a new word to the American language, and a new figure to world fiction, but had staked out the whole area of his own contribution to the national letters.

What we are about to study here, however, is the true nature of Lewis' literary cosmos: that American Middle-Class Empire whose ruling dynasty is the House of Babbitt and whose destiny forms a strange chapter in the national letters. For the fact that Lewis' true world is essentially a middle-class fantasy of life in America—rather than any sort of realistic picture of middle-class life in America—has been obscured simply because his superficial world, and particularly his visual world, are so concrete. Apparently one of the most immediate novelists of his period, Lewis is actually one of the most remote. We may notice, too, the curious intellectual framework of Lewis' work: its narrow limitations, its blind rigidity, its overtones of fear and almost willful ignorance. Probably the real fascination of Lewis' career lies just in the fact that this intrepid social rebel and fierce critic of the national manners is in the end so completely at one with his subject. This is not, indeed, America, but *his* America—that middle-middle portion of it with which Lewis is so absolutely involved, and from the values, beliefs, and illusions of which he will never, for an instant, be able to deviate. Not often before, in the history of our letters, has an artist been able to see so much and understand so little.

This has its own value, of course. Sinclair Lewis' novels, and the worst of them along with the best, form a remarkable diary of the middle-class mind in America.

But surely the Middle-Class Empire is one of the most limited phases of the innumerable phases of history—and not only of world history but of American history—and not only with respect to its time span but also as to its cultural values and aspirations. Furthermore, what has distinguished Lewis' own work as a whole has been the narrow view he has taken of even that narrow orbit of history. The fact is that he has presented the worst possible examples of his own theme.

Yet the actual limitations of Lewis' literary world do much to explain the final apotheosis of that world. As a matter of fact, they make it almost inevitable. Even in *Dodsworth* and *Ann Vickers* the accent on wealth, on material possessions, and on a polished "aristocracy" is the final as it was the initial note of

Lewis' literary scene. (Just so, the James Buck Titus of *It Can't Happen Here,* equally rich and suave—"as near to a country squire as one may find in America"—is at once the only major figure in the novel who hasn't the slightest interest in the revolutionary struggle and the one whom Lewis views with the least qualms.) And Lewis' aristocrats differ merely in degree from his middle-class figures and not in kind. They have more money, more social position, more culture. But their culture and their social position are simply used to proclaim the fact that they have money.

There are really no aristocrats in Lewis' work. There is not even, as in Dreiser, or Willa Cather, or Thomas Wolfe, any convincing middle-class aristocracy. Nor, on the opposite side of the social scale, does Lewis attempt to project a single working-class figure of any dimension. And, in the entire body of work by this major critic of middle-class manners in the United States, from Carol Kennicott to Doremus Jessup, there is hardly an effective or even attractive social rebel. Actually, of course, this writer, whose historical position is that of having established the "classes" in American literature, deals only with the establishment of the middle class in American literature. His theme is that "bourgeois colony" which, up to 1917, as Lewis says in a curious historical inversion, "was the only America," or which, anyhow, after 1917, considered itself as the only America. The real distinction is between the middle-class farmers, merchants, artisans of the early American Republic (whom Lewis never understood), and the new middle-class society of finance capitalism, whose product Lewis was.

It is interesting to notice the narrow social stratification of this colony. There are no musicians, dancers, painters, poets, or sculptors of consequence in Lewis' work. The Ora Teagle of *Work of Art,* who is the only full-length study of a writer, and who does at least write one honest novel—a novel which is "financially unnecessary," and which convinces Ora of the futility of serious writing—is Lewis' prototype of the artist in America. Furthermore, from the Raymond P. Wutherspoon of *Main Street* to the Lycurgus Watts of *Dodsworth,* are there any "intellectuals" in Lewis' work who are not also by inference dilettanti or perverts—that is, when they are not "radicals" and dangerous as rattlesnakes?

No, early and late, the only true hero of Lewis is the scientist. But *Arrowsmith,* too, reveals not merely the inadequate nature of Lewis' "scientific truth," but also his failure to project the native life and character which he had linked with this ideal. Right there was the very epitome of that petty, nagging, back-biting, provincial existence which the Western scene seems to be identified with in Lewis' mind when it isn't a stereotype of the frontier or a ghastly vision of suburban standardization. So, too, the town of "Catawba" in Lewis' novels, the upstate town of Winnemac which is intended to represent the best features of an older rural and democratic society, is actually a ghost town.

In the whole range of Lewis' work, where is there a view of life which could sustain a novelist's belief in life, or even in his own work? Perhaps this helps to explain the increasingly curious view that Lewis took of the Eastern metropolis itself. There are references to the Bohemians and anarchists, the "intellectual parasites" and "one hundred per cent mongrels" who have become the typical inhabitants of the metropolis. ("Russian Jews in London clothes," as Lewis tells us in *Dodsworth,* "going to Italian restaurants with Greek waiters and African music. . . .")

In these tones of superstition, as well as in his earlier tones of naïve yearning, Lewis clearly shows his own lack of cultural roots or of any historical perspective. The country people and the city people of his tales are neither true country people nor true city people. Just as every extreme of Lewis' inner world has been eliminated, and the whole gamut of human feeling has been reduced to what you might call the medium-priced emotions, so, in his whole outward scene also, the true poles of his society have been removed—or, more accurately, perhaps, have never been established. The central dramatic conflict of Lewis' work is precisely the conflict of these inadequate—or missing—extremes. I mean of a specious aristocracy and an almost invisible working class; of a romantic socialism and a visionary capitalism; of Westerners who are trying above all to be Easterners and of Easterners who in spite of everything are exactly like Westerners.

Now without cultural roots or abiding human values—without a sense of either the flesh or of the mind—perpetually oscillating between such extremes, none of which are satisfactory, none of which are really imagined or felt, none of which are actually *there,* how can a writer sustain himself? Marked by a thin past

and a narrow future, Lewis is indeed the Last Provincial of our
letters. A provincial who wanders, homeless, between a barren
and deteriorating hinterland and an increasingly appalling industrial order—a hinterland with which he feels no ties, an industrial order with which he cannot come to grips.

And it is interesting to realize just how little of the "real"
United States is in the work of a writer who is so full of its
manners, habits, and idioms.

I mean, of course, the United States which actually formed
and determined Lewis' whole literary world. The U.S.A. of the
corporations and the cartels, as well as of the factories, the
mines, and the slums, which is the source and conditioning factor
of Lewis' Middle-Class Empire and his Economic Man. If Lewis'
work is in the literary tradition of Frank Norris, Theodore
Dreiser, or Upton Sinclair, what a limited view it gives us, after
all, of the North American Continent, and with what a tender
and tardy sort of "realism." The U.A.C. of *Dodsworth*—the Unit
Automotive Corporation—is the true *deus ex machina* of Lewis'
world. But, showing as he did all its consequences at the dawn
of the 1920's, it was only at the outset of the 1930's, at the point
when the God of the Machine was Himself temporarily out of
order, that Lewis allowed himself to take another look at it.
Perhaps the most violent and brutal example of Lewis' social
satire in the later Twenties was directed, in *Elmer Gantry,*
against rural life and evangelical religion. Just as Lewis has
foreshortened the whole exterior scene of his people's activity,
so he ignores the basic determinants of the life which surrounds
them. The real institutions of finance capitalism lie outside his
world: a world of continuously worse results and no causes.

All through Lewis' work we may trace a curious transforma-
tion of that earlier and more intricate conflict of "East" and
"West" which has marked the national letters. Perhaps never before has the familiar and uneasy artistic search for the cultivated
and aristocratic "Eastern" life been so swiftly and surely trans-
posed into the search for financial security and the material
consequences of wealth. But what Lewis has done is to *bourgeois-
ize* this whole cultural conflict too; to make it completely middle
class, to remove both the upper and lower limits of this search—
to reduce it all again to another formula where the "East" simply
means a little more money and the "West" a little less money:

where the Easterners are the people who have got the money, and the Westerners are the people who are going to get the money.

So Zenith is Lewis' true home, after all. Zenith, which is in itself an in-between world, a by-product of the cartels, a psychological suburb of the new money society in America which lives on financial sufferance as well as on the nationally advertised brands—this middle world of derived goods and derived values which is the whole world of Lewis' literary achievement. Perhaps we can now appreciate the fascination of hotel life for Lewis, from the Una Golden of *The Job* who found her salvation in running the White Line Chain to the Myron Teagle of *Work of Art* whose lifelong aspiration is to manage the Perfect Inn. To Zenith's Child, at any rate, a good hotel is all that home should be.

Here, too, we can appreciate Lewis' curious relationship with the Younger Generation. In the last of the broken antitheses which form the real dialectic of Lewis' work, we should notice how the writer who sought after "youth" most fervently hardly expresses it with the greatest conviction. How prematurely sober Lewis' typical young people are, and how perennially gauche and infantile his adults are: almost as though, never having had a true youth, they can never achieve a true maturity. You might almost say that the typical Lewis hero is an adolescent with a paunch—and in this respect rather like those Western settlements which jumped from crude hamlets to ersatz cities, Lewis' people reflect the broken life line of the Middle-Class Empire itself. That Empire whose own youth in America was capped by a hurried and frantic maturity, and for whose brief flourishing Lewis was forced, in *The Prodigal Parents,* to substitute a mythical and timeless splendor.

Although Lewis' realism does not in the end compare with either Dreiser's or Dos Passos', although his values are quite inadequate when compared with Willa Cather's or Sherwood Anderson's, there is a curious sort of solidity in his work, a fundamental sense of human decency, and a fundamental human perversity which is at the base of any mature individualism. It isn't, moreover, that Lewis is not always serious about the craft of a novelist. It is simply that he doesn't always know how serious the craft of a novelist can be.

Yet all Lewis' wit and eloquence and artistic vitality operate in a sort of intellectual vacuum in the end. You could say that the whole import of Lewis' work shows that he has learned nothing, answered nothing, solved nothing. Those Lewis characters who, in his first novels, left the West for an imaginary East are the same characters who leave the East for the imaginary West of his last novels. And Lewis himself, like his most typical figures, is the Eternal Amateur of the national letters.

The point isn't that Lewis lives so completely in illusion. This is one of the prime sources of an artist's power and one of the reasons why Lewis' work, for all its limitations, has its own appalling validity. The point is that the illusion which nourished Lewis was so inadequate, and in the last analysis so transient.

For the Happy End to Lewis' unhappy historical vision—the vision of Middle-Class Bliss which marks the entire last period of Lewis' work—came at almost the precise historical moment which marked the crack-up of the Middle-Class Empire in America; at least in its first natural exuberant form. And if Lewis sees clearly enough the failure of the Horatio Alger tradition in American life, it is just as true that the brand of economic individualism for which he yearns was, almost from the very start of his career, more of a vestigial than a vital force in his society. It was even then, in the dawning age of the cartels, a myth and a memory of the past.

And doesn't George F. Babbitt himself, the Grand Mogul of the Middle-Class Empire, take on an added glory simply because he was allowed such a brief span on history's moving stage? The dupe of time as well as of the great American fortunes, Lewis' single big creation is a tragic clown in truth. The clock goes faster in the United States, too fast for both Lewis' many-volumed diary of the economic man and for the diarist too.

But it is interesting that the cultural lag in Lewis' work should be so marked. Just as the real social forces of his time are placed for the most part quite outside of his literary scene, so the real social changes of his time are reflected cursorily and late. The ordinary mark of a first-rank author is that his writing is generally in some degree ahead of its time. The typical characteristic of Lewis' writing is that it is generally, to a marked degree, behind its time. Very likely this is the final key to Lewis' achievement—

the key which opens the secret chamber in this otherwise absolutely uninspiring middle-class mansion.

For it would appear that Lewis' whole literary world, so
extraordinarily prosaic for the most part, so lacking in subtleties
and shadows, a world of perpetual daytime, on which night, with
its enigmas and mysteries, never falls—that this whole uniquely
commonplace literary universe of Lewis' *is* in the end haunted by
the sense of its own unreality. This is also a middle class which
is essentially without a home life, without children, without
religion, and, finally, without an economic status to speak of. It
is a middle class which is without all the historical props of a
middle class, and which, hardly established in power, has every
appearance of dissolving—including the escape into a dream
world of the middle class.

At any rate, that is the impression which Sinclair Lewis' work
leaves with us, as it turns from the barricades to the Land of
Faery, while the true and final fascination of his own career is
the degree to which he was identified with the illusions of his
class.

This condensation of the Sinclair Lewis chapter in
The Last of the Provincials (1947), published by
the *Saturday Review,* November 1, 1947, has been
revised for its appearance here.

A Postscript

*From Main Street to Stockholm: Letters of Sinclair Lewis 1919-
1930,* edited by Harrison Smith, interesting and illuminating in
many ways, deals with the first decade of his literary career. They
are letters to his publisher, Harcourt, Brace. But Lewis' relationship with this firm was so close—not only with Alfred Harcourt
but with Donald Brace, Harrison Smith, and other members of
the house—that they are also very personal and, as it were, even
family letters. They throw a strong light, and I must add at times
a rather curious light, upon the writer and his work.

It was the period of Lewis' beginnings, and of his greatest

success: *Main Street, Babbitt, Arrowsmith,* and *Elmer Gantry.*
These books brought the literary revolt of the 1920's into the
popular mind in a way that no other writer of the period had
succeeded in doing; in this sense too they were a culmination of
the realistic movement in our literature which had started a
quarter of a century before with *Maggie, McTeague,* and *Sister
Carrie.* Yet our first impression of Lewis himself—in the letters
at least—is that he was only concerned with publicity and
advertising campaigns. He objected to the ads for *Free Air,* his
romance of the automobile, because they did not stress that it
had "the dignity of realism." He wanted to put signs about the
novel on every garage in America.

He was imbued surely with that native conviction that the
machine would construct a new highway to paradise. After
Lindbergh's flight—and after he had written his serious books—
he remembered another early novel about airplanes and cabled
from Paris: "Why don't Grosset start intensive campaign Trail
Hawk which is really story Lindbergh. Can hook up with fact
we born forty miles apart." Indeed, when *Main Street* first began
to catch on with the popular audience, Lewis seemed to go
absolutely berserk with ideas—gags, angles, stunts—for pushing
the novel along even faster. What one misses in the early sections
of the letters is the sense of Lewis' position as a writer, or even
perhaps as a human being. There are few moments of reflection;
of his dealings with other people, or other books, there is almost
nothing except enthusiasm or rejection. "Since writing you the
most interesting person I've met has been Rebecca West. If she
proves not to be too tied up to Century, I may try to pinch her
off. Same with Norman Angell."

All the same, the letters are filled with fascinating side lights
and glimpses of the artist who was hidden away beneath all this.
One notices the early titles for *Babbitt,* which was originally to
be called "Burgess" or "Fitch"; while *Elmer Gantry* was at first
titled "Rev. Bloor." There is a delicate episode with Paul de
Kruif who wanted a more direct acknowledgment for his work
on *Arrowsmith.* Lewis was hurt by this, and could not perhaps
quite understand it. "Edna St. Vincent Millay is here, and I'm
trying to decide whether, as an agent of the firm, I want to tie
her up with a contract," he wrote from Rome later. "Her poetry
is splendid, and much worth having, and she is planning a novel.

But the devil of it is that she quite definitely plans to make this a novel that would be sure to be suppressed—and she wants enough advance to live on for four months while writing it!"

For a moment the two poles of the literary movement in the 1920's met and touched—there were sparks—and yet *this,* I think, somewhere in those buried depths, Lewis could understand. The statements on his rejection of both the National Institute of Arts and Letters and the Pulitzer Prize award were admirable, as was his Nobel Prize address. There was something appealing—something of the older village atheist and dissenter in our tradition—in the spectacle of a Lewis who defied God to strike him dead while he was writing *Elmer Gantry*—even though the Lord refused the challenge. There are very touching letters about the separation from his first wife, Grace Hegger Lewis; her own eloquent letters of despair are here, too. When Lewis first met Dorothy Thompson in Berlin, he noted that "I haven't had and, what is more curious, haven't wanted a drop of whiskey, gin, rum, brandy . . . for a long time now." He hoped he was going to be able to save money and live less expensively in his new life. Within a few months, fixing over their Vermont farmhouse, he was broke.

The rupture with Harcourt after the Nobel Prize comes as another one of the unexpected twists in the narrative; unexpected, distressing, and yet, quite logical. For the small-town world of Babbitry whose unique historical voice Lewis had been (this narrow, shadowy world which its petty potentates of commerce thought was the only world) had already disappeared from the center of the historical scene. The 1930's and 1940's were the beginning of a new epoch, where Lewis was never again to feel quite at home. But meanwhile he had made immortal the bustling phantoms of Zenith.

From the *Saturday Review,* November 15, 1952.

The Man From Main Street: A Sinclair Lewis Reader. Selected Essays and Other Writings, 1904-1950. Edited by Harry E. Maule and Melville H. Cane, assisted by Phillip Allan Friedman. As the somewhat imposing array of titles, subtitles, and credits makes clear, this is a collection of Sinclair Lewis' occasional writing, mostly journalism. It covers the years from his Yale education (and early passion for romances) to his solitary and tragic death in Italy. It is a useful companion volume to the Lewis letters which were recently published in Harrison Smith's *From Main Street to Stockholm*.

The editorial notes, like the titles, are generally helpful but have a tendency to inflate themselves or to describe Lewis' work in terms that are questionable. Looking back now, we can see that he was essentially a popularizer (at his best a great one) of the tradition of literary revolt which almost coincided with the span of his life. He was never a "philosophic" or even a very thoughtful writer. He was rebellious by nature and conservative or even authoritarian by deepest instinct. That is to say, he belonged to a tradition of native satirists, such as John P. Marquand, who need a strong tradition of authority to support their own revolt against it.

Thus, when the familiar outlines of Lewis' world disappeared in the 1930's—the world which had heaped fame upon him for excoriating it—he was lost, and spent the decade in confusion and irritation. Much of the interest of *The Man from Main Street* lies in the disclosure of these personal traits, revealed perhaps even more sharply in Lewis' articles and reviews than in his novels. There is the excellent Nobel Prize Address, where he defended the new literature of the 1920's against "an astonishing circus called the New Humanism," the predecessors and ancestors of the New Critics today. Toward the end of his career, Lewis was at his best again in a brilliant defense of his own period written in answer to Bernard DeVoto's "The Literary Fallacy."

He was a marvelous satirist when he was sure of himself, and one we could use, as we could use another H. L. Mencken today, to stand up against the new menace of self-appointed literary censors and obscene custodians of public morals. There is another good article here on Negro writers, such as Richard Wright, and on the race problem—far more incisive than the dubious romance through which he projected this theme into the pages of *Kingsblood Royal*. For even when the later Lewis' instincts were admirable and his intellectual position sound, his expression was often inadequate: a combination of jeers and wisecracks, at its worst, in a world of misery and social revolution.

There is no doubt also that Lewis' later versions of Dr. Will Kennicott (in another essay in this collection) and of George F. Babbitt (in a series of repentant novels) stressed solid virtues in these national types. The only trouble was that while they were admirable and even sympathetic figures in the original satire, they became objectionable as cultural heroes. Perhaps this was the final paradox in Lewis' career. A member of the older generation in American letters, as Mencken was too, who had accepted the gloss, the emancipation, the modern sophistication of the postwar writers in the 1920's, he was unable, finally, to return to those roots and values which he really cherished.

Among the later essays and articles in *The Man from Main Street* there are intimations that Lewis realized his dilemma. In his ironical obituary, written in 1941, he described himself as a forgotten figure, though at one time "of considerable notoriety"; as "inevitably lone and insulated"; and—in a familiar lament—as a chronic wanderer and outsider. But what strikes one, after reading both the collection of his letters and the present collection of essays, is how little this writer spoke about himself—or about that part of him which produced his best books.

From the *Saturday Review,* February 28, 1953.

THOMAS WOLFE

Introduction to a *Portable Wolfe*

IN ONE sense a Portable Thomas Wolfe *is* a tempest in a teapot. In his build and his inclinations alike there was little of the synoptical in this writer.

"Some day," he says in the story called "Gulliver," "someone will write a book about a man who was too tall"—who lived forever in a dimension that he did not fit, and for whom the proportions of everything—chairs, beds, doors, shirts, and socks, the berths of Pullman cars and the bunks of transatlantic liners, as well as the normal rations of food, drink, and love—were too small; a man who became the butt, a hundred times a day, of those tiresome jocularities to which a tall man must resign himself and which soon brought home to him the truth of Renan's observation that the only thing that can give you a conception of the infinite is the extent of human stupidity.

In much the same way he must have become resigned to the anecdotes about his habits. How, for instance, since he was so tall, he wrote, standing, upon the top of his icebox, for days on end, adding up episodes of 50,000 words each. Or how he filed his manuscripts in huge wooden packing cases—that is, when he was not recording the endless flow of his reveries in those huge accounting ledgers: ledgers that contained every impression of his lived and remembered experience, and packing cases that contained every ledger he had ever compiled. Or how, in the periods when he was not thus feverishly writing, he was just as feverishly eating—I mean when he was not racing up and down the vast American continent in the longest trains or dashing from one continent to another in the fastest boats he could find, etc.

This, more or less, is the general impression of Thomas Wolfe. How true it is, is another question—and meanwhile there is also another Tom Wolfe.

It is with the *other* Wolfe that this volume deals: a writer who, I think, can be expressed in a portable anthology, and to whom even these selections of only 250,000 words will give you at least a fair introduction. For Wolfe, eminently spatial as he seems at first glance, was by no means a sort of mechanized Anthony Trollope. Is it characteristic of a purely quantitative artist, as it were, to spend three years on his first novel, as Wolfe did on *Look Homeward, Angel*? To throw out his second novel entirely, as Wolfe did with *K 19*? To spend five years on his next novel, as Wolfe did with *Of Time and the River*? To add, as Wolfe then did, that it was hard for him to let go of the book even so because he was not entirely satisfied with it—and then to have the book sent to press by his editor in his absence because he had, in fact, refused to let go of it? To a certain degree Wolfe *was* devoured by an almost morbid hunger for life and consumed by a ravenous fear of time. As a young man he had been driven wild by the sight of the Harvard library—by the fact that volumes were appearing on the shelves faster than he could read them, and by the fact that simultaneously, while he was reading, outside, on the bare New England streets, were passing thousands of faces he had not seen, people he had not talked with, lives he had not known. Yet this turgescent youth could also spend days trying to remember the look of an iron railing on an American bridge, the sound of a milkman's horse clopping down an empty city street, the feel of the crumbling green paint on a little wooden shed "out in the country two miles from my home town where people waited for the streetcar."

It is the care that went into the planes and surfaces of Wolfe's work—the tactile areas—that makes it an inhabitable literary world, just as it was the continuous rehearsal of his experience in his own mind—and the slow discovery of the underlying substratum of meaning—that made it, finally, a durable world. He wrote in the large, to be sure. But what is chiefly responsible for the notion of Wolfe as a quantitative writer is, I think, a sort of quantitative reading of him. And, faced by these increasingly massive blocks of material, these steadily accumulating blue and red volumes, 6 by 8 inches, 500 words per page, 900 pages per volume, each volume somehow seeming much heavier than the last, it is probably difficult not to read him in a 6-by-8-inch way. Yet in such an episode as that of Starwick in Europe, which is probably the best single episode in Wolfe's work and which comes at the end of his best and also his biggest volume, you may suddenly realize the kind of craftsmanship that has gone into the hundreds of scenes within scenes which form the whole panorama of this world.

Wolfe may have been thinking of something like this when he remonstrated with Scott Fitzgerald, who had suggested more Flaubert and less Zola in the younger writer's work:

You have had to work and sweat blood yourself and you know what it is like to try to write a living word or create a living thing. So don't talk this foolish stuff to me about exuberance or being a conscious artist or not bringing things into emotional relief, or any of the rest of it. . . . The little fellows who don't know may picture a man as a great "exuberant" six-foot-six clodhopper straight out of nature who bites off half a plug of apple tobacco, tilts the corn liquor jug and lets half of it gurgle down his throat, wipes off his mouth with the back of one hairy paw, jumps three feet in the air and clacks his heels together four times before he hits the floor again and yells, "Whoopee, boys, I'm a rootin, tootin, shootin son of a gun from Buncombe County—out of my way now, here I come!"—and then wads up three hundred thousand words or so, hurls it at a blank page, puts covers on it and says, "Here's my book!" Now, Scott, the boys who write book reviews in New York may think it's done that way; but the man who wrote *Tender Is the Night* knows better. You know you never did it that way, you know I never did, you know that no one else who ever wrote a line worth reading ever did. . . . I want to be a better artist. I want to be a more selective artist. I want to be a more restrained artist. I want to use such talents as I have, control such forces as I may own, direct such energy as I may use more cleanly, more surely and to better purpose. But Flaubert me no Flauberts, Bovary me no Bovarys, Zola me no Zolas. And exuberance me no exuberances.*

And perhaps also these selections from Wolfe, standing on their own, will dispose of some other current notions about his writing.

The simplest thing to do with some of these statements is to

* Quoted from a letter to Fitzgerald, published in *The Crack-Up* (New Directions, 1945).

admit them. Was he an heir to the Southern rhetoricians, a pet
of poeticizers and an easy prey for choral arrangements? Yes,
naked and alone, he came into that agrarian society of Shakespearean Festivals and Stedman's Selections. But notice also, a
little later, the Wolfe of a trip North in *Of Time and the River*—
the Wolfe of Shakespearean take-offs, of a low and gaudy native
humor. Was he, again, in his youth, a prime case of the Rural
Romanticist—of the *Weltschmerz* of the Hinterland? Yes, but
even then he was writing chiefly of other twisted rural souls; he
soon wrote of Harvard aristocrats, Boston hoodlums, the Park
Avenue *bourgeoisie*. Caught up in the web of cosmopolitan
sophistication, was he also reminiscent, in opening accents at
once credulous and bigoted, of the familiar, even the stereotyped
Provincial in the Magic City—a semitropical cousin of Dreiser's
in our letters, and sometimes almost equally "flaccid and elephantine," as Henry Mencken noted in respect to Wolfe's literary
ancestor? Yet, as early as his second novel, he had summarized
the whole vexing cultural issue of Eastern ease and grace in, for
example, that fabulous Castle on the Hudson; or in those
"French" writers, Feuillet, Capus, Courteline and René Bazin;
or merely in his suggestion to the critics of sexual activity in
America that, even in Boston, on the Esplanade, at nighttime, in
the hot and sultry month of August, the noise of the kissing was
like the noise the wind makes through a leafy grove—and that
they were still selling cradles down in Georgia. At this point, too,
he began to see the Enfabled Rock, with all its enchantment and
all its bitterness, a little more clearly than Scott Fitzgerald himself, say, had ever seen his Lost City. During the course of the
1930's, in fact, Wolfe took on a cultural as well as a personal
perspective that was not entirely granted to some of the more
typical literary figures of the 1920's. It is even possible that this
writer, heavy-handed as he seemed among the whole group of
deft and delicate American moderns, was the one who changed
most sharply and surely. At any rate the rebellious and in-
troverted mind becomes one of the most acute and entertaining
social commentators of the decade—and a prime chronicler of
the national mind in the epoch of the bust and the hangover.

Yes; still—wasn't he finally, as was announced by some of our
more consistently disappointed students of the Literary Craft—
wasn't he, after all, a, so to speak, *professional* believer, an

optimist, a happy vulgarian among the disenchanted professors, and the blind Yea-Sayer of contemporary Belles Lettres? Well, he was also, as you might note for the record, a Yea-Sayer whose constant companions were despair and disease, whose closest friend was death; a poet of springtime in the hearts of men who was well acquainted with autumn and its shriveled forms; a seeker of sensuous beauty who had met "the sickening and abominable end of flesh"; a lover of all life who felt himself "life's monstrous outcast"; a naïve and resplendent enthusiast, in short, who came trailing visions of the abyss.

As a matter of fact these visions—of guilt and of horror; and these recurrent fears that he would "strangle like a mad dog in the tunnel's dark"—are at the center of Wolfe's work, and we ought to look into them in order to understand him.

II

In some ways, too, he was an unduly sensitive and difficult young man.

Probably that outsized carcass, nature's gift to him, was the initial factor. "The really important thing—the *truly* autobiographical thing," Wolfe wrote in respect to his later, "objective" novels, "was the fact of physical variation: to create a figure who would illustrate that variation and all the great human experiences that attend it." In any case this is a persistent theme in Wolfe's work from one of the earliest short stories, "No Cure for It," whose youthful hero resembles a monkey, to "Gulliver" itself, whose mature hero laments the accident of birth that had imprisoned a spirit "fierce and proud and swift as flight" in such a grotesque tenement.

But the fact of physical variation was complicated by the fact of physical disease. Some of the most remarkable passages in Wolfe's first novel deal with this, and Eugene Gant grows up under its shadow: the early sickness of his brother Grover, the final sickness of Ben, the cancerous infection of Gant himself which almost seems to grow and spread as the novel grows and spreads—this interminable diseased growth that outlasts the first novel and spreads well into the second, with the father's black arterial death blood flowing out over these pages just as the son's life blood went into them. *Look Homeward Angel* is first and foremost a study of the distorted and dissolving body.

I give thanks for every dirty lust and hunger that crawled through
the polluted blood of my noble ancestors. I give thanks for every
scrofulous token that may ever come upon me. I give thanks for the
love and mercy that kneaded me over the washtub the day before
my birth. I give thanks for the country slut who nursed me and let
my dirty bandage fester across my navel. . . . By God, I shall spend
the rest of my life getting my heart back, healing and forgetting every
scar you put upon me when I was a child.

Yet the festering Gant of the novel is balanced by Eliza Gant
and her almost equally cancerous spiritual sickness—her in-
sensate passion for property.

Mama, Mama, in God's name, what is it? What do you want? Are
you going to strangle and drown us all? Don't you own enough? Do
you want more string? Do you want more bottles? . . . Don't you
own enough? Do you want the town? What is it?

On this note the early Wolfean hero leaves the "rich and
mysterious South"—this barren spiritual wilderness, as Eugene
Gant then believes, with its cheap mythology, its swarming
superstitions, its "hostile and murderous entrenchment against
all new life."

Wolfe himself, however, was not so easily rid of his Southern
associations—and obligations. He was supported by his family
during the early years of his Northern education, and the sense
of debt to a society he had apparently repudiated forms a recurrent and uneasy motif in his letters home.* As early as 1917, at
Chapel Hill, he noted that expenses were much higher. "I try to
pay up every check I get and then, naturally, go broke. . . .
However, I'm as economical as possible"—a refrain, with its
element of truth and its element of absurdity, that is to echo
through these letters for the next twenty years. "Do you want me
home?" Wolfe again wrote to Julia Elizabeth Wolfe in 1919:

If so, let me know immediately. I shall need money—a considerable sum. Your last check—$25—did not cover my debts as my room
and board were $30 alone and I also had books equipment etc. So
there is debt of approx. $15 on last month together with $30 for this

* *Thomas Wolfe's Letters to His Mother,* edited by John S. Terry
(Charles Scribner's Sons, 1945) is an invaluable source book of the
writer's earlier years, and I have drawn heavily upon it for the biographi-
cal account that follows. *A Note on Thomas Wolfe,* by Edward Aswell
(Harper & Bros., 1941), is also informative and interesting.

month. . . . I'll need $70. Sorry bill is this large. If you think best I stay here deduct expense home and send rest. Pardon my lack of enthusiasm but I'm all in and must go to an English conference with my professor.

From now on, however, Wolfe wrote from Harvard in 1921, he really would practice strict economy.

I know I have wasted some money, which has worried me considerably, and which I will try to profit by. The rest of the family hold it against me, I know, that I have been to school so much and spent so much, and there is much truth in what they are saying about me. . . . I am in a delicate, trying position before you and the family [he said again in the same year] and I am trying to meet and solve the problem as honestly and courageously as I can. Of one thing I earnestly entreat you never to doubt: That is the sense of gratitude and loyalty I feel to you and Papa. That is stronger now in me than it ever was, stronger than, when as a little boy, we occupied the same room, stronger than when you took me on your trips to Florida and elsewhere. When I retire at night, when I wake in the morning I am conscious of the weight of my gratitude; it is the spur that drives me on.

And this was all in a sense true. He had gone north in the face of the family's suspicion and hostility. He intended to become a writer in the face of their belief that a writer was a man "like Lord Byron or Lord Tennyson or Longfellow or Percy Bysshe Shelley"—a man who was far away from them. Moreover, he had given up a respectable teaching job in Asheville to become such a man—and meanwhile to live off the family's bounty—and he had made this decision in the face of William Oliver Wolfe's mortal sickness. ("While I am absent Papa may die. I foresee these consequences. Do you think they have not been gouged in my very soul?") And the relationship with Julia Wolfe was a delicate one.

For, whether consciously or not, it was part of the mother's natural instinct, if not altogether to her natural interest, to continue to tie the son down; her gesture of generosity, in supporting the young Wolfe, was also an act of domination. While, on the other side of the partnership, by thus allowing himself to be supported—and over this period Wolfe seems curiously and even willfully unself-sufficient—the son may have been deliberately allowing himself to remain in this childhood pattern. It is pos-

sible that the very forms of Wolfe's opposition to the pattern—
he is always losing Julia's checks or overdrawing her account—
that these obvious gestures of revolt were also designed to keep
himself penniless and dependent. It was only later, with the
Angel, and with Julia still supporting him, that he was able to
free himself by destroying her—and by destroying her, created
her.

But even on the partial level of human behavior which people,
quite wisely, prefer to take for the whole, it is difficult to feel a
perpetual gratitude toward a ceaseless benefactor. And particularly, say, when the benefactor is buying real estate in Miami,
and when one, from the provinces, in the midst of the Boston
blue bloods, is using one's vest to patch one's trousers. (Later,
the ragged young Wolfe, venturing down to interview a Broadway
theatrical producer in respect to his new play, was given two
five-dollar bills as a handout.) In any case, the expressions of
indebtedness in these letters become a little stylized, while the
accents of bitterness become sharper. "You are the only one who
ever writes me from home now," Wolfe wrote to his mother in
1921, "and you have about deserted me."

Two weeks from today I will be twenty-one years old—legally the
beginning of manhood. If the time has come for me to go out on my
own, so be it, but please try not to treat me with the indifference that
has characterized your correspondence, or lack of it, for the last year.
You would not be intentionally guilty of cruelty to me but uninten-
tionally you have been. Uncle Henry says it is a family trait to forget
once out of sight—but how in God's name can I believe you would
forget me in a year's time?

You didn't want me at home [he added], you said nothing about
my returning and I shall see that your desires and those of the family
are satisfied.

This increasing bitterness extended from his family to his
friends.

As a matter of fact I almost have an aversion—natural or un-
natural, to seeing any of my old friends—unless, by God, I know
they are friends whether you bloom, or if you wither. . . . I couldn't
stand Asheville now—I couldn't stand the silly little grins on the
silly little drugstore faces. I couldn't stand the silly little questions of
"What're you doing now?"—And the silly little "oh" and the silly
little silence that follows when you say you are writing—as if they

could know—stupid little vermin as they are—the tragedy, and the heartbreak, and the travail of mind and spirit—that has kept me ragged.

And it was a bitterness that extended from his family and friends to his work itself:

To Langner's credit he did not ask me to retract a thing—I can keep all this—all he wants is a shorter, simpler play. Well, I will take one more chance and give him what he wants, in spite of the fact that Professor Baker will throw up his hands and say that I have "prostituted my art," and so on, when I see him. Well, "my art" has kept me ragged and driven me half mad;—I will see now if prostitution can put a few decent garments on my back and keep me housed. My good friends, Professor Baker included, have told me for years now of "my great talent," "my artistry," and so on—they have told me it would be a terrible thing for me to do anything else but write. They have said, "You have it—it's bound to come"—but not once has anyone given me advice on the simple little matter of keeping the breath of life in my body until the miracle does happen. That I can write better plays than most of those on Broadway I have no doubt— God help me if I can't—but to write such filthy, sexy twaddle, rot, and bunkum as this, I must cast all conscience to the winds. Well, I can and will do even that, for *money, money, money.*

Although there was now a question as to whether he could do even that. "My life being so up in the air, I find it hard to accomplish anything I want to write."

In part at least Wolfe had dug himself into this hole, too. Were his present fears somewhat extreme? His earlier hopes had been ever more so. He had worked with Frederick Koch and the Carolina Playmakers at Chapel Hill. He had gone on to the celebrated George Pierce Baker and the 47 Workshop at Cambridge, and there, grooming himself for the stage, along with the young Phillip Barry, he had almost persuaded himself that his early play, *The Mountaineers,* was going to be another *You and I.*

For a one-act play it is somewhat long, and will stand condensation and polishing, but it is the real thing and deals with a great tragedy. . . . It's the best play that has been written here this year simply because I have burned with eagerness and desire to have the truth out.

Well, a score of young provincials, watching the lights of Boston and New York, have written such letters home from the

time of Royall Tyler, and there is also unconscious comedy in
Wolfe's detailed summary of his next and even better play—and
of an earlier Eugene who is "wild with grief" as he bids farewell
to a rotting Southern aristocracy. "Master of Oakmont. Master of
a ruined kingdom, and a rotting Mansion— What a farce! Lord
of Misrule."

A similarly youthful tone, at once intense and inflated, marks
the "destiny" letter which Wolfe sent home two years later, in
1923:

The plays I am going to write may not be suited to the tender
bellies of old maids, sweet young girls, or Baptist Ministers but they
will be true and honest and courageous, and the rest doesn't matter.
If my play goes on I want you to be prepared for execrations upon
my head. I have stepped on toes right and left—I spared Boston with
its nigger-sentimentalists no more than the South, which I love, but
which I am nevertheless pounding. I am not interested in writing
what our pot-bellied member of the Rotary and Kiwanis call a "good
show"—I want to know life and understand it and interpret it without fear or favor. This, I feel, is a man's work and worthy of a man's
dignity. For life is not made up of sugary, sticky, sickening Edgar
A. Guest sentimentality, it is not made up of dishonest optimism,
God is *not* always in his Heaven, all is *not* always right with the
world. It is not all bad, but it is not all good, it is not all ugly, but it
is not all beautiful, it is life, life, life—the only thing that matters. It
is savage, cruel, kind, noble, passionate, selfish, generous, stupid,
ugly, beautiful, painful, joyous,—it is all these, and more, and it's all
these I want to know and, by God, I shall, though they crucify me
for it. I will go to the ends of the earth to find it, to understand it, I
will know this country when I am through as I know the palm of my
hand, and I will put it on paper and make it true and beautiful.

But there is also a new note. Did this early Wolfe, like any
Lardnerian song writer from Schenectady, consider himself "inevitable"? Did he earnestly believe that "the only thing that can
stop me now is insanity, disease, or death"—and go on, innocently, to proclaim that "I never forget; I have never forgotten"? He had nevertheless become aware of something which
Lardner's paranoiac yokels never quite realized: that he who is
inevitable is the victim of his inevitably—trapped and bound by
even the most beneficent sense of destiny. "That is what my life
means to me: I am at the mercy of this thing and I will do it or
die." Already he had plunged himself into that involved and in-

terminable evocation of his own life and backgrounds, that tortuous American remembrance of things past which formed the core of his work—and already disease and death formed the medium of approach, so to speak—the opaque psychological liquid through which he swam.

For as early as 1920, too, while he was still at Chapel Hill, Wolfe had developed a heavy cold which hung on persistently.

The thing got down into my chest and a week or two ago, I began to cough—at first a dry cough—then a rattling, tearing sort of cough, full of phlegm. I became worried. My right lung was sore. Of course I had to be out in all kinds of weather, and this didn't help. One night I started coughing here, in my room, and I put my handkerchief to my mouth. When I drew it away there was a tiny spot of blood on it. I was half sick with horror and I tried not to think of it. Thereafter when I coughed I kept my mouth closed and coughed in my throat. I swallowed pneumonia salve at night in huge balls, and rubbed my chest with the stuff. I ate cough drops.

And, remembering as he did his early family background—and his brother Ben had died of pneumonia—it is no wonder that the impoverished country man kept track of his health with an almost neurasthenic solicitude. "The meanest, most persistent cold I ever had," he wrote from Boston at "Xmas time," in 1923, "is slowly breaking up." He was "all nerves" in New York the year after, and had lost fifteen pounds during the summer. While he was teaching at New York University he noted that his eyes had gone bad. "I hope it is the cold, I don't know."—"I haven't wasted time by sleeping," he wrote again, "I am worked to a frazzle, and my left eye went bad about ten days ago." And his physical ailments, as Wolfe knew, were accentuated by his working habits—that is, by the fits of nervous frenzy and the spells of nervous exhaustion that followed each other during his work days, by his increasing sense of being deserted and alone ("I suppose I am one of the loneliest people in the world"), and by the dreams of time and guilt which now began to mark his nights: by all these symptoms of the heightened physical and spiritual intensity which had now become his normal routine. And now, too, as Julia Wolfe continued patiently and inexorably to accumulate her plots in Miami, the earlier accents of filial bitterness become those of exasperation, and almost of renunciation.

"I have no belief in your property or in anyone's property any more," Wolfe wrote from England in 1926. "I have no hope or belief or expectancy of getting anything from it now or hereafter —and he who ceases to hope or believe ceases to desire." "Money in our family," he said two months later, "has been a deadly poison—for it you have lost comfort, peace, and in the end, money itself; it has been a breeder of suspicion, of jealousy, of falsehood among brother and sister." His own life at home had ceased to be possible, he said the next year, and it had taken him twenty-seven years to rise above the hatreds of his childhood and the ugly and rancorous feeling which had existed in the family during his youth. "The next time we get hold of money let's put it in the bank, or on our back, or in our bellies—where it will do some good."

Yet, with this condemnation of his Southern home, there was no fond acceptance of his Northern life either. If the earlier Wolfe had displayed a certain impatience with Asheville's "little vermin" who awaited the proof of his dramatic talent; if what had actually stopped him at this point was not disease or death but the Theatre Guild, which had rejected his play; and if consequently these Northern intellectuals too, and indeed the entire Enfabled Rock, the whole glamorous pageantry of "that distant Babylon, cloud-capped and rosy-hued there in the smoke of his imagination," had turned stale and bitter for the provincial aspirant—now he had even more to say on the subject. Was his strongest impression of the Northern metropolis that of "thousands of inferior people undeveloped physically, dwarfed mentally"—from whom would grow the America of tomorrow, the hope of the world, which it was impossible to regard without a sinking of the heart? The nation itself now seemed compounded of such people, or of overgrown and ill-bred children, insolent to everything but money, servile, boastful and cowardly. "That, I am sorry to say, is my free opinion of this noble land—the amalgamated Boosters, Kiwanians, Lions, and, in general, the Federated Half Breeds of the World." If he remained in it at all, said this morose and peevish Wolfe, it was simply because other countries were not much better off—"the rabble everywhere is much the same— loud, ignorant, and cheap"—and when their leaders were not fools they were rascals. Furthermore, while he lived in New York, it was not for the sake of the hundred million who surrounded him, and whom he ignored unless they began to blow their bad breath and their superstitions in his face, but because New York was the money center and there was still a great deal of money in him:

I am sure I could make it out of advertising, the movies, or some form of publicity (fat, juicy, sugar-coated lies for our great Boob Public to swallow). I know a great deal about some things (not as much, it is true, as most of my fellow country men who know almost everything), but I have read and studied much and observed abundantly. Perhaps I shall end up by persuading the morons that the way to live forty years longer is to eat yeast every day, or to keep the voice beautiful by smoking Lucky Strikes. There is no limit apparently to what they are willing to believe, if you say it to them long enough.

Now, in fact, these accents of provincial superstition and arrogance, of vindictive envy and blind hatred, reach their climax in the young Wolfe. But now, of course, he was in the very midst of the first of that series of profound and agonizing creative struggles—those traumas of articulation—which marked, which actually *were,* his life. He was writing the *Angel.*

III

What was remarkable, moreover, was not that the young Wolfe was the sort of person he seemed to be—but that he wasn't.

For in a sense it seemed that almost everything around him—his origins, his temperament, the particular pattern his life fell into—conspired to make him into this sort of bigoted provincial; the real fascination of his story is by what sort of spiritual jujitsu he managed to slip out of fortune's iron collar—though perhaps that is the fascination of human life itself, and magic is its true medium, and in the realm of the psyche a Houdini is a piker.

What was a fact, anyhow, was that Wolfe's work was both a resolution to and at least a partial triumph over these native maladies and phobias—over his resemblance to Oedipus and his attachment to Mammon; over his romantic infatuation for and subsequent disenchantment with the Enfabled Rock; over that lingering but still very powerful tradition—and particularly for this child of Julia's "Old Kentucky Home" in North Carolina—of Southern gentility; over his aversion to the "Federated Half Breeds" of the world and his infatuation with Fame and the Fair

Medusa; and even over his initial handicap, that huge and hyper-
sensitive body which, just as it brought home to Wolfe the infinite
extent of human stupidity, very early showed to him "the barren
unity of life." This wound, too, became another entrance to experience, and similarly, through his work, built in spite of and
outside of Time, he trapped and made a friend of his last enemy
also. What was remarkable was that this harsh and arrogant
young man, whose proudest claim was that he had never forgotten, that he never forgot, *did* forget.

The resolution was not always quite complete, of course. The
broken accents of superstition are likely to recur in Wolfe's
weaker passages up to the end, just as his troubles did not quite
stop with the publication of *Look Homeward, Angel*—just as,
in fact, they seemed to be starting all over again. Like Bunyan's
Pilgrim, Wolfe took quite a while to arrive at the Celestial City,
and like Dante's he seemed, for a time, to be merely moving from
the simpler to the more involved circles of Life in the Inferno.
The six years between the *Angel* and *Of Time and the River,*
the years from 1929 to 1935, are almost the most involved and
the most interesting years of Wolfe's career; during this period
he passed from an apprentice to a craftsman and from revolt to
"discovery," and the account of this process which is contained
in *The Story of a Novel* forms a particularly illuminating diary of
the writer in America.

Some of these tortures were self-inflicted again—it would be
difficult to prove how many of them are not—and sometimes it
seemed that when Wolfe, like God, did not have any troubles he
was forced to invent them. Perhaps it was inevitable that the gas
heater in his New York apartment would leak—but was it inevitable that, waking up steadily with a headache, he should
never guess it was leaking? In Paris, down again with "a terrific
cold in the foggy weather," he entrusted his manuscript to a
perverse *concierge,* and it was Wolfe who ended up in a French
jail for abusing a French citizen. In Germany, in the midst of
those jolly Beer Festivals which appealed so bluntly to his nether
soul, he was beaten up and landed in a jolly German hospital.
Some years after his first novel Wolfe is still patching up his old
clothes—"I had really got to the point where I felt disgraced
every time I appeared in public"—and still working "ten, twelve
and fourteen hours a day here" for weeks on end, with his back

up to the wall. And when he had finally surmounted the almost
insuperable hurdle of his second novel, why, of all the literary
agents in New York, did Wolfe pick a young man who was as
temperamental as himself? In the lawsuit which followed, and
which dragged on endlessly, with its lurid charges and counter-
charges threatening whatever peace of mind Wolfe might have
achieved, lay the final stroke of this ludicrous and sometimes
almost heartbreaking drama of the country man and the arts: a
drama, really, which has in it all the elements of a crossroads
tragedy, and the central figures of which might appear as the
Hillbilly and the Furies. For this indigenous Orestes certainly had
a touch of the Doppus in him—this local Faustus was a kinsman
of Peter Schlemiel.

But maybe it was also this fundamental innocence that made
Wolfe what he was—a believer in humanity who wore down even
his own lawyers—and these continual afflictions that kept his
head bowed when it might have been turned. For there was no
doubt as to the attraction of the New York society Wolfe
describes in *The Web and the Rock*—and from Howells in
Boston to Cather in Chicago not many of our literary pilgrims
have described it more vividly. After his arrival, moreover, Wolfe
was a sort of literary sensation; surrounded as he was by his
circles of aesthetic admirers, owning the deep friendship of his
two celebrated artistic friends, he might well call this his "Magic
Year." So the Retreat to Brooklyn—the deliberate self-immolation and the return to darkness and anonymity; the halting efforts
of the hillman to comprehend the urban Brooklyn character and
to penetrate the barbaric Brooklyn accents; the final conviction
of this night-prowler among desolate alleys that here was his
second and in a sense even his true home—all this was a strategic
move of the highest order. And, just as Wolfe came to settle
here, so, too, for all his earlier exasperation, it was his continuing
bond with his first home and with the hill people themselves—his
recurrent complaint in the very arms of the Fair Medusa that he
was "still very homesick and lonely"—that helped him equally
to preserve a sort of balance on the pavements of the metropolis.

Were these country people among the benighted citizenry of
what Henry Mencken had just called the Sahara of the Bozart—
and, proud possessors of a low cunning, not altogether unrelated
to William Faulkner's later Bundrens and Snopeses? They were

also enigmatic, not without resources, full of tricks as well as
quirks—like Dashiell Hammett's Continental Op, they sometimes
took pleasure in playing the other half of a halfwit. *"Esse Quam
Videri."* Did Julia Wolfe herself, for example, show a certain
maternal naïveté, according to the most enlightened modern
standards, in her claim that her prodigy had slept with her "until
he was a great big boy"—and did she, further, go on to relate a
number of outrageous anecdotes about her boy's nursing habits?
(By these same modern standards, she was no doubt compensat-
ing, through this maternal possessiveness, for a wandering and
rhetorical husband.) Yet there was nothing untoward here in her
mind; while we would do well to keep in our minds the physical
frankness of these somewhat nonpuritanical and almost pre-
Victorian mountaineers—and to notice also their more intimate
contact with the Negro spirit. If Calvin and Knox finally reached
these Southern hills too, they had arrived, so to speak, through
the courtesy of Drake and Frobisher (and Thomas Otway was
as likely to be known in these regions as Alfred Tennyson), and
there was still that little detour through darkest Africa.

There was another interesting Southern strain here which
affected Faulkner and Caldwell as well as Wolfe, and which the
more cultivated Southern writers—the "superior" people—neglected at their own risk. There was, in these hill people with
their involved family histories and their back-country rituals,
their abundant hospitality and their endless talking, their mountain laughter and their clinging legends of sin and bloodshed, a
strain that probably comes closest, among all our rich regional
strains, to what we have labeled the "Russian" soul: I mean, of
course, merely the human soul, though at once more deeply
enslaved and freer, a soul, as it were, in fetters and in ecstasy.
And there is also a mountain mixture here that is not so noticeable in the Mississippi deltas or in the Georgia pinelands—of
primitive myth *and* equalitarian enlightenment; of voodoo and
the Bill of Rights.

"You belong to North Carolina," William Oliver Wolfe had
told his son when Tom wanted to go to the University of Virginia.
"And you must go to Chapel Hill. And that's a good school."
And so it was. For, while the hill people were suspicious of
"culture," they were not altogether averse to "learning"—Julia
Wolfe kept a sharp eye on her boy's Northern extravagances, but

she also bought a set of the Harvard Classics which her boy was reading. The Civil War, too, was part of their public conscious-ness as well as of their tribal memory; they had attended every presidential inauguration since McKinley, and every World's Fair. It was at St. Louis that Grover Cleveland Wolfe died of typhoid —his twin, the Ben of the novels, was Benjamin Harrison Wolfe —and Tom himself bought a low-rate ticket to Chicago in 1934. "I've done what all the rest of you have done and came to see the Fair." Although, during his apprenticeship, Wolfe had suffered the indignity of depending on these hill people for his financial support, it was also true that they *did* support him. And though, in his maturity, he had the shrewdness to draw upon them for the substance of his writing—for his mental capital—it was also true that he was less professionally and more directly and hu-manly involved with them.

"If people at home think they find some reference to them-selves and to Asheville in this story," he wrote about his last novel, "I hope they will feel this time that both my head and my heart are in the right place and that I have written as one of them." And the town's indignation over his first novel had at first shocked and then embittered Wolfe* precisely because he had always, at heart, felt himself "one of them"—because the rela-tionship of the writer and his people concerned Wolfe as it had not always concerned the esthetic rebels of the 1920's and as it would not always concern the social revolutionaries of the 1930's. You might almost say, in fact, that in Wolfe's work the American people came back into the American novel. At least, for all his hyperbole, he is the first major novelist of the Thirties to depict American family life in relatively normal terms—he may even be, coming on the heels of Fitzgerald, Hemingway and Dos Passos, the first novelist to depict family life at all. To some degree Wolfe marks the return of the "invisible roof" that Sherwood Anderson felt had once extended over the Ohio towns at the turn of the century: a roof that has hardly spread itself over contemporary letters.

And one, perhaps, in spite of all our technological additions, that seems hardly large enough to house both General Motors

---

* There are interesting accounts of Asheville and the *Angel* in both *The Story of a Novel* and *You Can't Go Home Again,* and this whole issue is a crucial one in Wolfe's mature thinking.

and the U.A.W. But in a more immediate sense it was surely there
for Tom Wolfe. "There are only fifteen hundred people in
Zebulon County," says the narrator in "The Return of the
Prodigal," "and we're all related somehow." "I would just like,
for example," Wolfe wrote his mother, "to get a list of the
twenty children or more that your grandfather had by his two
marriages and what happened to them and where they settled
and what parts of the country they move to, and so forth." There
were some lively relatives in Boston (the Bascom Pentlands of
Of Time and the River), there were Westalls and Penlands in
Oregon, and through all these numerous Eastern and Western
towns he would be almost sure, sooner or later, to run across a
wandering uncle, an eccentric aunt, a long-lost cousin. Perhaps
it was just this sense of kinfolk, extending over the width of a
continent and across the span of the Republic's history, that gave
Wolfe so sure a sense of his country; that allowed him, the
awkward provincial that he seemed, to move through the metropolitan salons with a sort of ease that a Dreiser or a Sinclair
Lewis, for example, could never quite manage (for there might
well be some forgotten Westall or Penland ensconced in these
chambers also)—and that, when Mrs. Jack's world went up in
the blaze of '29, enabled Wolfe to understand the Brooklyn
scene as well. For wasn't even the "pavement cypher," the
"dweller in mean streets," the "C. Green" of *You Can't Go
Home Again,* who finally makes his little impression upon an
impersonalized urban society by splashing his blood and bones
upon an American sidewalk from an open window twelve floors
up in a luxurious American hotel—wasn't even this anonymous
and starving Brooklynite a sort of kinsman, too?

At any rate, just as Wolfe's first novel had marked a shift in
that literary tide, always flowing east in the munificent Twenties,
from the Middle Western towns to Chicago, from Chicago to
New York, and from New York to London, Paris, and Capri—
so, by the time of his last novel, Wolfe had come to occupy a
special position among that new Younger Generation which came
of age in the economic distress of the Thirties. Did the Chicago
novelist, James T. Farrell, take Wolfe to task for his burgeoning
style during those lean years?—and use such a Wolfean phrase
as "in the green heart of June" as an example of sucking a dry
lemon? Still, whatever the diction, and there was something in

this sermon that recalled the pot and the kettle, it was precisely
the green heart of June that was lacking in Farrell himself and
in the majority of his colleagues of social crisis—these new urban
writers who seemed in many ways so closely identified with the
machine civilization they were attacking. It was possible, too, that
on the Chicago West Side—along those wide industrial thorough-
fares that ran, as Sherwood Anderson noticed, "on and on
forever, out of nowhere into nothing"—that there, there had
never been a month of June. So it was, after all, the whole web
of Wolfe's agrarian origins—his entire and immediate and intense
sense of the rich and varied nature of places, persons and things
—that allowed him to place the crack-up of contemporary city
culture within a wider framework of values.

During these years there was blind anger in Wolfe's work also
—those familiar accents of indignation and bewilderment that
mark the writing of the period.

Everywhere around me, during those years [Wolfe says] I saw the
evidence of an incalculable ruin and suffering. My own people, the
members of my own family, had been ruined, had lost all the material
wealth and accumulation of a life-time in what was called the "depression." And that universal calamity had somehow struck the life
of almost everyone I knew.

And prowling in his endless quest through the great web and
jungle of the city, he saw and felt the full weight of the calamity:

I saw acts of sickening violence and cruelty, the menace of brute
privilege, a cruel and corrupt authority trampling ruthlessly below its
feet the lives of the poor, the weak, the wretched, and defenseless of
the earth.
And the staggering impact of this black picture of man's inhu-
manity to his fellow man, the unending repercussions of these scenes
of suffering, violence, oppression, hunger, cold, and filth and poverty
going on unheeded in a world in which the rich were still rotten with
their wealth left a scar upon my life, a conviction in my soul which
I shall never lose.

But just as Wolfe had escaped from the neo-Menckenian twaddle
of the "mob" and the "aliens" who comprised the "Federated
Half Breeds"—and as he had watched the more sophisticated
members of the Lost Generation perform "as if there really were
a new and desolate race of youth"—so he now escaped from the

melodramatic and moralistic elements that marked the typical
social novelists of the period. He succumbed, moreover, to neither
of the two ideological extremes that ran through the literary
thinking of the 1930's—neither to a complete and blank personal
despair nor to a sweet and childlike trust in the revolutionary
utopia—but merely to a reasonable belief in the fortitude of man:
"his ability to suffer and somehow to survive."

For a somewhat verbose young man, Wolfe expressed a
similar notion with a curious simplicity just before his death*—
in those final letters written to the "Fox":

Your own philosophy has led you to accept the order of things as
they are because you have no hope of changing them; and if you
could change them, you feel that any other order would be just as
bad. In everlasting terms—those of eternity—you and the Preacher
may be right: for there is no greater wisdom than the wisdom of
Ecclesiastes, no acceptance finally so true as the stern fatalism of the
rock. Man was born to live, to suffer, and to die, and what befalls
him is a tragic lot. There is no denying this in the final end. *But we
must, dear Fox, deny it all along the way.*

Where were the provincial accents now? You *could* say he
had gained a sort of rationale for that earlier lyricism on the
"promise" of America.

And everywhere, through the immortal dark, something moving
in the night, and something stirring in the hearts of men, and something crying in their wild, unuttered blood, the wild unuttered
tongues of its huge prophecies—so soon the morning, soon the morning: O America.

At least that celebrated Wolfean door, that long-sought-for
door, opened out now not merely upon a personal exit but on
a communal vista. And just as Wolfe had joined that whole
earlier pilgrimage of East and West in our literature—that long
quest of our hinterland Jasons for the Gilded Fleece—so now he
linked himself to that later sequence of writers who saw the Magic
City no longer as the center of ease and grace but as the symbol
of industrial conquest. The symbol, I mean, of that whole new

---

* In July, 1938, after having delivered a new manuscript of more than
a million words, Wolfe became ill with pneumonia. He died that September, at the age of thirty-eight.

mechanized and standardized social arrangement whose triumph was complete when Woolworths came to Winesburg, and whose typical human products—the pavement cipher and the man-swarm atom—were separated by our historical tradition but *not* by our technological progress from what Wolfe, for all his love of the German people, had very early felt to be "the beast with the swine-face and the quenchless thirst."

Yes, Wolfe also remained at times the black and bitter Yea-Sayer of the new novelists of social crisis. And the fears and hatreds that still marked his work, the dark Faustian frenzies, the sense of disease and the almost morbid apprehensiveness of time's passing—these, too, were in the end a little more than strictly personal. With his corrosive doubts as to our future as well as his lyrical hope for the wild unuttered tongues of our huge prophecies, he belongs among those other artists in the national letters—from Melville and Whitman to Dreiser and Sherwood Anderson himself: those who were expansive by nature and constrained by necessity.

Introduction to *The Portable Thomas Wolfe;*
The Viking Press, 1946.

The Letters

Thomas Wolfe spent the years from 1924 to 1930 teaching at the Washington Square College of New York University. These were the crucial years of his apprenticeship when he gave up playwriting and turned to the novel form. Still uncertain of himself, unknown, and possessed—a ragged Faust first meeting the enchantment of the "enfabled rock"—he prowled through the city's streets. They were difficult years when he might turn upon friends and acquaintances all the huge emotional shock of his own suffering.

Because of this *Thomas Wolfe at Washington Square* by Thomas Clark Pollock and Oscar Cargill and *The Correspond-ence of Thomas Wolfe and Homer Watt,* edited by the same two authors, have a greater value and interest than many similar collections. And there is a central irony that pervades them. Homer Watt, the chairman of the English department at that time, was particularly fond of Wolfe, as their correspondence shows. In fact the impassioned Southerner was a privileged character among the other struggling young instructors. Yet Wolfe later lampooned his whole experience at New York University in a famous section of *Of Time and the River* on the "School for Utility Cultures."

This is a common experience, of course, of those who have dealt with writers—who have experienced the monster that lurks behind the child. Young Tom Wolfe was arrogant, ruthless, demonic—if not, as he later admitted, almost demented, during this period of gestation. To a certain extent he inflicted even worse wounds upon the two closest friends and literary influences of these years, Aline Bernstein and Maxwell Perkins. But this is the human price that is forgotten—or rather, memorialized— in the long vistas of art. Perhaps the essay by Oscar Cargill in *Thomas Wolfe at Washington Square* tends to soothe the ruffled vanity of Wolfe's former students and academic associates, and thus to emphasize the monster rather than the poet. It ignores the true meaning of the social satire in Wolfe's novels.

This satiric vein was becoming increasingly important in his work—to the point of supplanting his original lyricism. If the portrait of that invincible student, Abe Jones, was overdone in *Of Time and the River,* if Wolfe repaid his friend John Terry's devotion by creating the character of Jerry Alsop in *The Web and the Rock,* these are nevertheless memorable figures, and not just "objects of ridicule." The point is that Wolfe's satire at its best was not merely fashionable; it cut deep, it was based on solid human values—and we feel its absence in the national letters today. In my own judgment, too, the anti-Semitism which Mr. Cargill stresses was not nearly so pernicious in Wolfe's work as it was in that of certain contemporaries who were less obvious, perhaps, and more prejudiced.

At least Wolfe could almost always see through his own spells of hysteria in the end. This "crazy and tormented weaver," as he called himself in the novels, could also describe the core of his own black hatreds. There is further evidence of this among the other letters and essays contributed to *Thomas Wolfe at*

Washington Square by former faculty and students alike. Henry Volkening has written a sympathetic account of his friendship with Wolfe during this period. Vardis Fisher has a psychological analysis that, if it sometimes projects the neurosis of one novelist upon another, also throws real light upon Wolfe's inner motivation. It is interesting, finally, to compare these two volumes of personal reminiscences with Richard Walser's recent collection of critical essays about Wolfe's work. Which of these two personalities—the tormented young English teacher or the author of *Look Homeward, Angel*—was the real one?

From the *New York Times,* November 14, 1954.

What American literature at the mid-century lacks and needs is a vital center—though I do not mean conformity. The glittering virtuoso talents of the 1920's—the Hemingways, Fitzgeralds, and Faulkners—derived from and were preceded by a solid core of earlier native realists all the way from William Dean Howells to Theodore Dreiser.

Thomas Wolfe himself, for all his romantic egoism, his verbal frenzies, and exacerbated emotions, belonged precisely to the central and solid middle ground of American fiction. The first value of *The Letters of Thomas Wolfe,* edited by Elizabeth Nowell, is to clarify his true literary position.

There are other values in this collection. Like the author of the letters, it is massive, varied, illuminating, and entertaining in turn; and somehow Elizabeth Nowell has managed to keep out much of what was ponderous and repetitious in Wolfe's work. The book is described as a form of autobiography, but most Wolfean autobiography is also a form of fiction. It might almost be called the last of Wolfe's novels, since he often used these letters—many of which he never sent to his ostensible correspondents—as a kind of preliminary sketchbook for his ideas, scenes, portraits, or what his later editor called Wolfe's "dithyrambs."

Thus the central focus of the present book is on certain very sharply defined areas of American life and society, quite as much as it is on the rebellious and provincial artist-hero. If the forward movement in Wolfe's life was to attain freedom and originality for himself and his writing, the backward and binding tie—in what he called the web of memory—was with his own early origins and environment. Unlike the expatriate generation of the postwar period, Wolfe never disdained and never looked down upon—though he might often rant about—his homely provincial ties. He continued to write to his family, to his childhood and college friends, throughout his life. He was horrified, after the publication of *Look Homeward, Angel* in 1929, when Asheville, North Carolina, nearly repudiated *him!* His realism was devouring and ruthless, and almost unconscious. He could never understand why his relatives and friends protested—and sometimes brought libel suits—at having been "caricatured."

Since Wolfe's letters to his mother—perhaps the least engaging aspect of his personality—have already been published in a separate volume, the present collection moves almost directly into the Harvard years, when Wolfe had set out to be a playwright and received his first literary defeat. (Very likely the lingering prejudice with which he always viewed New York theatrical and literary society stemmed from this first wound.) Meanwhile his mother kept reminding him of the "wasted money" that was being spent on his education—and here, after his break with the great Professor Baker of the Drama Workshop, began the first of a famous series of Wolfe's farewell letters.

This pattern of idolization and disenchantment was to continue through Wolfe's mature emotional life. He was never one to let a friendship pass in sorrow and silence. He moved on to New York University, where his first novel, the *Angel* itself, was taken by Maxwell Perkins of Scribner's, and where he found in Aline Bernstein (the Mrs. Jack of the novels) the central love affair of his life. These were the years of the fame and glory which the young artist had craved beyond all else; how bright they were, and how brief! For Wolf was already obsessed by a series of future novels he had planned: gigantic and impossible projects which brought him to the brink of desperation. And then came the breakup with Mrs. Bernstein herself, in "the black spring of love."

The more personal letters of this relationship are not included in the present volume; but certainly Wolfe's inner despair contributed to the difficulties which surrounded his second novel. *Of Time and the River* took six years of turmoil, which later Wolfe himself brilliantly described in *The Story of a Novel*. He was always poor. His family had been wiped out in the Depression; and during most of this period he lived in and prowled through the Brooklyn slums. When he did not have troubles, one might add, he appeared to invent them. There is the anonymous and dreadful young man of these letters who became the "agent" for Wolfe's manuscripts, and then threatened (in another of the tragicomic lawsuits which marked Wolfe's meteoric career) to publish obscene sections from them.

The European trips were almost Wolfe's only moments of relaxation and pleasure; though he managed to get involved in a nightmarish brawl at the Munich Oktoberfest. He had always been drawn to Germany, where he had been lionized in the middle Thirties. It was another wrench to his spirit, as well as to his vanity and pocketbook, when he realized the nature of the Nazi terror. And meanwhile his deep relationship with Maxwell Perkins —who was a kind of foster father as well as editor and friend to him—was drawing to a close. The letters to Perkins form a central stand in this volume. The dissolution of the friendship is even more complex, tortuous, harried, distraught, and unhappy than anything which has gone before.

I have hardly had time to mention the scores of letters which Wolfe wrote to such constant friends as Olin Dows, James Boyd, John Hall Wheelock, Henry Volkening, A. S. Frere, Jonathan Daniels, Alfred Dashiell and many others. Nor have I had space to mention the famous interchange with Scott Fitzgerald—a dialogue between two generations in which Wolfe established his claim to speak for the writing of the 1930's. That he did; and that he does over and over again in the present book.

During the writing of his last two novels—*The Web and the Rock* and *You Can't Go Home Again*—Wolfe almost felt that he had lost everything. He doubted even his physical vitality, his fading looks. His paranoid visions assailed him constantly. This was the black side of grief and melancholia in the poet of the American dream; just as there is a very similar darkness in the inner thought, say, of Melville or Whitman. And what Wolfe had gained during these years of lonely and tormented struggle was the experience and the perspective, the central view of life, which put his novels in the main stream of our literature.

Like his illustrious literary ancestors of the nineteenth and twentieth centuries, he had an insatiable appetite for life and a fixed purpose to tell the truth about it. The letters bring this all back to us, and how we could use it again today!

From the *New York Times,* October 7, 1956.

BY COZZENS POSSESSED

I AM interested in the fact that *Critique* is preparing a special
issue on the work of James Gould Cozzens. It is a good idea in
general, and I hope the magazine will do the same thing for other
American writers. There might be a special issue, for example,
on some of the new novelists like William Styron or John Howard
Griffin and the rest, whose books haven't yet achieved the almost
universal acclaim of *By Love Possessed*.

He, James Gould Cozzens, is certainly due for some of the
attention he has recently received. Both *The Just and the Unjust*
(1942) and *Guard of Honor* (1948) were reputable and highly
intelligent novels which failed in popular impact but received
critical approval. Being a slow writer myself, I like the amount of
time, thought, and effort that Mr. Cozzens puts into his books.
They are a rebuke to the standardized bestsellers, one a year, of
the professional novelists we know all too well; they show the
admirable dedication of a serious craftsman. In the new book,
too, we know that every detail is solidly worked in, that in the
fictional context it is *right*.

Reading the novel, we can admire its ingenuity, its technical
proficiency, its humor, tolerance, and wisdom. I confess I rather
like the involved style which Mr. Cozzens has lately taken up.
Can anybody, moreover, really question the theme—or the moral
—of *By Love Possessed*? It is a graceful sermon on, and a hard
rebuke to, the present age of emotionalism and hysteria, of
commercialized or supernatural panaceas, of false education
and slippery success. From the vantage point of old-fashioned
American small-town society—the "best we have produced"
—the novel shows up, quite brilliantly, the whole contemporary
drift.

There is Mr. Woolf, the New York lawyer, obviously Jewish and converted to Episcopalianism, who at first looks down upon the whole pattern of society in Brocton. There is Jerry Brophy, the Irish Catholic district attorney, son of a saloon keeper on Water Street, who wants so desperately to become a judge, and is so naturally and intuitively a politician. There is Helen Detweiler who has devoted her virginal life for the cheap pleasures of her weak and spoiled younger brother Ralph.

These are the lower-class figures in the novel. (Though Helen Detweiler comes originally from a "good" family, and it is suggested that her uncritical form of mother-sister love for Ralph is the cause of his ruin.) Moreover, through the lawsuits and legal processes of the story, which are skillfully narrated, the central action moves downward to the very lowest depths of Brocton society—to the idiot girl Caroline Dummer, who has murdered her illegitimate baby, and who turns out to be the ironic counterpart of the rich, showy, sensuous, and "mystic" Catholic, Mrs. Pratt. A seeker after secondhand sexuality under the guise of God and Sin, insinuating, bosomy, and scatter-brained, Mrs. Pratt is a marvelous minor figure.

Arthur Winner is the mediator between these upper and lower ranges of Brocton life. An eminent middle-class figure, a man of honor and propriety as well as of reason, yet tolerant, forgiving and fair-minded, he is the real prop of his society, perhaps one of the best portraits of the average American (upper-income) man in our recent fiction. Yet this estimable hero, within the two days of the novel's time, discovers that his whole reputation, his professional career, his social position, have been based on the financial chicanery of his senior law-partner, Noah Tuttle. Moreover, his other partner and best friend, the crippled, cynical Julius Penrose, has known this from the very beginning, and is an accessory to the crime. When Arthur Winner, in righteous indignation, proposes to reveal the facts of the situation immediately, and pay the penalty, Julius suggests that after all he, Arthur, has had a turbulent love affair with his, Julius' nympho-maniac wife which he has never thought it quite necessary to reveal to the world or to Julius himself.

The respectable hero is forced to carry on as before, but as the shell of the man he was. In the long bout with fate which we call life, this "winner" is a loser too, like all the other ruined

souls around him whose broken destinies he alone has tried to
salvage. The Reason Machine itself, as Cozzens says, is based
on the dirt of human experience, and can hardly rise above it.
And if *By Love Possessed* must be classified as belonging to the
conservative side of our literature, if its closest affinity is perhaps
with Ellen Glasgow's Southern tragicomedies, I don't think either
that its central vision of life coincides with the *Time-Life* eulogy
of the novel and its author.

The critical furor over the novel has, however, some curious
aspects. All unsuspecting, perhaps, like the peeping shepherd on
the gilded clock who opens and closes the novel, Mr. Cozzens
has fallen into the trap, not indeed of love, but of the time spirit.
On the part of the Luce publications, at least, the high praise
of *By Love Possessed* is not unrelated to the recent adulation of
Herman Wouk. Here it is the exaltation of mediocrity which is
being sought after. The approval of Mr. Cozzens' book implies
a return to "reason," which somehow means a return to conservatism, conformity, and the rest. (In one sense, this is accurate, of course, and how much bigger a literary fish have these
wily anglers caught now than the entertainment-minded Mr.
Wouk.) It signifies a return to normalcy, decency, sobriety, etc.,
in our literary trends. No love, no passion, no divorces, no unhappiness; or what is the same thing in the moral of the present
novel, that these impulses are dangerous or destructive, as indeed
they are.

The sexual drives, which are so natural and so powerful, can be
gratified safely, so Mr. Cozzens indicates, only within the bounds
of a respectable marriage, and a stern, moral upbringing for your
children. (True, it is a second marriage for Arthur Winner, with
a much younger wife who is a daughter symbol and a fine tennis
player.) Mr. T. S. Eliot gave us the same moral recently in *The
Cocktail Party* (though devoutly religious, while Mr. Cozzens is
only skeptically so). But for myself I still prefer the old Dreiserian view, or Walt Whitman's view, that these dangerous and
powerful human feelings—our illicit impulses, I mean—are what
make life interesting, valuable, and instructive. Indeed, they *are*
life.

Mr. Cozzens (to whom I must apologize for making him in
turn a symbol of the time spirit, when after all he is mainly a
writer) is a rationalist and a classicist by temperament. This is

a valuable strain in our literature, and we always have had and
will have writers who uphold this tradition. (Though Cozzens'
mode of classic rationalism is rather eighteenth centuryish, a
little quaint, old-fashioned, and bookish; closer, again, to the
Edith Wharton–Henry James school, which also shared his literary preconceptions, say, of "*the* Jew.") Now the fact is, until the
1940's and Fifties, that contemporary American writing was
nearer the other pole of the literary spectrum: rebellious, wild,
subjective, and romantic in general.

But is the issue, then, that of Cozzens versus American literature, as it was put in the glowing (and rather sweeping) review
by the editor of *Harper's* magazine? Does the latest novel by
James Gould Cozzens really show up, and wipe out, all of Hemingway, Faulkner, Dos Passos, Sinclair Lewis, Tom Wolfe, at their
peak, not to mention Nelson Algren at this end of the literary panorama, and Theodore Dreiser at the other? No; perhaps Mr.
Cozzens looks so good at the moment, like Mr. Nixon in the
political arena, only because the others look so bad. Perhaps
the success of *By Love Possessed* is only the final confirmation
of our literary failure in the Fifties.

Once we have escaped from the magic of the novel's craftsmanship, indeed, we have an increasing sense of disappointment,
of inadequacy, almost of sterility. It is a good novel, but it is not
a great novel, because all the great novels, whatever their type
or genre, increase our sense of life, and this one, in a very curious
way, decreases it. It is a contractive, not an expansive document;
and one almost suspects that beneath its measured harmony lies
an anguished, perhaps a morbid or neurotic fear of life. It is
not only that Mr. Cozzens' conservatism, high-minded as it is,
cuts him off from things, that his ascetic temperament leads him
to scholarly rather than to profound conclusions, that his dedication to his craft (and to reason) is at the expense of experience
itself. There is something else. What?

In his previous work there has always been a certain lack of
primary feeling; he is a cold writer who has needed a recharge,
say, of human sympathy. To a certain degree *By Love Possessed*
is probably the attempt to get at just this issue in his own work
and career—but an attempt which, rather than enlarging the
writer's capacity to feel, simply confirms his prejudice against
feeling. It is a treatise on the different kinds of love—parental,

oedipal, sibling, self-love or vanity, religious, sexual. But why is it that all these types of love are only destructive and never even momentarily rewarding? Why is the sexual act itself always described in such forbidding and perhaps really obscene terms: the horror and shame of menstruation, the masculine fear of being trapped by pregnancy, the "bumping bellies," the "crisis of connection," or the "mucid encompassment," the "clandestine lechery," and "the slippery lovers." Now let me quote:

Deaf as yesterday to all representations of right, he purposed further perfidy, once more pawning his honor to obtain his lust. Deaf as yesterday to all representations of reason, he purposed to sell himself over again to buy venery's disappearing dross—some moments of transient dallying with eye or hand, to which untied impatience quickly set a term; some impassioned moments of the now engendered beast of two backs, of that acting androgyne whose he-half was excitedly prodding and probing, whose she-half was excitingly prodded and probed. The little life span of the beast soon sped, its death was died. At the she-half's flings-about in her extremity, the he-half's spoonful of phrenetic sensation was tweaked to spend itself —and there! There was the buy, the bargain, the prize, the pearl of price! All possible gain now realized; and, in sum, but loss, would the fallen rider, fallen steed still under him, contract another time for such a run? Yes (if flesh could); a hundred times. In proof, was the truth of fact that, until a day or two before Julius was due home, the indoor turfman had his sport as often as opportunity (his mount was much of one week menstruating) could be afforded him.

Well, this is rather good—isn't it?—as prose, or as the description of a grotesque biological process. But in the central love affair of Arthur Winner and the uterinely enraged Marjorie Penrose (of which it is the climax), why is it, again, that between these impassioned if slippery lovers there is not one word of conversation, of mutual affection, or even, say, of thank you and good-by? Why is it that Arthur burns the semen-stained mattress at the end, and then, in the retrospect of this passion, feels obliged to decapitate a poisonous snake with a hoe? Is love then merely a matter of glandular secretions, of aroused gristle, of muscular contractions, and dripping fluids? No, the point is that *By Love Possessed* has no love in it, nor does it understand, for all its rationalism, the meaning of the sexual love which it describes so anatomically. For if life is indeed viewed as the "dirt" which supports the reasoning faculty, and if sexual love is only a prodding he-part and a prodded she-part (a tweak and a spoonful of phrenetic sensation!), how is any further and full concept of human love, or ordinary human understanding, possible?

It is not. And what Mr. Cozzens does not seem to understand, for all his classical lore, is that the Goddess of Love, whatever her cruel demands on her afflicted subjects, is also the Goddess of Life. Now one more comment might be pertinent to the current vogue of "By Cozzens Possessed." Despite the photographic or microscopic sexual descriptions in the novel (and the curious scenes of voyeurism), I have met very few readers of the book, including the young writers studying Mr. Cozzens' craft, who have really enjoyed it. I wonder whether it is the fault of these readers, or perhaps some deeper instinct to preserve the great life-giving illusions of nature. For this novel also lacks all the gaiety, the pleasure, the luxury, yes, the comfort and the exaltation of spirit which—along with the tortures and torments—belong to the realm of "love." Good God, has that become dull, too?

An essay written for *Critique* magazine in 1958.

FURTHER DECLINE OF THE MODERNS

John Steinbeck

The Pearl is an old Mexican folk tale which John Steinbeck has recast in his familiar paisano vein. It originally appeared in the *Woman's Home Companion* under the title of "The Pearl of the World" and now, with five full-page original drawings by José Clemente Orozco, it forms a modest and attractive little volume. But it also raises some serious questions about Steinbeck's recent books and his work as a whole.

The story deals with a Mexican fisherman named Kino who is devoted to his wife, Juana, and his child, Coyotito. The child is bitten by a scorpion and the white doctor refuses to treat it. Kino discovers a huge pearl, the greatest pearl in the world according to his Mexican neighbors. The doctor tries to steal it. The pearl merchants (also white) try to cheat him out of it, and Kino is forced to flee from his village and to murder the "trackers" who come after him. In the end he has lost his home, his child, and his happiness, and he flings the pearl back into the sea.

"If this story is a parable," Steinbeck says, "perhaps everyone takes his own meaning from it and reads his own life into it." Indeed, as in most of Steinbeck's allegories, there are several meanings implicit in *The Pearl,* not all of which, perhaps, are what the author consciously intended.

The writing is very good, as are the descriptions of village life and Mexican types, and the Gulf scene itself: the land, the climate, even the various hours of the day. There is less of Steinbeck's romantic whimsicality, too, although one still could do without some of his Mexican "songs." And what one notices again is how much more interested Steinbeck really is in the nat-

151

ural scene, and in animal life, than in the people or the human
emotions of his narratives.

It is not particularly important that the "whites" of his primitive tales are always complete villains. "As with all retold tales,"
Steinbeck also tells us, "there are only good and bad things and
black and white things . . . and no in-between anywhere."
But the quality that has marked Steinbeck's work as a whole is
precisely the sense of black and white things, and good and bad
things—that is to say, the sense of a fabulist or a propagandist,
rather than the insight of an artist. Moreover, we have now come
to understand that even primitive souls are highly complicated.
It is probably harder for a modern writer to understand them
than to understand a man of his own time and place. The doctor
of *The Pearl* speaks to all of Kino's race "as though they were
simple animals." But the doctor's main fault is that he apparently
considers all Mexican Indians bad, while Steinbeck considers all
Mexican Indians good.

At the climax of this fable, one notices that this native fisherman is described as "a terrible machine." In Kino's moment of
anger he becomes "as cold and deadly as steel." One has only
to compare Steinbeck's primitive types with those of D. H.
Lawrence, say, or his studies of peasant character with those of
the Italian writer Silone, to realize his limits. Of all the ranking
modern writers who have gone back to primitive material as a
protest against and a solace for contemporary society, Steinbeck
is, as a matter of fact, the least well endowed. What he usually
does is to ascribe a peculiar sort of suburban American romanticism to these native types. "Go with God," Juana says to her
husband as he prepares to murder the trackers, but one wonders
just which God Kino is supposed to go with.

The most important point in Steinbeck's earlier career was the
change, around 1935, from such pagan excursions as *To a God
Unknown* or *Tortilla Flat* to the novels of social criticism, *In
Dubious Battle* and *The Grapes of Wrath*. It is interesting to
speculate on the reasons why Steinbeck has now returned to this
earlier and less satisfactory vein of his work. And, without stressing the fact that our national history did not end with the Second
World War, one would like to remind this gifted and volatile
American novelist that his recent works do mark a reversionary
tendency in his career.

One might say that the artist, too, must discover and cherish his own pearl. He cannot reject it for a state of false innocence.

From the *Saturday Review,* November 22, 1947.

John Steinbeck's new "play-novelette" *Burning Bright* is a flat failure as a novelette at least. I think it is correct to add that he has not written an important work of fiction since *The Grapes of Wrath,* more than ten years ago.

What has happened to the career of this writer who was, along with Tom Wolfe, one of the major figures to emerge during the 1930's? *Burning Bright,* as you might guess, is actually a play in three acts—a play that is "easy to read," as Steinbeck says, or a short novel that can be played simply by "lifting out the dialogue," and something of this facile and mechanical approach pervades the whole tone of the writing. It is practically a gadget, and you can also lift out any of the central characters without doing great harm to the script.

Another feature: the main characters are a group of circus acrobats in the first act, and remain as the same personages throughout the story. In the second act, however, they are farmers, in the third, sailors. This is symbolic, and at a quick guess the shift in scene from air to land to sea involves the three main areas of human or animal existence in the evolutionary process.

But I am still trying to work out the connection of this symbolism with the story, and why Steinbeck's characters should start out as birds and end up as fish. The hero, Joe Saul, is starvingly in love with his wife, Mordeen, who is, as we are also told, a burning flower in his heart. But he craves a son to carry on his bloodline. Mordeen, who knows that he is sterile, is determined to give him a child by any means, and for this purpose selects Joe Saul's assistant, Victor, another acrobat, who represents animal vitality and complete sterility of spirit.

The drama is now under way, and from this point on everything drops into place with a nice, sharp, clean click. There is no attempt to define any of these characters beyond their symbolic roles in the play—whatever happens to them is formulated by the plot and not by temperament or character. Mordeen is, of course,

one of Steinbeck's recurrent fantasies of the Eternal Woman or
the Cosmic Mother—a type I myself have never personally met.
Even Victor, the brute-man, is affected by the aura of supreme
love that radiates from her; so much so that he quite naturally
wants to claim his own son. Jealous, frustrated, and in human
terms the only credible character in the play, he has to be murdered, of course, to preserve Mordeen's secret.

What is one to make, incidentally, of this episode in which an
innocent human being, however unpleasant, is bumped off so
casually—an episode that has undertones of the California vigi-
lantes as well as of maternal bliss? It is good stage, probably,
but is it nice? Are the peculiar means of Mordeen really justified
by the altruistic climax of the drama, in which Joe Saul discovers
(in another improbable episode) that what counts is not his own
son, but, as it were, anybody's child, or the gift of life itself, which
Mordeen in her infinite, if witless compassion has granted to him.

In the final "big scene" of the drama Joe Saul appears in the
hospital, next to Mordeen and the new child, as only a voice and
a white facelessness. "Where is your face?" Mordeen asks.
"What's happened to your face, Joe Saul?" "It's not important,"
he says, "just a face."

Now here, perhaps, in the revealing unconscious which so
often tells the truth about a writer's work, is the clue to the deterioration of Steinbeck's work in the last decade. For the whole
purpose of art, if not of evolution, is to create human faces which
are important, and which cannot be lifted off and on in the
interests of the loftiest message or the most startling stage effect.

That voice, indeed, and that "white facelessness" are symptomatic of a writer who is concerned only with grandiloquent
themes and mechanical people. Steinbeck's work has always been
uneven, and one had to measure such an excellent early book as
The Pastures of Heaven against such poor works as *Cup of Gold*
or *To a God Unknown*. The success of his later works was due
primarily to the essential force and vitality of the writing, which
often obscured the false, sentimental, or banal concepts of life
which Steinbeck still carried along with him.

And this "success" in terms of the commercial stage, the movie
scenario, the bestseller, has apparently led Steinbeck to develop
the least satisfactory elements of his previous work. One can still

hope that he will throw off the adolescent philosophy, the facile emotions, the final subordination of any genuine interest in human beings as such to a tricky theme or a theatrical climax. (These are typical characteristics of the California school of writing from Jack London and Frank Norris to Steinbeck himself, and of a cultural atmosphere in which writers somehow never seem quite to grow up.) But this is, judging from Steinbeck's present work, a poor and desperate hope.

> From the *Saturday Review,* October 21, 1950. This review was considered so severe (or so wrong) that the *Saturday Review* published a rebuttal in the editorial column the following week. The later stage production of *Burning Bright* was a failure. Perhaps music might have helped it.

The real question about John Steinbeck is what has happened to John Steinbeck. When I first wrote about him in the 1940's he was, along with Tom Wolfe, one of the bright lights in the literary firmament. He had then written *The Grapes of Wrath, In Dubious Battle, The Long Valley, The Red Pony,* and the lyrical short stories of *The Pastures of Heaven.*

Another early hit of his was *Of Mice and Men,* and one could forgive the ham in that novel-play, or digest it, just as one realized that the paisanos of *Tortilla Flat* were not quite authentic. (Steinbeck's primitivism, an antidote for the machine age, is tinged with adolescent notions of "fun," "anarchy," "sex.") But since that time almost all of Steinbeck's works, from *Cannery Row* to *Sweet Thursday,* can be classified only in the category of entertainment —that is to say, hits and ham.

The present book *The Short Reign of Pippin IV* is better than most, perhaps, because it is a "fabrication," and deals with imaginary people in an absurd situation. It is a satire on contemporary French politics, and reflects on the one hand, Steinbeck's inner yearning for cosmopolitanism, royalty, and nobility, and on the other hand, his perhaps atavistic fantasies of social justice. M. Pippin Arnulf Héristal is a French astronomer who happens to be related to the line of Charlemagne. He is selected as the new French king, in the interest of national stability, when the various French political parties have no other solution.

Pippin IV has a devoted wife, an uncle named Charles Martel who runs a shady art gallery, a daughter named Clotilde who has just written a bestseller called *Adieu Ma Vie*. She is a post-Existentialist who loves American jazz, cowboys, hooligans and hoods, and then meets an American Chicken Prince whose dynasty dates back to F.D.R. Pippin IV also takes a mistress, in accordance with French custom, but his best female friend turns out to be Sister Hyacinthe, formerly of the Folies Bergère, until her arches went flat.

All of this is entertaining enough if you are looking for light reading. Steinbeck still writes with a charmed pen—that is the real loss—while the humor of the book rests in the political and social satire, both French and American. When Pippin IV takes his job seriously and inaugurates a New Deal program, revolution ensues. Yes, it is only when we compare this satire with a book, say, like Simone de Beauvoir's *The Mandarins,* that we realize just how inadequate and trivial John Steinbeck's present vision of France, or of the world, can be.

Is there nothing left for him to take seriously? And I mean seriously even in the sense of satire which is directed at something more than laughs. Men are like children, says Sister Hyacinthe to Mrs. Pippin. "The ones who really truly grow up . . . are no good because men are either children or old—there is nothing in between." This is a sample of Steinbeck's philosophy. But what lies in between childhood and age, is maturity.

From the Chicago *Sun-Times,* April, 1957.

J. P. Marquand

John P. Marquand is a novelist of talent in the technical area of his craft, and for this reason alone he deserves consideration. There are other reasons, although *B. F.'s Daughter,* his last novel, was also one of his weakest and this new one is not altogether a success. But *Point of No Return* is marvelously clever in design and execution and it is a pleasure to read, if in some respects it is painful to think about.

Money is the central theme of the novel, just as money has haunted so much modern writing from *The Great Gatsby* to *Tucker's People*. Perhaps no theme could be more valid or more difficult to handle. Money is the source and center of much of the national character today. Yet only Dreiser, in the older generation, and Dos Passos, among the moderns, have had the stamina to deal with it directly, and Mr. Marquand himself uses an oblique attack.

The Stuyvesant Bank in uptown New York, where Charles Gray works, is a conservative institution. "The employes of the Stuyvesant understood rich clients and knew all the pains and drawbacks of being rich, although they were not rich men themselves." Charles has developed the discipline and the attitude for this—"a priestly, untouchable, ascetic attitude."

Charles and Nancy Gray have a house in Sycamore Park, they belong to the Oak Knoll Club, which is not quite as good as Hawthorn Hill, but is still not cheap. Like most suburban Americans, they are just getting by on their income, although Charles would have thought it handsome in the old days. But now, in his early forties, he is suddenly afraid of things. He has reached the point of no return.

Mr. Marquand's skill in telling the novel is that of balancing or weaving together the subordinate themes in a contrapuntal effect, and in this case themes of a discordant nature. What Charles dislikes about the office work is the continual caution, the restraint of feeling, the constant substitution of discretion for impulse. He will not crawl, but the instinct to please has almost become second nature—and his second nature has become his first.

Another of Mr. Marquand's fortes is the minor drama of domestic strain—the conversations that are always verging on the brink of a quarrel, the jokes that turn out to be not funny, the areas of silence, the general friction that is the normal environment of two people who have once loved each other and still perhaps do. Nancy is a good wife. She is a little too efficient about getting Charles to the station on time, and she doesn't like her hair disturbed when she is being kissed. She has become sharper, more anxious, in the competitive climate of Sycamore Park.

It is mainly the problem of the children being able to go to Exeter which bothers her. Charles himself went to public school in Clyde, Massachusetts, and here is the throwback into the past. The town of Clyde is the late nineteenth-century American small town and Mr. Marquand, tracing the early history of his hero, uses it as a contrast for his cutthroat suburban scene. Yet the story of Charles Gray's family is a rather familiar Marquand chronicle of lower upper-class society among the "upper-uppers" —of the Scott Fitzgerald type hero who is just on the fringe of the real thing. (It is really not the real thing, of course, or is it?) In his defense of this old-fashioned American town, Mr. Marquand succeeds mainly in evading the real point of his story.

For Charles does succeed in the bank. And all the true implications of his life, and the sensitive, acute observations about his career, are somehow toned down or actually ignored in the end. Mr. Marquand belongs to the ranks of the traditional novelists rather than the discoverers and rebels. He is among the "conservators of heritage," such as Willa Cather or Ellen Glasgow. But this does not mean that he must sacrifice, as he does here, everything he knows about American life and expresses so well, to the demands of a sentimental and romantic tale. True enough, Charles accepts his advancement with the acrid knowledge that he has lost his freedom forever, and this takes character. But it is character that lacks the real courage to make the break, whose virtue is compromise, and whose discipline is the discipline of submission.

Isn't this true of all Mr. Marquand's heroes from George Apley to the upright, if not righteous, Bob Tasmin of *B. F.'s Daughter*? And doesn't Mr. Marquand usually end by celebrating the life he pretends to satirize? Take the present case of Tony Burton, the bank president who is first viewed as a mock father and, somehow, during the course of the novel, becomes a real father. The note of rebellion in all Mr. Marquand's novels is always ironic because the rebellion is always ineffectual. The theme of the lost life—which is the central theme of his work—is less poignant than it should be simply because his characters are actually very well suited to the life they do lead. Charles Gray is a perfect, and perpetual, vice-president.

In this sense *Point of No Return* disappoints us, and leaves us with an impression of legerdemain, not art. Mr. Marquand knows all the little answers. He avoids the larger questions.

From the *New York Times,* March 6, 1949

Melville Goodwin, U.S.A. seems to me one of the poorer Marquand novels—but is there any point in comparing them, lately? You always start them with pleasure and admiration, and end with the same sense of disappointment. They are good reading, but somewhere along the line there has been an "upward twist," a cunning piece of literary magic through which the real story has disappeared and something else—a white rabbit, a handkerchief, an empty box—has been handed to us.

The thing to do is to enjoy them while you can. *Melville Goodwin* opens with the same fine flourish. Sidney Skelton is a famous radio commentator. The "integrity" of his voice has brought him a national audience, a wealthy sponsor, an estate in Connecticut, an ambitious wife, and a French poodle named Farouche whom he really likes. He is a typical Marquand figure, too bright for his environment, too weak to resist it. The opening survey of the entertainment field—to which apparently the broadcasting of news has now been assigned—is a high spot of the book.

The trouble is that Sid knows Melville Goodwin, a two-star general who has become newsworthy through his behavior with a Russian patrol in Berlin. The Army needs a hero to compete with the Navy and the Air Force, and Sid is in the position of protecting the general from making a fool of himself, which would ruin the effect. The main story is the gradual disclosure of Goodwin's true character through a feature newspaper interview in the style of *Time* and *Life,* and through a series of typical Marquand cutbacks into his past. There is also an enterprising career woman named Dottie Peale whose affair with Melville Goodwin is a serious handicap to his career.

The narrative of present action is handled very well indeed. The cutbacks into the simple small-town life of Mel Goodwin are to me, as almost always in Marquand's work, sentimental, unreal. This older native scene did—and does—exist, but Marquand has never been able to catch it except through nostalgia and romance. When he is faced here with the problem of character and human relationships in themselves—not for the purpose of social satire—or of some kind of serious experience, he almost always loses his grip. Melville Goodwin as a typical American adolescent is, to be frank, a bore.

So are his wife and children, later on in the story. Except perhaps for the single trait of getting ahead, of not sticking their necks out, which seems to buoy them all up in the meticulous and rigid—and if I dare say so—almost Chinese etiquette of the Army hierarchy. But then we begin to realize that Marquand is absolutely serious about this. General Goodwin is a true hero whose simple virtues of character influence everybody else in the story, including the cynical Phil Bentley, the feature writer who has come to take him apart.

Even Sid Skelton obeys the General's final directive, to make good in the radio racket for the sake of his wife and kiddies. The story which opened as a satirical study of both the entertainment industry and the military mind—the two poles of play and work in modern life—ends with the illusive warmth of an inspirational tract. For all I know this may be necessary in the present world crisis, but it is a curious conclusion to a central conflict in Marquand's own career as an artist. For Sidney Skelton himself is another one of Marquand's "outsiders" who is fighting for power in a business he disapproves of, and in a social tradition to which he does not belong.

The whole point about Melville Goodwin as an Army officer is that his code of behavior is honest. He believes in his career completely and puts it to the test in the field of combat. A good man if kept in his place; but is this the only possible solution for the problem of belief in a commercial society without established forms of tradition? It might have taken more guts, a word which Marquand's General approves of, if Sid had really abandoned his voice and put his mind to work, or if Melville Goodwin himself had really gone through with his disastrous affair with Dottie Peale. But in the struggle with "authority" that runs through Marquand's work, authority, even if stale or false, always wins. The soldier's code is a logical refuge for his disgruntled bankers and despairing playwrights.

It's odd that both Hemingway and Marquand have recently

put in a defense for professional soldiers (officers, of course). Perhaps the younger writers like Norman Mailer or James Jones will finally have to take their stand against the literary ancestors who first showed them the path of revolt. Meanwhile this is probably all too solemn about a book which is meant primarily for popular entertainment, and an author whose destiny has constrained him to do only what he can do so well.

From the *Saturday Review,* September 19, 1951.

Summary

Though Mr. Marquand was unaware of it, the novelist and the critic were in a contretemps sometime after *Melville Goodwin, U.S.A.* (Now looking back on the novel, was it really a plea for the provincial goodness of the Eisenhower-type personality in the modern age?) It seemed to me that he was writing the same book over and over again, and I found myself writing the same review. It was better to discontinue our formal literary relationship, and for the critic to continue reading the Marquand productions privately, as he had always done since first meeting Mr. Moto in his youth.

Maybe Marquand was better off than Steinbeck, in this respect, because he had never professed to be more than a superior kind of entertainment. That was his early training, his whole approach to literature. It was the high quality of the first few novels, like *The Late George Apley* and *Wickford Point,* which had stirred up the critics' aspirations. It was only because Marquand could do some things so well, that we believed he could do the other things. And by demanding of him the major values of literature, perhaps we had minimized the real, if minor, virtues of his work.

There is no doubt he is an acute and often brilliant observer of middle-class manners. He should be classed with John O'Hara in this respect: the merciless eye of a born reporter, the sensitive ear for speech, the gift of creating atmosphere and social types. These are fine assets for any writer, which Marquand puts to

good use. Add irony, which he in a familiar class of native
satirists from William Dean Howells down, substitutes for the
intellectual boldness of the major writers, the moral hardness, and
the depth insights. Perhaps the real barrier in this type of popular satirist is primarily psychological.

It was true of the early Howells, at least. And when that
writer refused to be the well-paid literary entertainer of the
American people any longer, he was still faced with the psychic
repressions in his own view of life. In Marquand's case, the novel
which followed *Melville Goodwin* is a good example. (*Thirty
Years,* in 1954, was a collection of articles and tales.) *Sincerely,
Willis Wayde* (1955) belongs to the new class of "business
novels" in the middle of the decade, and it is interesting for the
light it throws on this genre. The brief flurry of debunking novels,
written mainly by ex-Luce editors, it seemed, or overalcoholic
advertising men who had always wanted to be artists, was followed by a more sober series of novels and studies which ex-
amined the stresses and strains of modern business, and the new
role of the "organization man" in the age of corporate capitalism.

The Luce publications played their part in this. They had
earlier denounced the literary "vilification" of the American businessman by, it seemed, almost all the major American writers.
The vilification was true, unfortunately, and the new group of
writers in the mid-Fifties who were engaged in the program of
"reconstruction" unfortunately showed not much literary talent.
Marquand's craft was more secure. His central point of view
derived from a somewhat nostalgic feeling for small-town American life, in which the "lower-upper-class" hero hovered on the
fringes of the "upper-upper" New England aristocracy. (Perhaps
here we touch on Marquand's inability ever really to "cut
through" the social authority he satirizes.) And this was the
central formula in *Willis Wayde.*

The scene was the familiar town of Clyde, Massachusetts. The
industry was machine belting. The Harcourt mills represented
the old-fashioned type of individual business; and Henry Harcourt, the founder, was another example of the merchant prince,
or the "good millionaire" whom Howells celebrated in Silas
Lapham. But Silas was a rude newcomer in Boston society; the
Harcourts are rich, old, and established. The present intruder is
Willis Wayde himself, who represents scientific business methods

and the large corporations. Willis is a type of perfect executive, whose shortcomings Marquand sees, but whose moral conflicts, or real inner drives, are never made clear. He is destined to take over, or drive out the Harcourt business fortune. He is snubbed and finally cut by the outraged Harcourt heiress whom he loves; and he himself, never happy or satisfied with his life, becomes a sort of business legend.

He is the "successful" new corporation man who sets the tone for the "white-collar" classes beneath him; he is the lonely boss of the lonely crowd. (And how well up Marquand always is on the latest trends in social and cultural analysis!) But saying all this, one must add that *Sincerely, Willis Wayde* misses the final implications of its theme, even those presented in the popular textbooks. Where it might also have been linked, by virtue of Marquand's talent, to Ellen Glasgow's *Virginia,* Sinclair Lewis' *Dodsworth,* or Dreiser's *The Titan* and *The Financier,* as studies of the American businessman, it was simply another transient bestseller.

Marquand seems to be getting tired in these later novels. (Though I have not read *Life at Happy Knoll* [1957].) They are getting poor even for their type, and the burst of energy and talent with which they open is followed by the routine development of a formula romance. Even Marquand's realism and satire play a less significant part—for who knows just what might offend the susceptibilities of the audience which this artist has staked out for his own?

It is hard for a humorist always to be funny, and it must get pretty tedious, too. The personal history of popular authors is often a very harrowing affair. The point is that Marquand is at his best an old-fashioned artisan in the craft of letters. But in terms of the mass media, he must also compete with the "literary trusts," which, like the Simcoe Belting of *Willis Wayde,* are simply more efficient organizations. In the wake of Hollywood, and of the *Time-Life* research staffs, the new biographies, the new histories, and eventually—why not?—the novels designed for the mass audience will be largely collective productions. The incorporation of Herman Wouk is another sign of the times; and perhaps J. P. Marquand's work already shows the falling-off of "handicraft entertainment" in the age of automation.

It is an ironic fate for an artist to be dragged along by the conveyor belt of bestsellers; perhaps there is a final Marquand novel here. But saying this of his work, one must add that somehow he is still "himself," while just who, in the mid-Fifties, is the writer called John Steinbeck? Looking over the earlier reviews, I see that I was casting about for the more complex causes of his decline. Well, perhaps the simple fact is, as in the central philosophy of *Pippin,* that he has never matured. There were strong evidences of a romantic and belated adolescence in his literary history before *The Grapes of Wrath.* And even in that novel, we had to forgive and to accept the failure in the central characters and in the human relationships for the sake of its larger promise. But that is a serious failure; it is the core of an artist's art; and perhaps the critics who have stressed Steinbeck's attraction to animal life and to nature, to the biological currents of evolution, are correct.

Is there also an underlying ignorance of, and perhaps a contempt for, the highest realm of the evolutionary process: man himself—whom Steinbeck, at least, still insists on seeing in the mechanistic-scientific terminology of Social Darwinian thought? And is this at base a philosophic error or a human one, since what a writer "thinks" is hardly so important as how he feels? Or did the Broadway success of *Of Mice and Men,* the movie productions of Steinbeck's later books, the Book-of-the-Month choice of *The Wayward Bus,* in 1947, confirm Steinbeck in all the more theatrical, the least rewarding, the least hopeful aspects, of his literary personality? Even when he was considered in the same category of American writers as Tom Wolfe, Dos Passos, Hemingway, and Faulkner, in the early Forties, it was hard to take him as seriously as the others. Now it is almost impossible to take him seriously at all. In his chosen category of entertainment, rather than art, his work is dubious. *The Moon Is Down* was a novel. *The Moon Is Down* was a play. In neither form was it really successful. And this divided focus of Steinbeck, from *Of Mice and Men* to *Burning Bright,* is another aspect of a writer who is trying to make the best of both worlds. Literature is not an interchangeable slot machine, with spare parts furnished on request by the mechanic-inventor.

The most solid, important, and widely heralded work of Steinbeck's later years was *East of Eden,* in 1952. (The publishers keep on telling us that this writer is endlessly fertile, imaginative, versatile.) And the novel was surely intended to be an American saga from the time of the Civil War to the First World War. But let me quote from the jacket of the novel.

The scope of *East of Eden* can hardly be suggested by an outline of the story. Adam Trask brings his strange wife, in 1900, to settle in the Salinas Valley. John Steinbeck's own forebears, the Hamiltons —a wonderfully gusty and varied crew—had been in the valley for years before, and through them we already know its history, its colors, and its moods. . . . We also know the story of the calculating girl whom Adam had found on his Connecticut doorstep and married. After twin sons are born Cathy leaves, to return to a career more familiar to her, and eventually to become the fabulous Kate, owner of Salinas's fanciest brothel. Cathy is possibly one of the most fascinating hateful characters in modern fiction. Her story might have been a novel in itself.

The rich and respected Adam, blighted within, rears his sons with the help of a worldly-wise Chinese, and with friendly advice from the Hamiltons. As the boys grow older, the inevitable disclosure threatens, and the reader watches with mounting tension to see how Aron, the "good" son, and Caleb, who carries the strains of both good and evil, will stand up under the blow.

Now one might simply conclude the discussion of Steinbeck with this statement, which is an accurate description of the novel. One might add that only a romantic and adolescent mind could have conceived this "plot," and only a great writer could have brought it off. Steinbeck doesn't, and if the novel is written with one eye on the Hollywood picture, which was later produced, the other eye is directed steadily at the audience for popular romances.

Yet there are curious and discordant undertones in this novel, which make it of more than passing interest. It is also written around the Cain and Abel story. Adam Trask's brother is named Charles. (And like Thomas Mann, if less successfully, Steinbeck, stressing Adam and Abel, uses one myth to recapitulate others.) The sons of Cathy and Adam are named, as we know, Caleb and Aron repeating the mythical pattern (C. and A.). The theme of sibling rivalry is recurrent and dominant in the Old Testament itself. It is subject to many levels of interpretation, from the moral, ethical, or social import, to the deepest levels of psychology, where both Mann and Freud found it so fascinating.

Moreover, Cathy has tempted and then seduced Adam Trask's brother Charles: the twins are more than likely derived from this source. Is Cathy herself (another "C" name) a feminine form of the Cain principle? Or is she, again, a "temptress" indeed, preying upon this toiling and sweating Adam progenitor, more directly related to the conventional notion of Eve, or Lilith?

The story is thus deliberately intricate and incestuous, like its Old Testament backgrounds, like the childhood of the race, or of the individual. The "inner" or true plot, of these involved human relationships, might also have interested a Hawthorne, a Faulkner, a Robinson Jeffers, in our American line of literary descent; but here again Steinbeck himself rouses our interest only to juggle, to toss, to manipulate, and to let slip his real theme. In the early figure of Cathy, we see only what is a puritanical or infantile fear and hatred of the "sexual" woman, who uses her skill and charm to destroy "decent" men. (The obverse side of this coin in Steinbeck's work is the Mary Magdalene figure: the "pure-hearted" prostitute.) In the later figure of Cathy-Kate, who becomes the criminal and corrupt proprietor of a "decadent" brothel which caters to the most depraved forms of vice, we see what is in effect Steinbeck's form of "punishment" for the evil and sexual woman.

But this brothel is boring. (Compare the very human scenes and broad sexual comedy in the similar sections of James Jones's *From Here to Eternity*.) Cathy-Kate herself is an unreal, flat symbol of malevolence. At the climax of the story, Adam's son Caleb (or Charles's) destroys his brother Aron—but where is Moses?—by revealing the truth about their sinful "mother." Yet Caleb, it turns out, is not really Cain at all, in this popularized modern American version of the legend. Or at least he is not really evil. He is guilty and repentent; he did not "mean" his crime. He begs forgiveness from his dying father, and is in effect a subject for social rehabilitation. The true moral of the novel, says Steinbeck, is "the only one man has ever used as his theme —the existence, the balance, the battle, and the victory in the permanent war between wisdom and ignorance, light and darkness—good and evil." But God save us, as the saying goes, from any more such victories in our literature.

Thus *East of Eden* is a tricky and meaningless parable—on the conscious level—of man's "fall" through woman's vice. On

the unconscious level—in this case, unconscious to the author—
we may feel beneath the novel's sentimentality, and even below
the humanitarian principles which are the remaining link with
the best period of Steinbeck's work, a certain malice and hostility
toward human life itself. The good writers often acknowledge
this in their own literary vision, and build upon it. The lesser
ones write romances which both reveal and deny it, and sometimes it comes to dominate or destroy their spirit.

Part Three: NEWCOMERS

NORMAN MAILER: THE BOHEMIAN
OF THE NATIONAL LETTERS

JUST WHEN we have stopped talking about the new literary
voices of the period, they seem to be appearing. Norman Mailer
is a young American writer who grew up in Brooklyn, went to
Harvard, and found himself, as a rifleman, in Leyte and Japan.
His earlier work has appeared in *Story* magazine and *Cross
Section,* but *The Naked and the Dead* is his first novel. It is a
solid and interesting story of the capture of Anopopei, a typical
Japanese island in the Pacific.

Mr. Mailer uses some of the technical devices which John Dos
Passos initiated in the American novel, while there is also an
influence of tone. But *Three Soldiers,* like most of the typical
stories of World War I, was essentially a novel of individual
protest. The military organization was something to escape from,
not to understand. The virtue of *The Naked and the Dead*—and I
think it will be the typical pattern of the new war novels—is that
it sees the individual within the military organization. It attempts
to evaluate the whole complex structure of the American Army
in war and peace, as a manifestation of contemporary society, as
well as a weapon of conquest and destruction. Or perhaps even,
in the Tolstoian sense, as one-half of our "natural" existence.

That doesn't mean Mr. Mailer particularly approves of army
life, or that the campaign on Anopopei was an idyl of human
decency. The novel opens with an amphibious assault upon the
island. The central group of characters are members of a recon-
naissance squad. The slow, blundering, and tortured progress of
the military action also marks their physical and moral disintegration as human beings. The plump and foul-mouthed Wilson,
the superstitious and embittered Gallagher, the ambitious and

171

servile Brown, the tough and rebellious Red Valsen, all are
partially or completely destroyed by their ordeal. To live through
it is not necessarily to have survived. Only the slow-thinking
farm boy, Ridges, and the "intellectual" Brooklyn Jew, Goldstein,
seem to have the necessary resources, whether of sheer animal
vitality or of spiritual comprehension, to endure the impervious
jungle, the sickening climate, the steady, demoralizing contact
with filth, pain, and terror even more than the actual and para-
lyzing shock of combat.

Staff Sergeant Croft, an excellent soldier to begin with, becomes a rigid and implacable tyrant. If he has accepted the
hatred of his men as part of his job, he soon begins to nourish it.
As the novel moves up through the ranks of the military hierarchy, it is particularly good on the relationship of these men with
the commissioned officers. There is an ironical episode in which
Major Dalleson, a typical disciplinarian and drillmaster, goes
into panic because the Japs have given him a chance for a break-
through, and he is forced to use his troops. Lieutenant Hearn is
a social rebel who has broken away from the conventions and
prejudices of the ruling class, financial or military. General
Cummings, who has given up human relationships completely,
for the sake of organization and efficiency, who believes that the
only value of a human soul is the use it can be put to, also
believes that, after the war with Russia, the next century will
belong to the reactionaries and the capitalists. And why not?

The antagonism between these last two figures, both human
and theoretical, gives Mr. Mailer a chance to build up, often very
eloquently, the historical and philosophical connotations of the
war. In the end Hearn is broken and killed. Perhaps this represents Mr. Mailer's own conclusion about the future, yet Hearn
is a curiously vapid character, and the ordinary soldiers in *The
Naked and the Dead* lack the vitality and originality they should
really have. Mr. Mailer leans rather heavily on the sexual experiences of his lower-class figures, too. These may be a solace
for the common man, and even a source of strength, but they
don't constitute his only achievement.

I think this is the main weakness of the novel, for there is no
real balance of the dramatic forces in it, just as there is a final
lack of emotional impact. The story ought to be more impressive

than it is. Within these limits, however, *The Naked and the Dead* is a substantial work, and Mr. Mailer is a new novelist of consequence.

From the *Saturday Review*, January 8, 1949.

The Naked and the Dead was a solid job of realism and social criticism in one of the main traditions of American writing. Mr. Mailer's second novel *Barbary Shore* is a drama of ideas that is held together by a symbolic framework of complete human frustration. It is fashionable, it is literary by current standards, it is well done, but I think it is a mistake.

The scene is a rooming house in Brooklyn Heights. The hero is a young writer who has lost his identity in the war. He is the anonymous man of the contemporary period, and through his search for his "identity" he is of course seeking for his salvation. His landlady, Mrs. Guinevere, turns out to be a combination of vamp and slut. In more polite terms she is a nymphomaniac who has, according to the modern definition, small use for sex, while her young daughter is a terrifying parody of a Hollywood starlet.

This is the effect of mass entertainment upon the feminine psyche in the United States; and in parts it is pretty good as satire and prophecy. Mr. Mailer's hero also discovers two more curious neighbors in the boardinghouse. Mrs. Guinevere's husband is a disillusioned intellectual who has been a figure of some importance in the Communist party. The soft-spoken, polite, ominous young "clerk," Hollingsworth, is an agent of the F.B.I. The ostensible heroine of the novel, Lannie, is on the edge of a nervous breakdown and still involved in the splits and schisms of revolutionary ideology. She is an incoherent disciple of Trotsky.

I have given away the plot to some degree, while the novel uses the elements of suspense and melodrama to carry the story along, but it is impossible to discuss *Barbary Shore* without making this clear. Even so, none of these people are quite what they seem to be, and the action of the story has further developments. As in *The Naked and the Dead,* there is no question of Mr. Mailer's craft and particularly his sense of narrative, even when his sense of character seems inadequate or to a certain degree artificial. In the present book the central question isn't of course whether these people are "real," but whether they are effective enough in symbolic terms to make us follow the course of Mr. Mailer's argument; and if we can to find out exactly what the argument is.

The answer seems to be that the people are inadequate as symbols, if not in the end utterly absurd. Mr. Mailer has used a Kafka-esque allegory of futility on the human level to support what is a minor version of Koestler's *Darkness at Noon* on the political issues of our time. At the novel's climax Hollingsworth, the Government agent who is also a sadist and repressed homosexual, forces McLeod, the revolutionary Socialist, to betray all that he has left—his conscience and his integrity.

The young writer, still searching for his identity or a meaning to his life, unable to find a satisfactory love relationship with either Guinevere or Lannie (who are equally unpleasant alternatives), has only the memory of McLeod's heroism and the prospect of an evolutionary socialism after Russia and the United States have destroyed each other. "So the blind will lead the blind, and the deaf shout warnings to one another until their voices are lost"—but this theme is never really made convincing. To reverse Freud's dictum, Mr. Mailer merely seems to be saying that no normal sex life is possible until the neurosis of history has been resolved.

Barbary Shore is deficient in both the biological and the cultural insights that are necessary for symbolism as well as for realism in literature. What is left is a novel of atmosphere and action, which has at its best something of the same gruesome fascination as Orwell's utopia of horrors. But this is not often, and it is not enough for a novelist of Mr. Mailer's stature and promise. Not half enough.

From the Saturday Review, May 26, 1951.

What is evident in *The Deer Park* (1955) is that Mailer reclaimed the central plot, or structure, of *Barbary Shore* for a better literary projection. And what was evident in both his first and second novels, or so I thought at the time, was that Mailer was a bright and sophisticated talent, well informed, up on things, with the "right" social values, and yet curiously lacking in some of the human feelings of a good novelist.

He was a cold writer, perhaps too intellectual (though American fiction has always been deficient in ideas), and too far removed from the common soldiers he described in *The Naked and the Dead*. That was still a good novel, but one recognized its literary sources in Dos Passos, Tom Wolfe, or Hemingway. It was almost as though the novelist had gone to war in search of a novel; and James Jones's *From Here to Eternity,* where army life was all of life, made this clear. Mailer might still go further than Jones in the literary arena, but he would never write as good a novel; unless, at least, something—but what?—would change sharply in the writer's temperament.

Meanwhile, in the early Fifties, he had become a "voice." He was a contributor to the pages of *Dissent,* the socialist magazine which had been started in opposition to the dead-end policies of the ex-socialist and now mainly Trotskyist magazine, *The New Leader*. The Stalinist-Trotskyist debate, arid and bitter, and of so little consequence for an American novelist, continued in the pages of both these magazines. It seemed curiously old-fashioned now, or even Talmudic in many of these articles, and lay in a sense behind the failure of *Barbary Shore* itself. I still remember, during these years, that the editor of a "liberal" New York newspaper censored my review of George Orwell's *Catalonia* on the ground that is was not sufficiently anti-Stalinist. When this editor was later called up before a Congressional committee, I thought of volunteering my personal knowledge of his devout and fanatical anticommunism; no question of it on the part of my confused liberalism.

But Mailer, caught up in the same controversy, was intelligent and often entertaining, and his column in the Greenwich Village *Voice,* devoted to more immediate local issues, proved, at least, that the Silent Generation could be very vocal. All the same, when a novelist became Spokesman, as in the case of James T. Farrell. it was at the expense of his creative energies; and in this sense *The Deer Park* was a reassuring document. Was it really better than *The Naked and the Dead,* as Malcolm Cowley declared? Could only a writer of "the greatest and most reckless talents

. . . have flung this book between covers," as the *New Yorker* said, somewhat equivocally. But there was no question that the novel was big and solid enough, that it contained valid and sharp social commentary, and that the descriptions of Hollywood's more intimate forms of recreation were often penetrating.

The "Deer Park," as we know, was the play-pen of Louis XV, the famous scene of depravity, debauchery, and vice, though Mailer's description of the historical episode was rather lurid, and his modern re-creation lacked a certain glamour. (Or do the French always do these things better?) As in *Barbary Shore,* the hero-narrator is another war veteran; this time a handsome, sensitive, and hard-boiled lad, an Air-Force hero, who arrives at the town of Desert D'or with fourteen thousand dollars to spare. The real protagonist of the narrative—or at least the hero-victim —is Charles Francis Eitel, a Hollywood screen-writer and producer of great talent, who has been ruined by the Congressional committees because he will not "inform."

The *salon* of the new American royalty of power and cash, if not of heredity, of these oil men, clothing merchants, movie magnates, and their attendant columnists, models, entertainers, and pimps, is at Dorothea O'Faye's home, which she calls "The Hangover." Collie Munshin, the son-in-law and heir presumptive of Supreme Pictures, comes down to it with both hands full. He wants to get rid of an embarrassing mistress, and he wants to exploit the fact that Eitel's talent is now on the black market. (Both Munshin and his father-in-law, Herman Teppis, represent the highest echelons of Hollywood "art," and are amusing, if not entirely creations.) The problem is solved. Munshin hands over his girl to Eitel, and arranges to take over and produce Eitel's script under his own name.

For Eitel this is both success and failure. He has wanted to take advantage of his enforced isolation from the pictures to write a "sincere" movie, and discovers he no longer is able to. But the girl Elena is fantastic in bed; her skill and energy revive Eitel's waning faith in his own physical prowess. Meanwhile, the subhero and later author of the book, Sergius, wanders to a lavish movie party, meets Lulu Meyers, the famous actress who is Eitel's ex-wife, and learns how a star makes love. These two affairs run along simultaneously in *The Deer Park:* the revelations of "innocence," and of declining maturity, form the counterpoint of the novel.

At the party, Sergius has met Teddy Pope, the homosexual star whom Teppis wants to marry off to Lulu for the sake of their joint picture (and to preserve the moral standard of his studio). On the fringe of all this is the desperate dope-pusher and pimp, Marion Faye, who has his eye on Elena for business reasons, who worships the artistic talent of Eitel, and who instructs Sergius as to the subtleties of "entertaining" the entertainment industry. Faye is, so to speak, the keeper of the deer park. There are obvious echoes of Scott Fitzgerald's *Last Tycoon* in the portrait of the gifted movie producer Eitel, and his disintegration. (The movie script he is writing is a curious version of *Miss Lonelyhearts;* one may presume that Mailer has also read *The Day of the Locust.*) But the central scene of the novel is far more corrupt and decadent than the innocent and lyrical Fitzgerald could conceive of; it is much more literally and flatly "realistic" than Nathanael West.

The real literary connection here is with the merciless, nagging, true and yet false realism of John Dos Passos. (Mailer has other resemblances to Dos Passos, in his college background, his sharp intelligence, his reportorial talent, and his verbal facility.) Everything goes bad in *The Deer Park,* slowly, inevitably, without dignity, and finally without tragedy. Elena is a failure in life, and as a woman; she is insecure, clumsy, neurotic, and trivial. "No wonder she took her talents to bed," Eitel reflects about her. "Love was for amateurs"—and perhaps this is the key to the emotional failure of a novel which is centered around sex and love. Love is also for life, for comfort, pleasure, and human delight. The central view of it here is certainly "professional": hard, cold, wise, in the worst Hollywood sense. It is almost medicinal. The male figures are all on the edge of impotence; their virility is revived by a temporary passion, but the woman who "cures" them is also the agent of their destruction.

Thus Eitel's purely sexual passion for Elena leads them both on to orgies: "sandwiches," *parties-à-trois, à quatre,* and "balls" —which in turn destroy Eitel's own trembling faith in himself. Sergius' Lulu Meyers turns out to be the perfect American "baby doll," infatuated by her own narcissistic image, playing her role

of the charming little girl while she manipulates everything for
her own advantage, including her lovers. When Eitel finally
surrenders to the social blackmail of his profession, and "tells
all" to the Congressional committee—which is to say that he
gives them the information they already have, or that they are
fabricating for the sake of their own publicity—and when Elena
finally leaves him to become one of Faye's call girls—there is
nothing left in *The Deer Park*. But was there anything there to
begin with? If the opening of the novel is clever and promising,
and potentially rich in material, the development of the story is
empty and flat.

As to sex, surely the original eighteenth-century French version of the Deer Park had subtlety and charm; one feels at least
that love was still an art, rather than, as here, a dubious profession. As to Hollywood's business ethics, manners, and morals, a
neglected novel, Jay Kennedy's *Prince Bart,* has far more real
knowledge and insight. The curious thing about Mailer's whole
group of central figures is that they, too, are in the end "amateurs." They are not credible, they are not interesting either as
people or as social types. They remind us of nothing so much as
the Bohemian Art Novels of the Twenties; their locale should be
Greenwich Village; and the novel's central vision of life is that
of a sophisticated adolescence.

There are still fine episodes in the novel, as when Lulu, Teddy
Pope, and Herman Teppis pose as a "happy family" for the
press-release photos; what a family! Or when, in the denouement,
Lulu tells Teppis she has just married a new movie athlete, and
Munshin, blamed for this catastrophe, sends in a call girl to
relieve his father-in-law's "tension." But there is no human
center in *The Deer Park;* no balancing episodes of warmth,
affection, or generosity. Love is indeed a dirty word; and we read
through the story in much the same way that we follow the
movie scandals in the magazine called *Confidential;* this also is
clever journalism. Like his closest literary forebear, Dos Passos,
Mailer has no confidence in human nature itself, and perhaps no
mature experience with it. The social values in this novel, too, if
they are intelligent, decent, liberal, are based on a biological
void.

How tragic it is to be without illusions, even if they exist, in a writer's craft, only to be dispelled. That is probably Norman Mailer's central flaw, his central need; and meanwhile curious undertones of juvenile malice also appear in his work. He may be the latest type of Bad Boy in our national letters, whose problem is to grow up.

JOHN HERSEY: THE REVIVAL OF CONSCIENCE

The Wall is a novel based on the martyrdom of Polish Jewry during the Nazi occupation. It is the most complex and brilliant of John Hersey's books so far.

First of all it is an achievement in scholarship and study in human understanding. The culture of the Polish Jews extended back to the fourteenth century, when Casimir the Great invited them to develop the crafts and trades of his community. This was in many respects a feudal and medieval society; in moral terms it was the link between the origins of Western culture and modern Europe—the living testament of God. *The Wall* somehow manages to suggest these historical dimensions without a trace of pedagogy and even catches the peculiar tone of this society—righteous, devout, melancholy, cunning, and ironic—that we usually associate with such authors as Peretz or Sholem Aleichem.

The Nazis were determined to wipe out this culture in toto—its records, books, libraries, temples, social institutions, men, women, and, particularly, children. Perhaps because this society was the clearest evidence of the religious and moral values which they opposed. And in effect they did. *The Wall* is the fictional account of this experiment in genocide from the point of view of the Jews who lived in Warsaw, and on the technical level, too, that of sheer exposition and narrative, the story is excellent. Mr. Hersey has brought together the flow of historical events, the routines of daily life in the ghetto which the Nazis set up, the levels of Jewish society which operated there, and the most diverse types of personality. This is a panorama of souls who, condemned to hunger, disease, torture, and obliteration, either broke down completely or flowered even more vividly.

The form of the novel is that of a diary, broken and episodic on the surface. It combines melodrama and intrigue, scenes of domestic life or social organization, profiles, portraits, studies in character development, with the group scenes of hunger, typhus, mob terror, the organized manhunts, the mass executions. The technique is that of "inner exposition"—the record of these events as they are perceived by the victims of the trap or as they are conveyed through individual stories. The keeper of the diary is Noach Levinson, a Jewish historian who is determined to preserve every detail of Jewish life during these years, since curiosity and understanding are all that he has left. "Above all, we must keep a record. . . . There is nothing to leave behind but history."

So Noach is everywhere in the ghetto, preserving this final record of extermination, from the most intimate details in the lives of his people to their political stratagems and philosophical speculations. From a solitary observer he becomes a "family man," living with the Apts, who have previously belonged to the wealthy merchant class, and the Mazurs, who are devout Hasidic Jews. Family life in the ghetto was, of course, an ironical and tragic euphemism. The German system broke down all ordinary values of a decent life. It was intended to dehumanize the Jews before they were liquidated. The son of Reb Yechiel Mazur is forced to ask his father to volunteer for "resettlement" (the death chamber) in order to save his own wife. The mother, Froi Mazur, accepts this task voluntarily in order to save her children, bringing with her "nothing but a pair of slippers, symbolizing readiness for death, and a pair of candles, to make her prayers go straight to God."

The Nazis, indeed, took everything of value—property, clothes, rings, jewelry, gold inlays from teeth—before they sent the naked bodies into the sealed railway cars, the steam chambers, the gas room, the common grave.

Yet Noach Levinson's "family" continued to increase, until it included Berson, the amateur and dilettante; Slonim, the cold, analytical theorist; Rappaport, the old socialist lion; Menkes, the baker; Fein, the rough worker; Schpunt, the "clown" whose antics delighted the Germans whom he hated, and a host of others. When Froi Mazur reported for death, Rachel Apt became the new mother of the group, just as new members replaced those who had disappeared daily.

There are very touching and lyrical scenes of ordinary life in the early sections of *The Wall,* for everything that had been common and ordinary now became precious. There are scenes of violence, of increasing corruption and dissension among the Jews, too, for the Nazis set up what was in effect a forced survival struggle among the survivors in the ghetto. Pan Apt, the jeweler, decides to trust the generosity of his Polish friends; young David, the brother of Rachel, "takes a walk" to Palestine. Meanwhile the "reduction" of the Jewish population continues. In the last stages of the process, "it is safe to say," says the cautious Noach Levinson, "that more than 300,000 Jews have been liquidated in a period of about two and a half months."

In April, 1943, the Jewish underground fighters put up their last desperate resistance against the Nazi tanks, flame throwers, and heavy artillery, and the Battle of the Warsaw Ghetto takes up the last quarter of *The Wall.* In a way, this is the least successful part of the novel, perhaps because Mr. Hersey can't quite bring himself to describe the full extent of the Nazi terror. This was surely a nightmare world from its inception to the flaming inferno of its finale, and what *The Wall* lacks is just this final sense of horror and evil. Its tone is almost too rational, fluid, delicate, and tender. Nevertheless, it is an urgent and remarkable novel on a grand scale.

From the *Saturday Review,* March 4, 1950.

Looking back at this review, which was a trifle fervent, I would nevertheless agree with it. *The Wall,* if it is atypical Hersey, is still his best and most solid work, where his virtuosity as a craftsman met a large moral and social drama. It was indeed the first American novel of the Forties and Fifties to seize upon such a theme. It brought back echoes of Frank Norris' *The Octopus,* or *The Grapes of Wrath* itself, the period when American writing was directly concerned with social justice. And part of the critical resistance to Hersey's book in our literary journals proceeded directly from the fact that "social themes" in general were now equated with the Russian Revolution, and were therefore suspect.

What a dreadful philosophical and literary position we had

really arrived at by the early Fifties, where the stultifying domestic phenomenon of McCarthyism itself was condoned by our intellectuals under the same general premises. To be "social" in any way was to be vaguely in sympathy with the Communists, or at best a "misguided liberal"—or was the word "confused"? It was safer, so the time drift went, to avoid all such heresies, to confine oneself to questions of "taste." To remind us, as Hersey did so poignantly and directly in *The Wall* of the Nazi Terror was somehow to link oneself with the Red Tyranny. Since the Germans were now our strongest European allies, it was better to ignore their past foibles.

Yet the systematic and methodical extermination of over five million innocent people, mainly Jewish, on the part of the most "advanced" (scientifically, technically) European nation, could not just be forgotten. It was not just an aberration on the part of a few German "leaders"; it was an immense human crime with which every German was inextricably involved. It presaged at least the moral collapse of western European "culture," the advent of barbarism; even the final "resolution," perhaps, of the atomic bomb itself, which could accomplish in one fine careless gesture what the Nazis had done with infinite pains. Yes, the Bomb was "cleaner" in the moral sense, taking one and all with it, taking everything, not just hounding down certain separate human beings.

During this period I remember there were certain documentary accounts (*The Black Book of Polish Jewry,* for example) of the Nazi methods, and their scientific "experiments" in the concentration camps, the ingenuities of fiendish cruelty, that I could barely bring myself to read—even to touch. The mark of the Devil was on them, and one shrank from their revelations. The trouble, after all, with Hersey's novel was not that it was a "documentary" (the standard charge against it). It was not documentary enough. It excluded the real levels of evil in this demonic Nazi conspiracy against the Jews; and levels of personal behavior which had released every distorted human impulse. And once this Pandora's box of perversion had been opened, could it ever really be closed again? If God existed, the God of the Old Testament, only another cataclysm could purge the infamous soul.

Hersey's book missed on this level, as I thought at the time of the review, but at least he himself, like his historian Noach (suggesting Noah, and the Flood), had put down the intellectual "record" of this event in the annals of art. The American conscience still survived in his novel, as a "witness" to the crime against humanity. The lack in the story was surely not in the moral or intellectual or technical areas but, if anywhere, in the range of emotions; and the effect of this European experience on the writer was not to be discounted in imaginative terms. Hersey's next novel, *The Marmot Drive* (1953), was a sort of emotional postscript to *The Wall:* a study of evil itself, in terms of our own American society.

"As such, *The Marmot Drive* is interesting and illuminating," I said in the *Nation* that fall, "a tour de force in sadism and malice that is very unlike Hersey's other books. A city girl visits a typical Connecticut country town in order to inspect the family of the man she wants to marry. She meets a variety of rugged, dour, self-reliant, salty New England characters who seem the very essence of their tradition. The novel opens with the homely and typical touches which mark the 'return to the soil' sagas, or more lately those touching vistas of native democracy which writers like Granville Hicks have been describing with such fervor. About halfway through I was ready to give the whole thing up. The twist in the narrative comes just here; and Mr. Hersey does quite a job in revealing the personal frustration and mass cruelty which also exist in this idyllic village scene.

"Nobody comes out very well, least of all the 'heroine,' whose capacity for stray sexual adventures is matched by her inability to love. Yet Hersey is almost writing a parable—a warning—rather than a novel. Afterward, the characters are a little thin; the writer has not really submerged himself in his material."

Well, looking back at this novel in the sequence of Hersey's work to date, one sees more clearly that his moral conscience was running against the grain, again, as it should. In the period of mass hysteria and political witch-hunts, he—at least—was probing into the native sources of such behavior, whose price we are still paying. But this literary son of a Chinese missionary, who was at home equally with the survivors of Bataan, of Hiroshima or, later, of the Hungarian revolt against Russia, was not really at ease in Connecticut itself. Hersey has a special kind of lyric tenderness in his writing, along with a formal grace of style that may remind us rather of Willa Cather's romantic spells. But in the area of the unattractive emotions—frustration, perversion, sadism, and the rest—he was still curiously wooden or melodramatic. Or one might say that the Christian humility and sweetness in Hersey's soul had no pagan base, or that he had repressed even the Freudian repressions.

The village types in *The Marmot Drive* were rather wooden, or deliberately exotic. We have the impression at times that Nathaniel Hawthorne is visiting Tunxis, and hauling out the whipping post. The heroine, who is indeed called Hester, is both disillusioned and horrified at the slow revelation of the village's inner spirit, but she herself never gains our real sympathy. As a fable, Hersey's next novel, or novelette, *A Single Pebble,* in 1956, was far more effective, if it also returned to the emotional area to which this writer's talent is almost restricted. The tale concerned an American engineer who sails up the Yangtze River during the 1920's. During the course of the trip on a Chinese junk, he gets to know something about the ship's owner, the young wife, the cook, the heroic head-tracker, and the other "coolie" workers and sailors. At the end he is not sure about his own scientific achievements as a method of "transforming" this backward culture.

He recognizes, in fact, the depths of his own abysmal ignorance as to the "lower" races—or the human heart. Perhaps indeed this tribe of primitive, savage, and heroic river people—who are described and evoked in the tale by a kind of brilliant impressionism—will succeed in taming and transforming the achievements, the "progress," of modern science and technology. Perhaps it is they who now embody the "human verities," as against the abstractions of social engineering. And perhaps in time they will survive even, what is in their view, the transient modes of Chinese communism itself? But what is Hersey really suggesting here? Like the writing in *A Single Pebble,* the "moral" of the fable is beautifully fluid—too fluid. Absorbing as the story is while we read it, it is still somehow a romantic tale; it tends to disappear from our consciousness afterward. *The Wall* remains as Hersey's most solid work, the most concerned with reality, the best; while the two shorter novels after it are somewhat disappointing in retrospect.

This writer, who is a master in a very high form of journalistic fiction (as in *Hiroshima*), who is really so intelligent, civilized, and "right" in his moral values, who is so graceful a practitioner of the craft of writing itself, has a curious deficiency in the area of pure fiction. He is admirable also in his most recent tales, but not memorable. He belongs perhaps with those novelists of sensibility who are masters of illusion, but not of life. One may suspect that there is a whole psychic area roped off from Hersey's consciousness, and that he sees people in terms of a situation— or a crisis—rather than in and for themselves. Certainly this pattern emerged with his first popular success, *A Bell for Adano,* in 1944, and it lies behind the "fable form" of Hersey's most recent books. But the major works in our literary tradition, from *Moby Dick* to *An American Tragedy,* are primarily human documents, and then only fables if you want to make them so.

Even Hawthorne's brooding "romances" contain a rich and complex sense of emotional states, of human character, and particularly of that haunted unconscious which colors human behavior. This is as close as I can get, anyway, to what John Hersey lacks and needs as a novelist, and where, in a general sense, the future of his work lies. Freeing himself, as he has, from the jungle of journalism in the *Time-Life* area, and from the trim gardens of the *New Yorker* school, he may still have to face the special disciplines, the peculiar ordeals, the unending and enigmatic challenges which the craft of fiction imposes for its own sake. Among the newer voices in our literature, however, and those who deserve our admiration and continued concern, this writer ranks high.

NELSON ALGREN: THE IRON SANCTUARY

WHEN I first looked at Nelson Algren's *The Man with the Golden Arm,* after it had won the National Book Award in 1950, I regarded it as a piece of virtuoso prose writing. I was wrong. Having just read it again, along with the rest of his books, I realize now that, like most serious works of literature, it asks the reader to participate also. A writer can never be better than his audience; but you must pay the price of admission he has set. Such books as *Moby Dick* or *The Financier,* as well as the classic modern example, *Ulysses*—all such novels have their special language which you must translate, as it were, to learn the real intention of the artist.

Yet to live completely in Nelson Algren's world is a strange and somewhat exhausting experience. This is very different from the standard tours around the Lake Country of the English poets or that of Hardy's Wessex. This is a world of ruins—but living ones. And prison is the safest place for Nelson Algren's people to be. It is the "iron sanctuary" which puts at rest their fevered and distorted hopes. It is, as he says, "the play for which all had rehearsed many times," and whose chorus consists of snickerers:

Already the snickerers were waiting restlessly, in darkened rows, to identify the man who'd slugged the night watchman and the one who'd snatched the purse through the window of the moving El; for he who'd chased somebody's virgin daughter down a blind alley or forged her daddy's signature; tapped a gas main or pulled a firebox; slit the janitor's throat in the coalbin or performed a casual abortion on the landlord's wife in lieu of paying the rent. All the things that had to be done to help someone else out of a jam. The little things done in simple fun and the big things done for love.

These prison scenes are remarkable achievements in Algren's

work; they are recurrent and almost nightmarish episodes in which the writer, like the police captain Bednar in *The Golden Arm,* is haunted by an eternal procession of "bucket workers and bail jumpers, till tappers and assistant pickpockets, square johns and copper johns; lamisters and hallroom boys, ancient pious perverts and old blown parolees, rapoes and record-men; the damned and the undaunted, the jaunty and condemned." They come on and on and on, and where they come from no captain knows.

I am being polite and omitting the more flagrant cases of crime and vice who record their twisted destinies on the prison walls toward which they have moved just as surely as the young executives of middle-class American life aspire to join the country club. As early as 1935, in *Somebody in Boots,* his first novel, Algren had confronted the standard interpretation of American life— prosperity and success—with his own chronicles of poverty and failure. His first hero, a "poor-white" Texas boy, growing up during the depression years, takes to the road and becomes a vagabond and petty criminal. The book is dedicated to "those innumerable thousands: the homeless boys of America." It may remind you of Jack London's earlier study of American tramps and vagabonds called *The Road,* or of certain parts of John Dos Passos' *The 42nd Parallel.* There is indeed a whole body of literature dealing with this area of the national scene, as far back as the 1890's.

The emphasis of Algren's first novel is on the scenes of brutality which mark the life of the "lumpen-proletariat," the social scum, the passively rotting mass of people who lie at the bottom of the social scale. A boy is beaten up and crippled by a drunken father, a little Mexican child is crushed by the wheels of a train, a Negro woman gives birth to a stillborn baby in a sealed boxcar, a cat's head is twisted off, and worse. Those in "boots" represent authority: the police, the owners of property, the system of capitalism itself. But the novel is also in the straight documentary style of the 1930's: a thesis novel of social protest in which the characters are social types—if they are lucky. The prose is "poetic" in the bad sense; the tone of the novel is sentimental and melodramatic. *Never Come Morning,* seven years later, in 1942, was a very different story.

What happened to Nelson Algren himself during these seven

years, I have been unable to find out. We are told he was born
in Detroit, has lived in Chicago for many years, is an ex-GI, and
a graduate of the life he depicts. He has been called the "Poet of
the Chicago Slums" by Malcolm Cowley. Both Ernest Hemingway and Carl Sandburg have praised his work highly. But for a
writer who has no scruples of gentility or false refinement, who is
tough and blunt and calls a spade a spade only when he is at a
loss for a richer phrase, he is extraordinarily reticent, it seems,
about his own life. The hero of *Never Come Morning* is Bruno
Lefty Bicek, a young Polish boxer—or rather a young Polish
hoodlum who dreams about being a champion in the way it is
done in the movies and the comic strips. The early sections of
the novel describe the plight of the Polish immigrants and their
children in the barbaric slums of the new world.

The Polacks are on the ropes, though "Iron Man Bicek"
doesn't know it yet. The immigrants, Algren is saying, have been
betrayed, too. The barber Bonifacy is no longer sure about anything. "They were always trying to cheat him in this country."
What is this fight business, the Widow Rostenkowski asks Bruno.
"Is *crooked* business?"

"Ever'thin's crooked, Widow," he says easily, and glibly, for
he has just passed from boyhood to manhood, from vandalism to
hoodlumhood. The old people are bitter and despairing; the
young people—starved, warped, ignorant little egoisms—are still
warmed by the celluloid light of fame and wealth the quick way.
The new city light glares on the "old-world face" of Steffi Rostenkowski, when she is seduced by Bruno, and then abandoned
by him, in fear and drunken frustration, to the wolf pack of
tougher hoodlums whom he calls his friends.

There is only one thing that Bruno Lefty Bicek is wary about.
"The slot machine syndicate was big business—and big business
didn't fool." (And one remembers Jack London's prophecy of
the great battle between the business community and organized
crime.) But Bruno is haunted by Steffi's ruin; he has killed her in
his heart. The actual murder of the Greek, which he has committed in a blind fury of rage and revenge for Steffi, seems to him
the best thing he has ever done. "For once he had done something
right in his life." His visit to the prison is inevitable. "Knew I'd
never get t' be twenty-one anyhow," he thinks—"And the bell."

"To the greater understanding of our times, *Never Come*

Morning portrays what actually exists in the nerve, brain, and blood of our boys on the street, be they black, white, native, or foreign-born," Richard Wright said in his introduction to the novel. Perhaps the best comparisons are with the Chicago Irish of James T. Farrell's novels and the tormented black souls of Wright's own work; but you get in Algren's book even more clearly the sense of stunted (and potentially vicious) children. Bruno Lefty Bicek tears apart a doll he has won at the circus because he hates "stuffed things," while to the police captain Tenczara of the story he is just a "strange animal." The realism is cold and brutal. It is only indeed in the love affair of Steffi and Bruno—in the range of normal emotions—that the novel falters and becomes somewhat artificial or theatrical. But in this literary orbit of bitter, angry lusts, of stunted emotions and stuffed lives, it may be that love itself is a luxury—or another path to crime.

The stories in *The Neon Wilderness* (1948) are in a softer vein: provided that you have read the other Algren books. For the first time women appear here, not only as credible human beings, but as a source of comfort and aid, however briefly, in the fast run between the womb and the grave. There is the sketch, reminiscent of Sherwood Anderson's Midwestern vein, of the workingman who gambles and drinks his week's pay away on Saturday night because his wife had not been home to meet him; but she comforts him with her flesh at the end. "So nothing important has been lost after all." There is the stupid miserable creature who calls herself "the girl that men forgot awright," but there is also Wilma who gave all her love to another of Algren's boxers, and kept him straight, until her past caught up with her. There is the gambler who believes in "lucky bucks, fast money, and good women"—this glittering vista of Algren's Chicago slum world at its highest peak. And there is the tale of Railroad Shorty—a "halfy" or legless man—who clubs a young bartender to death in a casual brawl.

Algren's powerful effects are usually in his big scenes rather than in the portrayal or development of character. He is almost at his best in this volume of short stories where he can suggest the whole contour of a human life in a few terse pages. There is more warmth and humor here, too, than in the earlier books. It is, all in all, an excellent collection of short stories, perhaps one of the best we had in the 1940's. And, opening the new decade

of the 1950's, *The Man with the Golden Arm* brought together
the various strains in Algren's work.

The hero is Frankie Machine, in the Americanized version of
Francis Majcinek, whose golden arm has brought him local fame
as the "Dealer" in a gambling club. His pal and protégé is the
"Sparrow," unnoticed by God, as Algren implies, befriended by
Frankie; and the doorman or "steerer" in the same club. One of
the Sparrow's other rackets is dog-stealing. His close little room
has never lost "the special smell of shanghaied dogflesh," where
poodles would emerge looking like debauched terriers or "Cocky
Spaniards." There is a satiric episode of the Sparrow's love affair
with Violet, who, inflamed with passion, drives her "Old Husband" into the clothes closet and finally out of the window. Other
characters include the Jailor, the landlord of the Division Arms
Hotel; the bartender Antek, called Owner; the blind man
Piggy-O; and Nifty Louie, the morphine peddler at the Safari
Club.

It takes quite a while to discover all this; almost as long as in
a Faulkner novel perhaps. The structure of the book is panoramic; there are a host of minor characters. The language is rich,
if not ornate with the idiom of punks, cranks, and petty
gangsters. This is a *Winesburg, Ohio* of the slum dwellers; and
one remembers that Sherwood Anderson wrote his nostalgic
country tales while living in these miserable Chicago buildings,
at the ragged end of life, where the streets run on and on, "out
of nowhere into nothing." For Frankie Machine has cracked up
an automobile while he was drunk. His crippled wife uses the
accident as her revenge upon him. He has become a "junkie"—
has taken to dope—and not even his love for Molly Novotny can
save him from the inevitable trip—the classic denouement of all
Nelson Algren's novels—to see the police captain. Record Head
Bednar is the recording angel, the weary voice of justice and of
destiny, in this subluminous world of frustration.

The point is that Algren's typical figures are failures even at
vice. They are the underdogs of sin, the small souls of corruption,
the fools of poverty, not of wealth and power. Even the murders
they commit, out of blind rage or through sheer accident—or
through another ironic twist of their impoverished destiny—are
not important. It is a political feud in an election year which
dooms Frankie Machine, not justice. The police are no more

interested in him than are the social workers or penal psychologists whom Nelson Algren loves to take for a ride. Or than the respectable citizens of the Republic, who read and then forget these chronicles of violence; or who say, conveniently, that such a world doesn't really exist, or that nothing can be done about it anyhow. But in one sense, this is almost true. For when Algren's hero does finally reach the iron sanctuary which promises a relief from both his hopes and his vices, you almost get the impression, to paraphrase Freud's morose dictum, that his whole life has merely been the attempt to choose his own method of dying. His final act of human dignity is to hang himself through the cunning of the golden arm.

Thus Algren's work represents an extreme phase of the native American realism which opened, in the 1900's, with Stephen Crane's *Maggie,* Frank Norris' *McTeague,* and Dreiser's *Sister Carrie.* All these authors were concerned with the dispossessed, but still retained the notion of hope and chance in a blind and very often hostile but not absolutely fatal universe. These writers believed that human character was both a social and a biological (or hereditary) product. Or rather, they did not see character as a "product" at all, but as that "mystery of personality" which continued to fascinate the older generation of American artists up to Sherwood Anderson and Ellen Glasgow. (Nor should I exclude, in the "aristocratic" branch of our letters, Edith Wharton and Henry James himself.) Algren moves on a much narrower base than this—the range from the documentary novel of social misery in the 1930's to the later depiction of human beings who are caught in the trap of social circumstance. The scale is always weighted, in his view, the odds are too heavy, the universe *is* fatal.

He is the poet of this underworld, a high verbal talent, and one is not sure that he is even interested in character, or his characters, except in so far as they contribute another off-beat dissonance. (The true comparison of Algren's work may be with jazz, or bebop, or rock 'n roll.) At least *A Walk on the Wild Side* (1956), Algren's sequel to *The Man with the Golden Arm,* contributes to this impression. It is a loose-jointed picaresque novel of the New Orleans underworld during the Depression. It is an ironical parody of the American success story, then and now. And appropriately the tone of the book is no longer that of the Marxist morality which Algren shared with other writers in the 1930's, but often of ludicrous and demented farce.

The point is that the new "novel" was in fact the result of an attempt which Algren made to revise *Somebody in Boots*. The change in subject, tone, and method illuminates the difference between two ages as well as the change in the writer himself. Here, the bitter, ironic comedy, which supported Algren's earlier visions of doom, has become dominant, and the outlaw Bohemianism is refreshing as the reaction to a new age of prosperity and conformity. And if you get far enough under the norms of society, probably all morality is a farce. The tale centers around the sporting house on Perdido Street where the "hero" makes a living by displaying his sexual prowess. The narrative is filled with brilliant little profiles of very dubious characters indeed. There are passages of inimitable dialogue. There are comic interludes of a Rabelaisian hilarity, marked by a deliberate sensationalism which is also a take-off on our conventional notions of romantic love.

Algren has moved closer here to the San Francisco school of "Zen hipsters," as Herbert Gold has described them. ("Zen Strikes Back.") This is the group centered around jazz music— progressive or rocky—those sick sounds and weird reverberations whose newest spokesman is Jack Kerouac, whose philosopher- poet is Kenneth Rexroth, whose aging prophet is Henry Miller. But both Miller and Algren are mature artists, deriving from other periods and other roots. For Algren himself, *A Walk on the Wild Side* is also a kind of hit-and-run book. The trouble is that very often the poetic inspiration—exuberant, gay, outrageous as it is—runs away with the narrative; sometimes the narrative seems to be only inspiration. Here the earlier limitations in the writer's work also become dominant; and in a sense he seems indifferent to them.

Is this also the end of the whole tradition of social protest which, as we have seen, Algren has embodied in his previous work and career? That tradition is unfashionable today (though half the world is in the throes of social revolution.) A writer like Algren must at times regard himself as an isolated figure. It is easier to give up; it is easier to become the popularizer of the lower depths, rather than the poet—or to move in the direction of Steinbeck and make theatrical "primitives" out of these native

American paisanos. To a certain degree Henry Miller has also done this in his later "sex" books, which are diluted summaries of his earlier ones. The humor of *A Walk on the Wild Side* is a little too facile; the people are abstracted; their tragedy is muted. The writer is relying on his verbal talent to cover the loss of human material. (A book much in the same vein, Erich Remarque's *The Black Obelisk* [1957], a satiric and poetic chronicle of post-World-War-I Germany, has much more humanity and warmth.)

Nor is it, God knows, that I am against humor, as the final recourse against life. What would we do without it? But Nelson Algren should remind himself that he represents a solid and enduring part of the American literary heritage; that he derives from this past, and writes not for the contemporary stage alone. That Iron Sanctuary, the source and center of his earlier work, still haunts our civilization. And Algren, like John Hersey, is a writer who carries with him our hope and concern for something more than entertainment.

With matter added, from *College English*, March, 1953.

J. D. SALINGER: THE WISE CHILD AND THE *NEW YORKER* SCHOOL OF FICTION

HE WORKED on *The Catcher in the Rye* for about ten years, J. D. Salinger told us, and when it appeared in 1951, it evoked both critical and popular acclaim. Here was a fresh voice, said Clifton Fadiman in the Book-of-the-Month Club *News*. "One can actually hear it speaking, and what it has to say is uncannily true, perceptive and compassionate." The novel was brilliant, funny, meaningful, said S. N. Behrman. It was probably the most distinguished first novel of the year, said Charles Poore in *Harper's* magazine. The real catch in the *Catcher*, said *Time*, was novelist Salinger himself, who could understand the adolescent mind without displaying one.

Salinger's short stories in the *New Yorker* had already created a stir. In undergraduate circles, and particularly in the women's colleges, this fresh voice, which plainly showed its debt to Ring Lardner, but had its own idiom and message, began to sound prophetic. Salinger was the spokesman of the Ivy League Rebellion during the early Fifties. He had come to express, apparently, the values and aspirations of college youth in a way that nobody since Scott Fitzgerald (the other major influence in his work) had done as well. He is interesting to read for this reason, and because he is a leading light in the *New Yorker* school of writing. (He is probably their *ultimate* artist.) And besides, Salinger's talent is interesting for its own sake.

But just what is the time spirit that he expresses? The *Catcher's* hero has been expelled from Pencey Prep as the climax of a long adolescent protest. The history teacher who tries to get at the causes of Holden Caulfield's discontent emerges as a moralistic pedagogue, who picks his nose. ("He was really get-

195

ting the old thumb right in there.") During his farewell lecture, Holden is restless, bored—"I moved my ass a little bit on the bed"—and then suddenly uneasy. "I felt sorry as hell for him all of a sudden. But I just couldn't hang around there any longer." This refrain echoes through the narrative; and the rebellious young hero ends up by being "sorry" for all the jerks, morons, and queers who seem to populate the fashionable and rich preparatory school world.

He is also scornful of all the established conventions as "very big deal." (Another standard refrain in the story.) He seems to be the only truly creative personage in this world, and, though he has failed all his courses except English, he has his own high, almost absolute, standards of literature, at least.

"They gave me *Out of Africa* by Isak Dinesen. I thought it was going to stink, but it didn't. It was a very good book. I'm quite illiterate, but I read a lot." By comparison, *A Farewell to Arms* is really a phony book, so we are told. As in Saul Bellow's work, the very human hero of *The Catcher,* who is a physical weakling, who knows that he is at least half "yellow," is also a symbol of protest against the compulsive virility of the Hemingway school of fiction.

The action of the novel is in fact centered around the athlete Stradlater, who is "a very sexy bastard," and who has borrowed Holden Caulfield's jacket and his girl. Stradlater is "unscrupulous" with girls; he has a very *sincere* voice which he uses to snow them with, while he gives them the time, usually in the back seat of the car. Thinking about all this, Holden gets nervous ("I damn near puked"). In his room, he puts on his pajamas, and the old hunting hat which is his talisman of true rebellion and creativity, and starts out to write the English theme (which Stradlater will use as his own) about his dead brother Allie's baseball mitt. Yet when the athlete returns from his date, full of complacency about Holden's girl and of contempt for Holden's essay, this weakling-hero provokes him into a fight. "Get your dirty stinking moron knees off my chest," says Caulfield to Stradlater. "If I letcha up," says Strad, "willya keep your mouth shut?" "You're a dirty stupid sonuvabitch of a moron," says Holden Caulfield.

Later, nursing a bloody nose as the price of his defiant tongue, he wanders in to old Ackley's room for companionship. "You

could also hear old Ackley snoring. Right through the goddam
shower curtains you could hear him. He had sinus trouble and
he couldn't breathe too hot when he was asleep. That guy had
just about everything. Sinus trouble, pimples, lousy teeth, hali-
tosis, crumby fingernails. You had to feel a little sorry for the
crazy sonuvabitch." But he can find no comfort or solace in the
room which stinks of dirty socks. Ackley is even more stupid
than Stradlater. "Stradlater was a goddam genius next to Ackley."
A familiar mood of loneliness and despair descends upon him.
"I felt so lonesome, all of sudden, I almost wished I was dead.
. . . Boy, did I feel rotten. I felt so damn lonesome." He counts
his dough ("I was pretty loaded. My grandmother'd just sent me
a wad about a week before.") and says good-by:

When I was all set to go, when I had my bags and all, I stood for a
while next to the stairs and took a last look down the goddam corri-
dor. I was sort of crying. I don't know why. I put my red hunting
hat on, and turned the peak around to the back, the way I liked it,
and then I yelled at the top of my goddam voice, *"Sleep tight, ya
morons!"* I'll bet I woke up every bastard on the whole floor. Then
I got the hell out. Some stupid guy had thrown peanut shells all over
the stairs, and I damn near broke my crazy neck.

These are handsome prose passages, and *The Catcher in the
Rye* is eminently readable and quotable in its tragicomic narrative of preadolescent revolt. Compact, taut, and colorful, the
first half of the novel presents in brief compass all the petty horrors, the banalities, the final mediocrity of the typical American
prep school. Very fine—and not sustained or fulfilled, as fiction.
For the later sections of the narrative are simply an episodic
account of Holden Caulfield's "lost week end" in New York City
which manages to sustain our interest but hardly deepens our
understanding.

There are very ambiguous elements, moreover, in the portrait
of this sad little screwed-up hero. His urban background is curiously shadowy, like the parents who never quite appear in the
story, like the one pure adolescent love affair which is now
"ruined" in his memory. The locale of the New York sections is
obviously that of a comfortable middle-class urban Jewish society
where, however, all the leading figures have become beautifully
Anglicized. Holden and Phoebe Caulfield: what perfect American social register names which are presented to us in both a

social and a psychological void! Just as the hero's interest in the ancient Egyptians extends only to the fact that they created mummies, so Salinger's own view of his hero's environment omits any reference to its real nature and dynamics.

Though the book is dedicated to Salinger's mother, the fictional mother in the narrative appears only as a voice through the wall. The touching note of affection between the brother and sister is partly a substitute for the missing child-parent relationships (which might indeed clarify the nature of the neurotic hero), and perhaps even a sentimental evasion of the true emotions in a sibling love. The only real creation (or half-creation) in this world is Holden Caulfield himself. And that "compassion," so much praised in the story, and always expressed in the key phrase, "You had to feel sorry"—for him, for her, for them— also implies the same sense of superiority. If this hero really represents the nonconformist rebellion of the Fifties, he is a rebel without a past, apparently, and without a cause.

The Catcher in the Rye protests, to be sure, against both the academic and social conformity of its period. But what does it argue *for?* When Holden mopes about the New York museum which is almost the true home of his discredited childhood, he remembers the Indian war-canoes "about as long as three goddam Cadillacs in a row." He refuses any longer to participate in the wealthy private boys' schools where "you have to keep making believe you give a damn if the football team loses, and all you do is talk about girls and liquor and sex all day, and everybody sticks together in these dirty little goddam cliques." Fair enough; while he also rejects the notion of a conventional future in which he would work in an office, make a lot of dough, ride in cabs, play bridge, or go to the movies. But in his own private vision of a better life, this little catcher in the rye sees only those "thousands of little children" all playing near the dangerous cliff, "and nobody's around—nobody big, I mean— except me" to rescue them from their morbid fate.

This is surely the differential revolt of the lonesome rich child, the conspicuous display of leisure-class emotions, the wounded affections, never quite faced, of the upper-class orphan. This is the *New Yorker* school of ambiguous finality at its best. But Holden Caulfield's real trouble, as he is told by the equally precocious Phoebe is that he doesn't like *any*thing that is happening. "You don't like any schools. You don't like a million things. You *don't*." This is also the peak of well-to-do and neurotic anarchism—the one world of cultivated negation in which all those thousands of innocent, pure little children are surely as doomed as their would-be and somewhat paranoid savior. "I have a feeling that you're riding for some kind of a terrible, terrible fall," says the last and best teacher in Holden's tormented academic career. But even this prophetic insight is vitiated by the fact that Mr. Antolini, too, is one of those flits and perverty guys from whom the adolescent hero escapes in shame and fear.

He is still, and forever, the innocent child in the evil and hostile universe, the child who can never grow up. And no wonder that he hears, in the final pages of the narrative, only a chorus of obscene sexual epithets which seem to surround the little moment of lyric happiness with his childlike sister. The real achievement of *The Catcher in the Rye* is that it manages so gracefully to evade just those central questions which it raises, and to preserve both its verbal brilliance and the charm of its emotions within the scope of its own dubious literary form. It is still Salinger's best work, if a highly artificial one, and the caesuras, the absences, the ambiguities at the base of this writer's work became more obvious in his subsequent books.

I am conscious of treating severely, or at least analytically, a book which is most entertaining, but which is also so typical and so illuminating as an example of its class. *Nine Stories*, in 1953, was a collection of the *New Yorker* stories which had already established Salinger's reputation with an elite group of magazine readers. Among these tales, "A Perfect Day for Bananafish" was notable for the unpleasant suicide of a disturbed war veteran.

Seymour Glass has shot himself, seated on the bed next to his sleeping wife. Shortly before this, while carrying on a whimsical conversation with one of Salinger's innocent little girls, he has pushed the child ever deeper into the Florida ocean. There are intimations of a murder before the suicide; and similarly in another well-known story in the collection called "Teddy," a jealous sister pushes a child prodigy into an empty swimming pool. Here the little genius has anticipated and even welcomed his own death, however, while here indeed the morbid, the more than

neurotic emotions which are implicit in Salinger's first novel take
a more prominent place in his writing. The obsessive affection for
little children has usually been accompanied, in the major writers,
by other untoward elements of the pysche (child seduction, child
rape), as witness Dostoevski, Dreiser, or Nabokov. But like the
post-Freudian and revisionist psychologists of the Fifties, Salinger has also attempted to deny or reject the darker urges that
are present in the idyl of pure childhood.

One of the best tales in the volume describes the drunken binge
of an unhappy exurbanite wife, whose lonely little daughter kills
her imaginary playmate, Jimmy Jimmereeno. Two other stories
deal with the comfortable bourgeois New York Jewish society in
which, again, the leading figures are called Ginie, Selena, Franklin, Eric, etc. That is to say, Jewish and not Jewish: this "assimilated" German-Jewish urban group, not wishing any longer to
be identified with their religious and cultural minority group,
whose bright children now attend the fashionable American
Christian schools like "Miss Basehoar's." If Salinger has primarily been concerned with the pure, the isolated, the *causeless*
child, one sees that he can describe the milieu of their origin very
well indeed when he chooses to, even under its pseudonymic and
self-protective coloring.

Or at least, up to a point. In "Down at the Dinghy," Boo Boo
Tannenbaum, who, we are told, is "a stunning and final girl,"
discovers that her son believes a "Kike" to be something that
flies in the sky: a tricky little bit of anti-anti-Semitism. (Boo Boo
and Seymour Glass are to be heard from again.) "For Esmé—
with Love and Squalor" concerns a beautiful, dignified, precocious
upper-class English maiden of thirteen who saves an American
soldier from a nervous breakdown. There is no doubt of Esmé's
grace and charm (or of her social standing), but only whether,
in this case, an adolescent's romantic affection can replace the
need for mental therapy. The young hero of "De Daumier-
Smith's Blue Period" has a similar background: disturbed and
Continental. The mother, divorced, remarried, has died in
Europe. Back in New York, the second husband and the lonesome son have gradually discovered "that we were both in love
with the same deceased woman."

What was curious about Holden Caulfield's chronicle, besides the shadowy mother, was the absence of any father relationship at all. Perhaps here, through the device of the second husband or the "false father," the writer can express humorously and even gaily what was more difficult to describe seriously. At nineteen, at any rate, the present hero invents a "deceased wife," a false name, a small estate in the south of France, a kinship with Daumier and "poor Picasso," and goes off to teach art at an obscure correspondence school in Canada. The school and its inscrutable Japanese owners, and the types of students who use it, are all brilliantly described in the story; the young hero is engagingly and wildly adolescent, and falls in love, by mail, with a certain Sister Irma of St. Joseph's whose portraits of Christ have caught his fancy.

On a walk through the provincial town he is also fascinated by the window display of the local orthopedic appliances shop:

> Then something altogether hideous happened. The thought was forced on me that no matter how coolly or sensibly or gracefully I might one day learn to live my life, I would always at best be a visitor in a garden of enamel urinals and bedpans, with a sightless wooden dummy-deity standing by in a marked down rupture truss.

This is engaging and illuminating imagery; and perhaps the rupture-truss deity, before whom the hero has his moment of mystic insight, leads directly to the Eastern *gurus* who are invoked in Salinger's later and more famous short story "Franny," which took up considerable space in the *New Yorker* of January 29, 1955, and caused another minor sensation in the undergraduate (feminine) academic world. The central question was whether the story's heroine was pregnant, or insane, or both—or neither.

As in any good Scott Fitzgerald tale, it is the week end of the Yale game. The young men are waiting on the station platform for their dates. In his Burberry raincoat, Lane Coutell is reading Franny's passionate love letter and thinking that station-platform kisses are "rather inhibited in the follow-through." (The collegiate atmosphere is done very well.) Yet their dinner at Sickler's —a symbolic name—turns into a catastrophe. Lane is talking about his paper on Flaubert's concern for the *mot juste*. Franny, listening to him "with a special semblance of absorption," is overcome by her distaste for his vanity, his complacency. He is indeed a dreadful portrait of a college intellectual, who will become a typical graduate student in English, a "section man," and then perhaps a minor contributor to the *Partisan Review*.

That is what Franny tells him in effect, as she feels her "destructive" impulses coming to the fore, with the disloyalty and guilt "which seemed to be the order of the day." (She has had to strain to write him her last [false] love letter.) Lane's self-absorbed egoism can't stand criticism; the conversation becomes a controversy. Up to this point the story is sharp and sensitive. Then comes the mysterious scene in Sickler's ladies' room, where Franny collapses:

Without any apparent regard to the suchness of her environment, she sat down. She brought her knees together very firmly, as if to make herself a smaller, more compact unit. Then she placed her hands, vertically, over her eyes and pressed the heels hard, as though to paralyze the optic nerve and drown all images in a voidlike black. . . . She held that tense, almost fetal position for a suspensory moment—then broke down. She cried for fully five minutes. She cried without trying to suppress any of the noisier manifestation of grief and confusion, with all the convulsive throat sounds that a hysterical child makes when the breath is trying to get up through a partly closed epiglotis. And yet, when finally she stopped, she merely stopped, without the painful, knifeless intakes of breath that usually follow a violent outburst-inburst. When she stopped, it was as though some momentous change of polarity had taken place inside her mind, one that had an immediate, pacifying effect on her body. Her face tear-streaked but quite expressionless, almost vacuous, she picked up her handbag from the floor, opened it, and took out the small pea-green clothbound book.

And, armed with this mysterious weapon of spiritual guidance, but periodically overcome by other symptoms of nervous collapse, she proceeds to tell her lover off.

It is not only him, it is his whole life of habits, values, standards that she cannot bear. She ends up not only with an indictment of upper-class American society, but almost of Western culture itself. "It's *everybody*, I mean. Everything everybody does is so—I don't know—not *wrong*. . . . But just so tiny and meaningless and—sad-making." She thinks she is going crazy, she says; she is sick of "ego, ego, ego." While her teeth chatter, she explains that her little green book, *The Way of a Pilgrim,* is the story of a Russian peasant's attempt to find salvation through prayer. "Lord Jesus Christ have mercy on me," is the prayer that Franny herself keeps repeating incessantly, while Lane, not impressed by her religious conversion, reeking of garlic from his frogs' legs, discusses his psychoanalytic paper on Flaubert, i.e., his own literary ego.

Here is the central conflict, in collegiate terms, of the life of renunciation versus—just what? For Lane is certainly not an artist (which also implies a form of self-renunciation) but closer to a boor. There are references in Franny's hysterical outbursts (she is more learned than one might suspect) to the Nembutsu sects of Buddhism and the Indian meditation on the "Om." "You get to see God. Something happens in some absolutely nonphysical part of the heart—where the Hindus say that Atman resides, if you ever took any Religion—and you see God, that's all." But Lane says it is really a matter of the most elementary psychology, and adds that she should take a rest in the room he has reserved for them. "When was that Friday night? Way the hell early last month, wasn't it?" And that maybe Franny's real trouble comes from another source. "Too long between drinks, to put it coarsely." Left alone, while he goes off to make the necessary arrangements, Franny begins to pray. "Her lips began to move, forming soundless words, and they continued to move." It is the Jesus prayer she is saying, to keep herself from fainting again; but then why does the story also leave such an unpleasant or disagreeable impression?

It is mainly of course, the trickiness. After Lane's parting words we are still left wondering whether the painful description of Franny's "fetal" position was the opening of pregnancy or of mystical incantation. The descriptions both of Western materialism and Eastern spiritualism in Franny's adolescent terminology are hardly convincing, and her insistent tone finally loses her the original sympathy she had gained in the story. Both the central characters become almost equally unpleasant toward the close; and there are still more personal elements of Salinger's own philosophic conflicts involved here. For the remaining obscurities in "Franny" were developed, if not entirely clarified, in its sequel, "Zooey," to which the *New Yorker* devoted even more space— almost the entire issue—about two years later, on May 4, 1957.*

* "Raise High the Roof Beam, Carpenters," in the *New Yorker* of November 19, 1955, tells the story of Seymour Glass's disastrous marriage to the girl, whose name is difficult to locate, on the other bed in "Banana-

"Zooey" is an interminable, an appallingly bad story. Like the latter part of "Franny," it lends itself so easily to burlesque that one wonders what the *New Yorker* wits were thinking of when they published it with such fanfare—or what they might not have done with it, were it published elsewhere. Yet in terms of Salinger's career, and of the fashionable school of writing which he represents, it is also a very illuminating story. One notices, first of all, the uneasy tone of the prose. The writer's artistic conscience is at war with the apparent urgency of his message. What is here offered, we are told, isn't really a short story at all, "but a sort of prose home movie, and those who have seen the footage have strongly advised me against nurturing any elaborate distribution plans for it."

True enough, and the tale is full of these uneasy insights; it has a kind of Woukish ambiguity where the artist both is and is not responsible for what he is saying. For the narrator of the "prose home movie" turns out to be Buddy Glass (at least Salinger won't say he isn't), a brother of the late Seymour Glass and of Boo Boo Tannenbaum, both of whom we have met.

Risking the "aesthetic evil" of a footnote, Salinger indeed gives us a detailed chronology of the entire Glass family, including the dead twin Walt, and Waker, a Roman Catholic priest. One begins to realize that this is a sort of Yoknapatawpha County on Park Avenue. All of the Glass children have starred on the famous radio program "It's a Wise Child." They are all, apparently prodigies (like the deceased and also famous Teddy, who should be related). And just as we remember that Boo Boo was "a stunning and final girl," so the present "hero" of the new story, Zooey, is "surpassingly handsome, even spectacularly so." Boo Boo has in fact described Zooey as "the blue-eyed Jewish-Irish Mohican scout"—an odd bit of childhood romance.

The Glass children all seem to admire each other no end. Zooey is indeed in the bathtub, reading Buddy's four-year-old letter, when the story finally begins to move (in its own static way), and when Mrs. Glass herself slips into the bathroom to

fish,"—his wife, I mean, when he commits suicide. This is in fictional terms the best story in the series, because Salinger's philosophical and mystic preoccupations had not yet got the better of his craftsmanship. But it is simply an entertaining tale, with rather morbid undertones, comment on which is omitted here since most of the material in it is repeated with far more emphasis in "Zooey."

have a family conference with her handsome, talented, and naked son. (There is a shower curtain drawn between them, which apparently obviates both the oedipal and the pornographic factors here.) Franny Glass is still pursuing her nervous breakdown in the living room, and Zooey now repeats, in greater detail, the nature of her spiritual conflict, and the meaning of her quest for what is now a clear case of Zen Buddhism.

While Bessie Glass would appear to have all the anxious, doting traits of a Jewish matriarch, she turns out in fact to be a sort of mystic Irish druidess. She is indeed the Ideal Mother, understanding, perceptive, wise in her eccentric way, hiding her grief for her two dead sons, and crossing and uncrossing her remarkable legs throughout this whole scene. But there are really only two people talking—or one—in any given area of "Zooey," and now the camera moves on to the prone and ailing Franny. Zooey has already dissuaded his mother from calling in a psychoanalyst ("Just think of what analysis did for Seymour.").* Now he instructs his sick sister that what is totally wrong in her personal revolt against the Western ego is her inadequate view of Buddha, the Indian Japam, and the Bible itself. (During this scene Franny continues to fondle the altered tomcat Bloomberg, who is apparently the only honest Jewish character in the tale.)

Zooey proceeds to explain that she has never understood Jesus himself from the time she was a child. "Your age has nothing to do with what I'm talking about. There are no big *changes* between ten and twenty—or ten and eighty, for that matter"— an interesting rationalization for the perennial world of childhood. "You keep talking about *ego*," he adds. "My God, it would take Christ himself to decide what's ego and what isn't. This is *God's* universe, buddy, not yours, and he has the final say about what's ego and what isn't." Moreover, Jesus was far superior to

* Salinger's description of a "good" analyst is couched, alas, in about the same terms that Graham Greene uses for the Catholic analyst (another servant of God) in *The Potting Shed*. But isn't this revisionist concept of psychoanalysis contrary to Freud's whole scientific and antireligious orientation—as is the modern fusion of depth psychology and Eastern mysticism in the disciples of Jung, or even the recent Zen Buddhism itself of the Erich Fromm school? But perhaps the primary historical function of psychoanalysis (to cut through all these forms of supernatural myths, fantasies, illusions and prejudices) was too ruthless, too cruel, for the civilizations which live on such illusions.

earlier prophets. Moses "was a nice man, and he kept in beautiful touch with his God and all that—but that's exactly the point. He had to keep in touch. Jesus realized there *is* no separation from God."

This is again an odd synthesis of Eastern and Western thought which might not have the approval of Christian or Jewish scholars; and yet Zooey's own final picture of Christ is closer to the religious fantasies of a John Steinbeck or a Bruce Barton. "Jesus was a supreme *adept,* by God, on a terribly important mission," he says:

This was no St. Francis, with enough time to knock out a few canticles, or to preach to the *birds,* or to do any of the other endearing things so close to Franny Glass's heart. I'm being serious now, God damn it. How can you miss seeing that? If God had wanted somebody with St. Francis's consistently winning personality for the job in the New Testament, he'd have picked him, you can be sure. As it was, he picked the best, the smartest, the most loving, the least sentimental, the most un*im*itative master, he could possibly have picked. And when you miss seeing that, I swear to you, you're missing the whole point of the Jesus Prayer.

Isn't it odd, too, in Salinger's synthesis of Eastern and Western religions, that only the Jewish faith, like the Jewish father of the family, should be barely mentioned, and in effect is omitted? Nevertheless Franny, under the spell of this therapeutic magic, or that of Buddy's continuous, insistent, repetitious, sermonizing lecture, somehow achieves her peace of mind, and falls asleep.

There is no doubt also that Salinger is deadly serious about all this, and that his continual use of collegiate phrases is no longer for the purposes of satire, but of persuasion of his mainly collegiate audience. Yet to read "Zooey" seriously is indeed like being in a lunatic asylum, as the heroine says about the Glass family, where it is difficult to distinguish between the doctors and the patients, as these self-appointed spiritual saviors play out their dubious roles. What is obvious of course is that these roles are all identical; and the literary "personages" in the narrative are merely the splintered parts of the same literary ego, persuading, opposing, convincing and arguing with itself. Thus there is the almost deliberately static effect of the story: the lack of all inner or outer action, the monotonous and repetitious use of the same trite and paralyzed gestures—as though, finally, we were hearing one voice speaking endlessly in an empty room. This is close to a catatonic tale.

And perhaps those buried monsters and horrors, always hinted at in Salinger's work, are having their say here. *"Yes. Yes. Yes. All right. Let me tell you something now, buddy . . . Are you listening . . . I'll tell you a terrible secret. Are you listening to me?"* And yet "Zooey" is also the logical climax of Salinger's career to this point. We have noticed the narrow range of his literary orbit, its uneasy base, its superstructure of sham. This predominantly Jewish middle-class urban circle, which ends up with its exotic Irish and druidic thespians! This inner psychological world of highly confused parental images, of effusive, sentimental and false sibling affection, which arrives at a Super Mother and a whole clan of brilliant child prodigies! The family name of Glass could hardly be better as a symbol of the pervading narcissism of all these identical "characters"—their ego-bound armor of self-vanity which is so illusory and so fragile.

Nowhere in this whole literary scene is there a genuine parent, or perhaps a genuine child. The true existence of the "glass" family is indeed on the perennial radio program of the Wise Child. And perhaps the almost compulsive naturalism of "things" in "Zooey" is the writer's unconscious attempt to substitute a material solidity of furnishings for the missing social, economic, and psychological bases of his craft. Very likely these stories represent the writer's search, too, for his lost origins. Yet this family is still so evasive in its origins, so histrionic in its nature, so unnaturally handsome, talented, beautiful, wise, and sensitive in all its component parts (parents, children, furnishings, atmosphere), and so brilliantly artificial in the end! It also represents the failure of the writer really to understand his own, true, life experience and to fulfill himself.

Is this indeed the "terrible secret" that is contained and never revealed in the tormented latest story of Salinger's? For a serious writer it could be. The buried depths of the past, which are the core, the source, the dark and ever-fresh quarry of his work, have failed. Thus, too, the satiric study of formal American education, with which Salinger opened his career, has its own limited focus. It is not really concerned with all those jerks, morons, and queers that Holden Caulfied feels sorry for. It is directed at the failure of this educational system to understand the solitary "creative" rebel who protests against it. And Salinger's scathing references to the "normalcy" of those people who read the *Times*, care about the H-bomb, join the Westport or Oyster Bay Parent-Teachers' Association (not Bronx, Brooklyn, or Manhattan) proceeds from the same source. This is an Exurbanite Radical Party of One.

We might say much the same thing about Salinger's disdain for the mass entertainment of Broadway and Hollywood from the superior vantage point of the *New Yorker* school of entertainment. Gifted, sensitive, perceptive, such high verbal talents as, say, John Cheever, Irwin Shaw or Edward Newhouse, among the *New Yorker* Impressionists exist in a cultivated and most knowledgeable void. Maybe Salinger's real trouble is simply to be the brightest of all these bright children. "Always, always, referring every goddam thing that happens right back to our lousy little egos," says Zooey, in sober truth. But what a perfect solution Salinger's mode of Zen Buddhism offers for this uneasy and unresolved conflict. In favor of a higher ego renunciation, it "transcends" all the solid material facts of environment and personality which this writer has ignored or evaded in his own literary career. In behalf of a kind of oceanic moral grandeur, it dispenses with any attempt at self-knowledge.

In a desperate spiritual revulsion against a devouring infantile egoism, is the answer really to repudiate our whole notion of Western individuality? Is there really no such thing (as Zooey tells Franny) as time or change or growth in our concept of human personality? In the Zen quest for "No-Knowledge" (as Buddy Glass tells his split-half Zooey), is it true that all legitimate religious study must lead to unlearning "the illusory differences between boys and girls, animals and stones, day and night, heat and cold?" Then indeed Lord Jesus Christ have mercy on us—and perhaps we should also invoke the practical, hard-headed, wrathful Jehovah whom Salinger has always repudiated. For the universe surely has a final transcendent unity. But meanwhile, here on earth, it is the legitimate business of the writer, in his mortal and un-Zenish career, to make clear just what those "illusory" differences are between boys and girls, day and night, animals and stones.

"Cleverness was his permanent affliction," the latter part of Salinger's literary personality (whom we might call Zen Buddy) has also announced, in another of those brilliant half-insights which never make an artistic whole. And we may remember that little Teddy himself, the first of these precocious Eastern mystics, was attracted to Oriental philosophy just because it negated the "mind" which had distinguished him in favor of the pure and primary world of childhood sensation. That lost world of childhood indeed to which somehow or other, Salinger, like the rest of the *New Yorker* school, always returns! That pre-Edenite community of yearned-for bliss, where knowledge is again the serpent of all evil: but a false and precocious show of knowledge, to be sure, which elevated without emancipating its innocent and often touching little victims. . . . The root of the matter is surely here, and perhaps all these wise children may yet emerge from the nursery of life and art.

SAUL BELLOW: NOVELIST OF
THE INTELLECTUALS

JUST AS J. D. Salinger, by the middle Fifties, was the literary spokesman of the college undergraduates, Saul Bellow was the favorite novelist of the American intellectuals. This is a heavy burden for a fiction-writer to bear, and Bellow's work is interesting to the degree that it conforms to the prevailing values and standards of his "class," and to the degree that it goes beyond them. This writer, as I have said elsewhere, is a novelist in spite of himself; part of our sympathy and concern with his career lies with his own struggle to break through a predominantly intellectual and moral approach to life.

His first book, *Dangling Man,* in 1944, was acclaimed by the critics of the Partisan-Kenyon Review orbit as an "unassailable moral effort" in its attempt to chart the uncertainty of modern man caught between the military and the civilian worlds. "One of the most honest pieces of testimony on the psychology of a whole generation," said Edmund Wilson. Beneath the contemporary surface of the novel, there were echoes and parallels from Dostoevski's *Notes from the Underground.*

Books—"these guarantors of an extended life"—are the primary life medium of the Dangling Man. But this early hero, in a state of demoralization, is waiting for his draft call in a war that he supports but refuses to profit from (a different stand from that in our World War I writing). He has become indifferent to his friends, his family; what point is there in getting or holding a job? In the solitude of his room, while his wife becomes the breadwinner, even his new-found "freedom" seems futile. He resigns himself to a "narcotic dullness," broken by fits of hysteri-

210

cal anger at those who do not understand his devotion to principle.

He is already a "moral casualty of the war," as he feels; he has assumed that "weariness of life" which Goethe described. If he finds urban life particularly hideous and joyless—and particularly the lower middle-class segment of society that he frequents—yet he still tries continually to find "clear signs of their common humanity." There must be a difference, he thinks, between things and persons and even between acts and persons. Otherwise the people who lived and died in these ugly modern American cities were actually a reflection of the conditions they lived among.

I had always striven to avoid blaming them [he adds] because I was involved with them; because, whether I liked it or not, they were my generation, my society, my world. We were figures in the same plot, eternally fixed together. I was aware, also, that their existence, just as it was, made mine possible. And if, as was often said, this part of the century was approaching the nether curve in a cycle, then I, too, would remain on the bottom and there, extinct, merely add my body, my life, to the base of a coming time.

This was probably a condemned age, the hero reflects, in which, among the violent political factions, even simple human communication had become impossible. At the dreadful parties of rootless middle-class intellectuals and Bohemians, which he attends, he sees only a modern parody of the Eleusinian spirit where "the charge of feeling in the pent heart" was now released without grace or mystery. Nor is he better off with his rich brother Amos, the complacent and comfortable Dolly, and their spoiled daughter Etta who wants Cugat, not Haydn, to be played on *her* phonograph.

Joseph finally spanks this brat in a rare act of aggression (after Etta claims he has attacked her sexually). For the Bellow protagonist has also rejected—along with the militant pacifism of our World War I literature, and the adolescent modes of social protest—the Hemingwayish code of dead-pan virility. "Do you have emotions? Strangle them," he thinks, ironically. But what is the fundamental cause of his moral despair and spiritual apathy? Is it really because, as we are told here, "God is dead," and we no longer operate in that medieval hierarchy where man's

place was given, fixed and immutable in a ceaseless conflict between good and evil, or between Satan and the redeeming
Church?

But, since, the stage has been reset and human beings only walk
on it, and, under this revision, we have, instead, history to answer to.
We were important enough then for our souls to be fought over.
Now, each of us is responsible for his own salvation, which is in his
greatness. And that, that greatness, is the rock our hearts are abraded
on. Great mind, great beauties, great lovers and criminals surround
us. From the great sadness and desperation of Werthers and Don
Juans we went to the great ruling images of Napoleons; from those
to murderers who had that right over victims because they were
greater than the victims; to men who felt privileged to approach
others with a whip; to schoolboys and clerks who roared like revolutionary lions; to those pimps and subway creatures, debaters in midnight cafeterias who believed they could be great in treachery and
catch the throats of those they felt were sound and well in the lassos
of their morbidity; to dreams of greatly beautiful shadows embracing
on a flawless screen. Because of these things we hate immoderately
and punish ourselves and one another immoderately. The fear of
lagging pursues and maddens us. The fear lies in us like a cloud.
It makes an inner climate of darkness.

Now this is beautifully said, with a certain truth—but it summarizes almost too neatly the prevalent post-Marxist, nostal-
gically semireligious American intellectual view of our modern
dilemma. Aren't these eloquent words a little odd, after all,
coming from a writer who bases his work firmly, as Bellow has,
on the social-environmental nexus? And particularly from a
writer (as we shall see in the subsequent novels) who has within
him a deep and primary core of Jewish feeling and of Biblical
righteousness? "If there is no God, anything is possible," said
Dostoevski, after he had returned to his own particular complex
of religious and nationalistic "authority." But what the devil are
the descendents of Jehovah and Jefferson doing in this gallery?
If indeed *Dangling Man* caught the notice of our intellectual and
literary journals, it was because it represented their own inner
world view so accurately and so smoothly. In this sense, the
early Saul Bellow was the Herman Wouk of the academic quarterlies; and there are other interesting comparisons in fact between these two assimilated (in their art) Jewish writers and

prophets, one speaking for the elite of the 1940's and '50's, and the other for the masses.

In the purely literary aspects of the novel, too, it was a youthful and ambiguous work, for all its expression of the time spirit. "It's months and months since you took an interest in me," says Joseph's despairing wife, and this indictment could extend to all the other characters in the book whom this hero regards with, so to speak, an enforced humanity. He is a narrow, a self-enclosed auctorial spokesman who is so concerned "with keeping intact and free from encumbrance a sense of his own being" that his separation from his own society seems as much personal as social. The integrity of the hero's moral principles is matched by the shallow penetration of those sensual or material levels of human experience on which a novelist's work usually rests. But this typical hero of isolated sensibility appears again in Bellow's subsequent books, and the constricted psychic syndrome at the center of the moral vision becomes tormented in his second novel.

Three years later, in 1947, *The Victim,* marked a sharp advance in Bellow's craft, even while it was an elaboration of *Dangling Man* in certain aspects. (Like William Dean Howells, this later fictionalist showed a certain caution, even timidity, in the development of his career.) There was again the use of a purely literary source for the new novel in Dostoevski's *The Eternal Husband*; there were literal repetitions of certain "effects," while the energy of the novel was transferred from the cuckold-lover to the Jew—anti-Semite theme. But who is really the "victim" in this ironic fable of a lower middle-class world of commercial journalism? The poor, pathetic, moralistic, and tormented "hero," Leventhal, is made to feel responsible for having ruined another man's life.

The ostensible "victim," Allbee, has lost his job through one of Leventhal's fits of anger; he has taken to drink and is at the edge of that bottomless social abyss that Leventhal himself fears and dreads. In revenge—or is it simple human need and elementary justice?—Allbee fastens himself upon Leventhal in a parasitical relationship. He moves into the apartment while Leventhal's wife is away, takes over Leventhal's affairs, pries into the most intimate affairs, brings a prostitute into Leventhal's marital bed, and finally attempts a "mutual suicide pact" without, however, first consulting Leventhal's wishes about the mat-

ter. The worst of it all is that Allbee, a decadent New Englander,
has a morbid curiosity about the Jews which he is at no pains
to conceal; he taunts Leventhal, whom he is slowly destroying
He is disgusting in his personal habits, and he is drawn to Leventhal physically; there are homosexual elements in this tangled
and macabre relationship.

Why must Leventhal feel the moral responsibility for rehabili-
tating this dreadful specimen of his people's historic enemy; why
does he come to believe some of the worst charges of anti-Semitism that Allbee levels at him? What burden of guilt does he carry
in his heavy, sweating, panting, hairy black carcass? He feels
responsible, too, for the death of his brother's child—the brother
he hardly knows, who has abandoned his own family—and for
his Catholic sister-in-law. His only pride comes from doing his
job well in the business magazine office where he works. His only
solace is in the love and care of his missing wife Mary, who is,
however, barely more than a shadow in the story. The memory
of his mad mother, his ineffectual father, haunts him also; his
own delicate, hypochondriacal physical system periodically erupts
into storms of hysteria.

Yet we feel all this spiritual agony in *The Victim,* and we know
there is a certain justice in it. Leventhal is the eternal Jew, accepting his moral responsibility for a world he never made. And,
overcome by illness, treachery, and malice in the social air around
him, struggling desperately, not indeed to "get ahead" but simply
to survive, he is also, in Bellow's view, a typical product of
modern urban life. He is the Dangling Man, as it were, at last
coming to grips with life. He is in part heroic in meeting all these
commonplace disasters of the poor—the white-collar poor—and
as pure fiction, this novel is effective. We feel both the world of
commercial journalism—dingy, drab, snide—in which the distraught Leventhal has achieved a tiny niche, and the inner psychological world of the novel, where all of Leventhal's precarious
security is suddenly threatened by "some freakish, insane process," which yet has some curious inner logic. The account of
of Leventhal's neurotic symptoms in meeting this threat is a psy-
chosomatic drama in itself.

This is indeed the fable of the persecuted Jewish spirit that
now must embrace and revive the fallen image of its would-be

persecutors. Yet as in *Dangling Man,* the hero's friends are still
the same group of "assimilated"—that is to say, of decultured
and deracinated Jewish souls. In this close, narrow, joyless lower
middle-class environment, indeed, the element of almost stifling
domestic piety is all that thus remains to these people of their
cultural heritage. It is only the old Yiddish journalist Schlossberg
who breathes that other air, that other source of life and culture
—literary, artistic, Bohemian, intellectual, often atheist, radical,
or socialist—which, rather than the dwindling orthodox religious
tradition marked the true contribution of the Jewish immigrants
to American society around the turn of the century.

But Schlossberg, alas, has also turned from his passionate love
of the theater to more modern "scientific topics." His successor
is the Hollywood agent, Shifcart, or the anglicized Jew Harkavy.
And Leventhal thinks of his own father to whom nothing mat-
tered except to be freed by money from the power of his enemies.
"And who were the enemies? The world, everyone. They were
imaginary. There was no advantage. He carried on like a merchant prince among his bolts and remnants, and was willing to
be a pack rat in order to become a lion. There was no advantage; he never became a lion. It gave Leventhal pain to think
about his father's sense of these things."

"Ruf mir Yoshke, ruf mir Moshke,
Aber gib mir die groschke"

his father had cried.—"Call me Ikey, call me Moe, but give me
the dough." No wonder the son had rejected and recoiled from
his father's vision of things, just as he had repudiated, as Bellow
himself does, the whole ethic of American success, power, and
money: the fear of lagging, the dark climate within. Yet the
father's generation had had its own form of defense, if only
through hatred, arrogance, and cunning, against the evil world,
and those "imaginary" enemies who were often actual enough.
What is the real meaning then of the ogres and demons and suc-
cubi that continue to inhabit this harassed hero Leventhal's own
world: these terrible fears and panics of inward collapse, these
sudden and unexpected apparitions of outward evil and disaster,
that the son can only accept and endure?

In a curious twist of the narrative, Allbee is more Jewish than

Leventhal himself. He taunts this sweating hero with perverted references to Jewish folklore and history that Leventhal is ignorant of; he is almost the symbol of the cultural heritage that the Bellow spokesman has cast aside unconsciously, and that now returns to strangle him in this twisted and evil form. Certainly Allbee is the odious "double" of Leventhal; and, in this modern melting pot of all religious modes, Leventhal seems to have inherited all the pain and suffering of his moral tradition with none of its resources. Is New York a "Jewish" city in his fevered imagination? But then it is a city in which, like olden Babel, no man can any longer speak to or understand another. And indeed the whole "Jewish" concept in this hero (and in the author?) is so close to paranoia and madness, so fraught with guilt, anxiety, and fear, so lacking in warmth, humor, and joy, that it is no longer, in the historic sense, Jewish. There is all the Jewish guilt without the Jewish pride, there is all the agony of life but no enjoyment, there is the heavy vestigial morality with none of the deep or wild human impulses which necessitated this morality.

One is reminded of nothing so much as that drab, dingy, and dreadful lower middle-class London world of George Orwell's (high above it the code of "gentlemanly" behavior, just below it the gaping social abyss), dying by inches of sheer spiritual malnutrition, but refined to the last: that world of genteel poverty in *Keep the Aspidistra Flying,* from which Orwell's hero took his own desperate plunge into the pit. This is the real background of Bellow's best-known and most popular book, *The Adventures of Augie March,* a bestseller in 1953, a Book-of-the-Month Club alternate selection, and then winner of the National Book Award as the best novel of the year. Was it? The *New York Times* critic, Robert Gorham Davis, compared it with John Dos Passos' *U.S.A.* Robert Penn Warren called it "rich, various, fascinating, and important." Other critics of contemporary fiction such as Harvey Swados and Harvey Curtis Webster agreed that it was "the most significant and remarkable novel to have been published in the United States in the past decade."

Well, it wasn't, not by a long shot. It was important perhaps only in the sense that Saul Bellow was now aware of, and was attempting to compensate for, the narrow world of solemn sorrow that he knew too well. It was a declaration of insight and intention, rather than a record of achievement. The novel's hero was a proletarian, not a middle-class figure: a symbol of joy, exuberance, experience, of Wolfean extravagance and the Comic Spirit, arising from the lower depths and touching the dizziest pinnacles of American success. That was the novel's plan, at least, and in Augie's Chicago origins, Bellow put himself where his sympathies had always lain: with the social realism school of Dreiser, of Thomas Wolfe himself, and of such later figures as Ira Wolfert, James T. Farrell, and Nelson Algren. The book reminds us that Bellow is indeed, by environment and inclination, another one of these few surviving figures of the 1930's who have not repudiated their heritage and their link with a central literary tradition of the past.

There were the battles, the defeats, and triumphs of civilian life too, in those days; whose echoes are dim and lost in the generation of World War II writers which moved only from adolescence to the martial orbit. (The true break in contemporary American literature occurred somewhere in the late 1940's and Fifties.) But one must add that if *Augie March* describes the range of Chicago slum life, poverty, and misery during the depression years well enough to evoke our sympathy, it does not really compel our interest. It is done from the outside, as though the writer had lived near, but never quite in this life, and knew all the traits of this society without knowing *it*. It is a literary survey, or an anthropological study—this belated proletarian picaresque account of the American social depths—which is accurate, informative, aware—everything but authentic. What is significant, too, is that the hero's immediate family is the weakest part of the book. The tyrannical Grandma Lausch from Odessa, the gentle, weak-willed mother abandoned by her husband, the idiot brother Georgie, the "successful" brother Simon: these are almost daguerreotypes, done by a conscientious but bored photographer.

The formative years of Augie's life as a slum kid, a petty criminal, an amateur lothario, are simply dull. The prose, almost the only time in Bellow's work, is turgid and wooden. Only with Einhorn, the crippled sensualist who becomes Augie's foster father, does the narrative pick up. From here Augie wanders on to become the protégé of Mrs. Renling (who also wants to adopt him), and then meets the intense if empty-minded "upper-class" siren, Thea Fenchel, while he is in love with her sister. Escaping this snare of wealth and society for the moment, he descends to crime with the killer Joe Gorman, and then finds his true milieu stealing books in order to attend the University of Chicago. Meanwhile the family has gone to ruin: the mother as well as the half-witted brother have been placed in an institution, and the cynical Simon stakes his all on a marriage with the bovine coal princess, Charlotte Magnus. The Magnus tribe, as symbols of crude, ignorant, solid material power, are well done; the savage frenzy of Simon on the way "up" in the family business is one of the high spots in the novel.

Augie, too, has a Magnus daughter lined up for him, but again he evades the trap of success in life, and drifts into a quixotic love for the emancipated little working girl Mimi. (Perhaps this is his single real relationship in the narrative.) But there is also his little Sophie. Sexual love, free, open, generous, is Augie's yearning here, just as it has been the single great area of life which has been missing in Bellow's previous novels. ("Does anyone faint from pleasure?" says the apartment-house superintendent in *The Victim* about his dog Smoke; but this ecstasy has been confined to the animal kingdom.) And then there comes that curious and prolonged episode in the novel where Thea Fenchel returns to Augie, overwhelms him with her desire, transports him to Mexico, and develops a subterranean passion for snakes.

Thus the novel which opens in the Chicago slums ends with the exotics and expatriates of Mexico and Europe: which is also a curious parable of the course of American literary realism during the last half-century. But what can we really make of all this? Perhaps the only compelling episode in the last half of *Augie March* is that of the cowardly eagle, Caligula, who simply refuses to play out his Darwinian and Hemingwayish role as an eagle. And with *Seize the Day,* in 1956 Bellow himself returned to more familiar territory.

The surface of this short novel, the brilliance of texture which marks all of Bellow's work except perhaps the Chicago tale itself, is even more impressive here. The upper West-Side New York scene is brilliantly described from the huge and gloomy hotels to the barbershops, the steam baths for the tired, flabby businessmen. and the local branch of the stock market which is the nerve center of this overdressed and overfed segment of middle-class urban society. With his marvelously acute details of social observation, Bellow has almost reached, in his own area, the gloss of a Scott Fitzgerald, a John O'Hara, or a J. P. Marquand. And this whole New York City scene is of course an ironic parody of American society as a whole; just as Tamkin, the "psychologist," is the poet, the philosopher, the "scientific observer," and the spokesman for this society. It is Tamkin who has a "calm rational approach" to the money-fever; who analyzes the "guilt-aggression cycles" behind the gambling in lard, who is full of atomic inventions, and who summarizes the new American credo. "The past is no good to us. The future is full of anxiety. Only the present is real—the here-and-now. Seize the day."

This nightmare vision of the upper West Side—a grotesque inferno of useless, pampered, empty, and ugly old age—is extended to the nation's metropolis itself, where money has replaced blood in human beings. "The money!" cries Tommy Wilhelm. "When I had it, I flowed money. They bled it away from me. I hemorrhaged money. But now it's almost all gone, and where am I supposed to turn for more?" Even more than to the agonized hero in *The Victim*, New York has become a Babel of isolated souls. "And it was the punishment of hell itself not to understand or be understood, not to know the crazy from the sane, the wise from the fools, the young from the old or the sick from the well. The fathers were no fathers and the sons no sons. You had to talk with yourself in the daytime and reason with yourself at night. Who else was there to talk to in a city like New York?"

This is indeed the mechanized lair of the lonely crowd, the fragmented individual. In the central figure of Tommy Wilhelm himself, who has lost his job with the Rojax Company, whose wife has abandoned him, whose children are strangers, and who now lives on Unicap and Coca-Cola, there is Bellow's central observation on the dark fear of "lagging" in the United States. Yet in other respects Tommy Wilhelm is an odd protagonist to personify this social concern. With his still boyish and impetuous manner, but his clumsy, overgrown, sloppy body, he is one of the natural misfits, the "loose objects" on the social scene. He has never finished college, he has had illusions of being a Hollywood star, his vanity has destroyed his career as a salesman. Now a stock-market "speculator" under the spell of Tamkin (and the electronic bookkeeping machines that do not allow you to get in debt), he is in fact completely dependent on his father for financial and spiritual support. In this uneasy relationship of father and son (as in the tangled sibling relation of the Jewish "oppressor" and the anti-Semitic "victim," earlier) we reach the psycho-center of *Seize the Day.*

But it is easier to say this, and to feel it, than quite to understand it, with the perhaps deliberately ambiguous material that the novelist has recorded. Tommy's father, Dr. Adler, is another instance of those respectable, conventional, "assimilated" Jews in Bellow's work. He is a retired professional man, eminently correct, fashionable; and successful. He is also selfish, vain, and cold. Disowning both his children, in effect, after his wife has conveniently died, he simply wants to live out his self-centered, narcissistic, comfort-loving existence in peace. He is ashamed of his son, not because Tommy has Americanized his name and life to an even further degree, but because he has failed. And what the son wants from this narrow, proper, hardhearted father is not money, after all, but the paternal love he thinks he has never had.

Is this at base a sociological issue of the immigrant folk cultures adapting to the cold, hard, abstract success pattern of American society?* Or is there a still deeper question of a psychobiological nature, oedipal in essence, which lies at the base of Bellow's work, as it has in the case of so many other writers of the Western world? Certainly the panting frenzy of Tommy Wilhelm's search for love is beautifully done in *Seize the Day,* clumsy, grotesque, self-defeating as it is. And one remembers the other panting, yearning, panicky and defeated heroes in his previous work, or the solitary, brooding, loveless, and self-imposed human exile of the dangling man: two facets of the same psychological projection. Even the superman *schlemihl,* Augie

* There is no doubt that the children of the foreign-born in the United States are "mother-protected" against the pressures of a strange and hostile society; and to some degree they carry on the softness of the dominant mother image in most older cultures out into the harsh patriarchal power patterns of American culture—where, in turn, the father image has been succeeded by the dollar sign.

March, is an orphan in his own thoughts, with recurrent fantasies of noble adopted parents, who seeks refuge with the foster father Einhorn, or the foster mother, Mrs. Renling. One parent or another is always missing in Bellow's human chronicles; or in effect they both are.

Here it is the mother that Tommy mourns ("As though he didn't know the year, the month, the day, the very hour of his mother's death."), just as the image of the mad mother haunts the consciousness of the victim Leventhal. But the father is lost also, that is the true and present sorrow, just as the father has deserted Augie March's family, and as Leventhal's own brother has deserted his family. Surely Tommy Wilhelm is seeking to re-create his lost, his imaginary family (though he in turn has abandoned his own wife and children) while the earlier Leventhal also takes on an assumed, a contrived paternal role by assuming the responsibility and the guilt for his brother's child. In a larger sense one feels that this shifting, ambiguous parental pattern at the base of Bellow's work is itself somewhat artificial and even false: as though the writer were seeking it out almost too consciously, feeling its absence, knowing its importance, and putting together the plausible and yet not the true parts.

Or as though the true issues in this tormented constellation of contrived parental and sibling relationships had not yet been resolved. For the hatreds, jealousies, angers, and desires, illicit, amoral, and profound, that also mark and accompany the oedipal complex of emotions, are curiously missing in Bellow's work, just as they are missing in, and as they delimit, his whole artistic vision of life. The suffering, the humility, the moral goodness in his books, the honest and ironic realization of human weakness: these are the traits that appeal to us. But this note of resignation, of acceptance, does not appear in Bellow's work after the violence and passions of life, as it commonly does in the work of major artists. It appears in Bellow's fiction *instead of* the emotional storm and stress it should transcend. The central image of the hero in his novels and stories is not indeed that of the rebellious son, but of the suffering, the tormented, and the conforming son.

To use the phraseology of Salinger, this hero is the good boy, the sad sack; or to use the terms of depth psychology, he is the castrated son. There is that curious scene in *Seize the Day* when

the desperate and frantic Tommy searches for his father in the
steam bath and there sees the proud young athlete with the virile
curve in his sexual organ and the cruel smile on his lips. (Reject-
ing the sadistic aspects of the cult of masculine virility, Bellow
also denies, in effect, its legitimate, normal, organic, pleasure-
seeking, and luxury-loving function.) There is the deliberately
ambiguous ending to the tale where Tommy first sees the crowds
of ordinary people in the streets (those Dreiserian and Whit-
manesque masses that this highly sensitive and withdrawn artist
has always yearned to link himself with):

And the great, great crowd, the inexhaustible current of millions of
every race and kind pouring out, pressing round, of every age, of
every genius, possessors of every human secret, antique and future,
in every face the refinement of one particular motive or essence—*I
labor, I spend, I strive, I design, I love, I cling, I uphold, I give way,
I envy, I long, I scorn, I die, I hide, I want*. Faster, much faster than
any man could make the tally.

And then when Tommy joins the funeral of the stranger, and
bursts into hysterical sobbing at the sight of the corpse:

The flowers and lights fused ecstatically in Wilhelm's blind, wet
eyes; the heavy sea-like music came up to his ears. It poured into him
where he had hidden himself in the center of a crowd by the great
and happy oblivion of tears. He heard it and sank deeper than sorrow
through torn sobs and cries toward the consummation of his heart's
ultimate need.

Now here Bellow's peculiarly lyric cry of compassion finds perfect utterance. But what really is that consummation of this hero's
ultimate need beyond the depths of sorrow and self-pity? Does
the anonymous corpse represent himself? Or his father, whom he
might indeed have wished to kill if he had ever allowed his feelings their true expression? Or simply the fate of all men—though
Tommy Wilhelm in this tale only lives the life of a belated adolescent? Just as the central psychological issue in Bellow's fiction
is left unresolved at the end of his most recent story, so too we
realize that the "Jewish" issue, which is partly a mask for and a
cultural projection of the human issue, has become more evasive
in proportion as it has become more dominant. Does old Dr.
Adler also despise his *schlemihlish* son because he has carried the

process of "assimilation" one step farther, the final step, by changing his family name for the purposes of Hollywood—that is to say, of "American" society today?

The father still calls the son Wilky, the diminutive of his real name; but to Tommy, aware dimly that he has two selves, Wilky only means failure, not affection, and he is ashamed of it. And behind that there are echoes of his old Jewish name, Velvel, by which his grandfather had called him: his third, buried, and perhaps true soul. But this soul, too, Tommy never attempts to meet and understand; it is an uneasy ghost from the past, rather than a source of life. Just as Bellow himself has always stressed the narrowest part of the Orthodox Jewish religious tradition—rather than the flowering of secular Jewish culture and art in the New World—so, too, all his heroes continue to be ashamed of and to repudiate their true religious heritage. Judaism in Bellow's work is a source of nostalgia, but also of guilt and anxiety rather than of pride and pleasure. It is a constrictive and disturbing, rather than an enlarging or emancipating force.

Yet saying all this, we cannot deny the accuracy of this social picture either, in so far as it relates to the assimilating of all immigrant cultures within the stereotypes of modern American society; while it is from the moral burden of a specifically Jewish heritage that Bellow himself has been able to assess the outlines of this society. What is the real business of life, his last hero asks himself, if not "to carry his peculiar burden, to feel shame and impotence, to taste those quelled tears. . . . Maybe the making of mistakes expressed the very purpose of his life and the essence of his being here." Yes, one may still wish that the business of life in Bellow's fiction could go beyond this shame and impotence, these quelled tears. One notices that even his vision of the great, great crowd (the matrix of humanity) excludes the motives of *I lust* or *I desire, I enjoy, I give pleasure and take pleasure;* or better yet, that *we* do all these things together which are good for life, which express life, and which alone often make it bearable or pleasant. But still we must not deny the value of Bellow's humanitarian view in an epoch of the utmost social savagery; nor yet the peculiar lyric sweetness of what seems to be the essence of a pure soul.

There is something in Bellow's accent that may remind us of

the innocent and childlike spirit of a Stephen Crane, consumed as the earlier writer was also by the flames of his own oedipal and religious conflict. If I have already made the comparison with another Jewish writer in the popular field, it should be clear, too, that Saul Bellow is genuinely concerned with, and even oppressed by, the moral values of his heritage—that he suffers from them—while Herman Wouk has cashed in on them.

JAMES JONES: AND THE AMERICAN
WAR NOVEL

IN SOME ways James Jones is close temperamentally to one of his own idols, Jack London, whose career should be a warning to him. Jones's work illustrates, too, the central paradox—or the pitfall—of the post-World-War-II writers who moved directly from school or college to the army and military life, who escaped, indeed, the ordeals of peacetime.

For this generation, the single great experience of the war took precedence over the cumulative power of civil life. What was blocked or constrained—or simply did not exist—was the writer's own process of ordinary experience and emotional development. As in the notable case of Ernest Hemingway in the older generation, a trauma—romantic, intense, obsessive—took the place of growth. And a certain scorn for domestic circumstance took the place of understanding. Simply to live would not always be easy after knowing death so well, and seeing life so cheap. This is the central issue behind the second novel by Jones; but meanwhile, saying all this, I should add that his first book, the memorable *From Here to Eternity*, in 1951, is still perhaps the best single novel of its period.

It is a big, solid, and formidable novel; and only upon reading it a second or third time, maybe, do we begin to realize the brilliance of its craft. Surely the respectable critics were put off by the frankness of its material and tone. The advance-guard critics of the literary magazines, conventional in another way, viewed this novel as an appalling specimen of the realism and naturalism they rejected. The popular and movie versions of the novel diluted its real essence, but all this is the fate of most classics. In point of fact, *Eternity* is a definitive novel of the

225

American peacetime Army. Despite the blasphemy of its content, the poetic obscenity of its speech (which becomes contagious), and its open description of certain sexual values which have not been prominent in our literature, it is both a heroic and an epic novel. Yes, and it upholds those "eternal verities" that are shared by novels of this class, and which the conservatives can never find in modern literature. Only the previous mold of thought has been broken here, and the new expression is momentarily surprising or shocking.

Rather like Melville's epic of the whaling trade, a century earlier, Jones's novel is a synthesis: of a whole area of social, economic, political events, of a professional occupation within this area—"soljering"—and of human behavior that both accepts and rebels against its particular chains of circumstance and destiny. Also like Melville's tale, this novel appeared toward the close of the human condition that it summarized and celebrated; just at the time when the regular army of the thirty-year men was being transformed into the permanent civilian army (if not the atomic army) of a new world power. Of that year before Pearl Harbor in Schofield Barracks on the Hawaiian Rock, *Eternity* tells us everything we need to know. There is the country, the seasons, the changing routines of military existence, the day's work, and the payday orgies. There are the crucial differences between officers and enlisted men, the separate paths of official advancement—and then the solitary and horrifying road to the Stockade.

The novel is correctly, if ironically, dedicated to the United States Army, and beside it, the war novels of writers such as Norman Mailer or Irwin Shaw are "lit'ry" or derivative or simply lacking in the knowledge which James Jones has absorbed through his rebellious blood and bones. Prewitt is his spokesman, whose mistake is believing that a man should not be kicked around. He knows the price of his beliefs, too. "You cant disagree with the adopted values of a bunch of people without they get pissed off at you." The question is, does a common soldier have any human rights at all; and Prewitt has a romantic sense of personal honor, perhaps. (His civilian background as a mountain boy during the depression years in Harlan County, Kentucky, is not altogether convincing.) When he refuses to box in his new company, because he has blinded a man, and Captain Holmes tells Sergeant Warden to give him the treatment, the real action of the novel begins.

Because Dynamite Holmes—"boxing coach, horseman, and number one brownnoser with our Great White Father, Colonel Delbert"—is out to win the regimental championships. G Company is run by the "jocks," like O'Hayer the gambler, while Milt Warden tries to make it an efficient military unit. Even the Mess Sergeant Preem "is passed out on his fartsack full a vanilla extrack all a time," as Angelo Maggio, the Italian boy from Gimbel's basement, tells Prewitt.

"Leave me give you a tip friend [says Maggio]. They's a war goin on here. And I can tell you who will win the friggin thing. If you're smart you'll learn to jockstrap, and learn quick, and get on the gravy train, if you want to be a successful sojer. I was smart, I'd of joined the CYO when I was young and learned to be a good jockstrap myself, instead of playing pool. . . . Then I would of been on Dynamite's good list, instead of on his shitlist. If only I'd of listened to my dear sainted mother," he said. "Balls to spuds. This is the Army, they can give it back to Custer."

It is a corrupt company, all right. Henderson, Dhom, and Bloom are all "fugitives from straight duty." The kitchen is a mess; the supply department, under O'Hayer, is actually run by Niccolo Leva; and there is the great comic portrait of Ike Galovitch—"platoon guide am I of dis platoon"—who also gives Prewitt the "lowdown setup" on his duties. Moving up the military hierarchy, we come to the portrait of young Lieutenant Culpepper, a true West Pointer, "son of Brigadier Culpepper, grandson of Lt. General Culpepper," who has to stay in shape for his eighteen holes and the big party at the officer's club that night. There is the scene between Colonel Delbert himself who, "when he smiled he was really, truly almost fatherly," and the anxiety-ridden Captain Holmes, who sees his majority glimmering before him—if he can come through with Bloom in the middleweight class, *if* he can force Prewitt to box—in the struggle for place among these officers and gentlemen. Colonel Delbert asks how Miss Karen is feeling, after inviting Holmes to another stag party with "nothing but rank there"—sex and power, Holmes reflects that he doesn't want his wife to sleep with Delbert, or anything like that, but just to be nice to him.

There is the Colonel's dog, fat, pampered, secure, on whom

the uneasy Holmes takes out his rage and impotence. No wonder
that Warden takes out his rage on the file-clerk Mazzioli (an
intellectual kid who reflects that the First Sarnt is a manic-
depressive-paranoid) or on his buddy, Pop Karelsen:

"I'm sick of it. I'm turning in my stripes. This is the goddamnedest
fuckedup outfit I was ever in. Man like Dynamite's a goddam disgrace to the goddam uniform he sports around. Him and that punk
Culpepper."

Warden's tirades and rages are fine in the narrative, and when
Pete's not uncommonly tender feelings are finally hurt, Warden
soothes him back to friendship; just as he plays upon Captain
Holmes's own vanity, complacency, prejudices, in order to get
done what he, Milt Warden, needs to get done to keep the company going. The masculine relationships are beautifully handled
in an all-male world of blind authority. There is the author's
comment on the "two classes" who inhabit this world: "The
clerks, the kings, the thinkers: they talked and with their talking
ran the world. The truckdrivers, the pyramid builders, the straight
duty men: the ones who could not talk, they built the world out
of their very tonguelessness." And we see that Warden's trouble
is that he stands halfway up on this scale of power.

With all the impulses, tastes, and instincts of the common man,
he must deal with the ruling class of army officers who run this
world. He must interpret their royal commands to men who quite
rightly prefer good food, cards, and women over such noble
concepts as patriotism and death. There is the first poker game
in the novel:

"I call," said Pvt. Julius Sussman, who had been losing steadily,
"but I don't know why. Where'd you learn to deal such stinking
hands?"—"I learn to deal these cards in Brooklyn, as you would
know if you had of ever got out of The Bronx for air. I'm a Card
Dealer. Queen is high."—"Bets five," Sussman said disgustedly.
"You're nutward material, Angelo, thats what you are. The original
Ward Eleven Kid. You better re-enlist."—"I'll re-enlist," Maggio
said. "Right in your eyes, with all six inches of it." He looked at his
hole card. "Two more weeks till payday. I'm gona hit Honolulu like
a fifty caliber. Look out, Service Rooms!" He picked up the deck.
"Last time around," he said. "Ha!" Sussman said. "A good piece
of ass and a ride on my motor would kill you, Angelo." "Listen to
him," Maggio said, looking around. "The Waikiki Beach Kid. Him

and his motorcycle and his one string git-tar. Last time around," he
said. "Last time around. Any cuts, burns, or bruises."—"Dealem,"
Prew said.—"The man says dealem. . . . I aim to win this, friends.
Oh, oh. Two Jacks to Andy. Jesus Christ! I closed my eyes. Two
Jacks bets."—"It's a ukelele," Sussman explained. "Originally Hawai-
ian instermint. And besides, it gets the wahines. Thats all I care.
My motor gets more pussy than all the dough in this compny."
"Then why don't you put the other three strings on it?" Maggio
said. "You cant even play it anyway." "I don't have to play it,"
Sussman said. "Its ony atmosphere."

But we see that these inarticulate workers and builders of the
world, to whom this huge narrative is an ironic encomium, are
very articulate indeed. *Eternity* has caught them to perfection:
their motives, their moods, their speech. The poker game is only
the first of the big scenes; it culminates in the murderous fight
between Angelo and Bloom, the arrogant and dumb athlete, who
has called Angelo's sister a hot piece (to be euphemistic). Early
in the story there is the retirement of Preem, the incompetent
mess sergeant who expresses the bitter philosophy of the common
man:

"If you love the kitchen like I loved the kitchen, then you ought to
get out of it, and do straight duty. If you like straight duty, then
you ought to get in the kitchen. If clerkn's what you hate, then thats
what you ought to do. That way you're safe, you'll be a success,
you'll get the ratings and you'll keep them, because you won't have
no weak spot where they can hurt you."

—or at least the inner philosophy of James Jones himself, which
is echoed by all the major figures in the novel.

But meanwhile there is the first whorehouse scene, where Mrs.
Kipfer is a brilliant satire of the respectable hostess. ("Am I a
good lay?" asks Maureen, the hustler. "Good," says Maylon
Stark, "but mechanical.") And where Prewitt meets and falls in
love with Lorene, the Virgin Princess of Waikiki, who is out to
make her pile and marry into respectable society. "I dint hear no
sounds of combat, so I figured you are takin ten," says Angelo
at one point. "Restin," says Prew, and the two friends gossip,
while Lorene huddles beneath the covers. With her serenity,
refinement, and "culture," she too is a parody of the respectable
American woman on the way up the social ladder; just as the
later scene of the whorehouse on payday is a brilliant take-off

on the American capacity for "production." It is here that
Prewitt, having desperately gambled for the cash to keep Lorene
to himself all night, and having lost, and then borrowing enough
for at least one visit with her—

He was also wondering at the humiliation men will suffer for a
woman that they will not suffer for any other thing, even for their
politics

—discovers that she has no time for love that night. "She lay
naked on the bed, waiting frenetically, her head bent forward
irritably to look at him. . . . 'You'll have to hurry, honey. If
you don't want to take a raincheck.' "

The New Congress Hotel is "like a defense plant assembly line
in full swing." The gracious Mrs. Kipfer is harried by the lack of
towels. Lorene explains to Prewitt with patience and much
practicality that the best she can do is to slip him in between
the three-minute men. Prewitt refuses the refund of his money,
just as he rejects the biological comfort offered by Maureen.
(" 'Next!' Maureen bawled, as he closed the door.") "But the
hard tight sour knot of indigestible outrage in his belly did not
dissolve."

The stress on pure sexuality is remarkably honest and bold in
From Here to Eternity; the tone is hard, flat, and ironic. The
tragicomedy of impotent love in an orgy of mechanized sex is
reminiscent of Henry Miller. These sections of the novel are a
memorable achievement, and perhaps the best things of their
kind in a national literature which has either avoided or sensa-
tionalized them.

Directly after this, it is Prewitt's indignation at Lorene, as well
as the ever-present need for cash in order to buy her favors,
which leads him into the nest of Angelo's "queer" friends. "Aw,
they all right. They just peculiar is all. They maladjusted. Besides,
they'll buy you preparation all night long," says the Italian boy.
Angelo has been pursuing this vice for purely economic reasons.
(This is a Marxian view of Freudian pathology.) But Prewitt's
presence makes him ashamed of his behavior. There is another
drunken scene in front of the Royal Hawaiian Hotel, and the
arrival of two MPs:

They came in pairs, at night, dogtrotting, heavy-footed, leggins
scraping softly, clubs swinging silently, wherever soldiers ever lived.

And the air of fear they carried with them went before them always, the Law, holding them inside it.

And then Angelo's suicidal battle with them which leads the indignant and equalitarian city child down the long road to the Stockade. The one-way road to his physical mutilation, insanity, and ruin: the road of no return.

These are terrible scenes, too; and Angelo is a friggin hero, as Prew thinks, who had never liked Italians or foreigners or city people. Then there is the mass round-up and investigation of the homosexual "ring" in the army, which has been more profitable and more certain than gambling, while the common man in the two truck loads of suspects, clams up, and puts on a great act of stupidity. Their talk, Jones says, was full of country humor, and we are reminded that Jones himself is another country writer in the urban age of American literature. What is a queer, the men ask each other, forming their strategy for the investigation, you know what a queer is? "Christ no," says Dusty Rhodes, the "scholar" of the outfit; "You shewn me a queer, I wunt even know one of em things from a woman." The men howl; but it is at this point that the narrative begins to tighten. Bloom is discharged from officers' training school because of his contact with the homosexual group. In the epic-size boxing match with Prewitt, this obnoxious Jewboy (in standard Army lingo) has displayed incredible physical courage. In his suicide, he becomes a tragic figure.

Only the Hundred Percent Americans like Jimmy Kaliponi or Ike Galovitch (who can barely speak English) insist on enjoying this spectacle. "Not heven an Hamurican you are," says Ike to Prewitt later on in the chronicle. "Not heven to be grateful for tings good men like da Gaptn Holmes are willing do for you. . . . Dat bites de hand dat feeds it dey shoot dogs for. Heven a Commonist is batter. Dan to stabbing in da back da best frien any man ever having hat hafter de breaks da Gaptn Holmes having giving you." Ike takes out his own knife to stab Prewitt in the back, in the midst of this eloquent patriotic discourse. And Prew, suddenly thinking he has found the real "enemy," as an outlet for his growing hatred of the army's corruption, injustice, and brutality—Prew, feeling guilty about his own part in sending Angelo to the Stockade, and knowing that they are bound to break him anyway, and seeing in Old Ike the perfect symbol of

ignorant and cruel authority—takes him on. He has at last
become the "Bolshevik and Fuckup" that they have insisted upon
making him.

During the trial he never mentions the knife that has been used
against him; he accepts his fate. The accents of personal doom
which are implicit in the tale of the "soljer" who insists on being
a man, too, begin to reverberate in the narrative. There follows
the brutal and terrifying and desolate Book of the Stockade—
one of the blackest episodes in the national letters—which completes Prewitt's outlawry. Yes, with its mixture of high comedy,
biting social satire, and tragic undertones, with its open, wild
emotions and obscene poetic language, *Eternity* is a fine book.
If I have summarized it in some detail, it is because this "dirty,"
"sensational," and "realistic" tale itself shares so much colorful,
refreshing, and acerbic life with us—because it is a living organism of the first class. Perhaps it is only in the "civilian relationships" of the novel—i.e., the male and female love relationships
which lie outside the martial orbit of authority and revolt—that
we have some cause for complaint. The domestic interludes of
Prewitt's affair with Lorene, née Alma Schmidt, which are his
only moments of luxury and delight, are curiously flat and
adolescent.

Very early in the story Prewitt has renounced the thought of
marrying his shackjob, Violet. "Because I am a soljer." "But you
still don't want to marry me," Violet says, and Prew gets mad:

"You goddam right I don't. . . . If I was gonna spend my life in
Wahoo it would be different. I'll be moving all over, goin all the
time. I'm a thirty year man. And I aint no officer to have the govmint
pay for transportin my lovin wife all over the goddam world. . . .
Why the hell do you think I got in the Army? Because I didn't want
to sweat my heart and pride out in a goddam coalmine all my life
and have a raft of snot-nosed brats who look like niggers in the
coaldirt, like my father and his father, and all the rest of them. What
the hell do you dames want? to take the heart out of a man and
tie it up in barbed wire and give it to your mother for Mother's
Day?"

And this is in fact the central refrain in both the love affairs in
the novel: this barely veiled hatred and fear of women, who are
so essential to men and so delicious, but whose sexuality is

designed to subdue and tame (and destroy) the masculine integrity, the masculine virility. "They do not want you to find yourself in them," Prew thinks, even while he mourns the loss of Violet. "They want instead that you should lose yourself in them."

Sexuality is sharp, acrid, angry, and bittersweet in Jones— powerful, antagonistic, and delightful, the highest pleasure in the world. But love enfeebles it, and marriage destroys it, one way or another; and all feminine sexuality aims at love and marriage. Net result: male impotence. There is the episode of Prew leafing through the slick magazines in the rainy season, not bothering with the silly stories, but pouring over the shunt pictures of women: "The heavy-lidded, fullpouting-lipped look . . . that women get when they really want it bad." The American Way, that exists only in the libidinous fancy of the advertising agencies. For the American Woman wants a higher form of life. When Prew finally becomes Lorene-Alma's lover, and lives in her apartment, and is in effect supported by her, and nursed back to health by her, after he has killed the Stockade Guard Fatso, it is her maternal love—and his own helpless, childlike role— that he fears and despises, and then deliberately destroys. Jones is very sharp indeed on the social conditioning of the American female that leads to respectability and refinement. (Alma is a deliberately outrageous portrait of this ambition.) Yet there are of course deeper psychobiological elements involved here.

Milt Warden, too, wants ruthless, savage, sensual love. Like Prewitt, he is willing to risk everything and sacrifice everything— even the welfare of his company and his own legendary reputation—for the sake of a woman. His jealousy of Stark, the mess sergeant, because Stark has also slept with Karen Holmes; a jealousy that he cannot show because he needs Stark in the company kitchen, but which he cannot also restrain, is a brilliant minor theme in the narrative. But when Warden finally gets his thirty-day furlough with Karen, the honeymoon for which he has worked and schemed so desperately, the whole love affair collapses. Again, Karen, a powerful woman, is determined to have her own way: the way of middle-class status and security.

Now James Jones himself surely belongs to the class of American "realists," such as Dreiser and O'Neill (and behind

them Melville and Whitman), whose basic affinities are in fact
close to the romantic school of intense emotions. It is probably
this mixture of "romantic" emotion and the solid, realistic facts
(and farce) of life which makes *Eternity* so good. Yet the major
writers, while acknowledging all the vulnerable and destructive
aspects of love which Jones describes, also stress the human
relationships, even of lovers, which are so weak here. Does love
always lead, as Jones implies, to a form of entrapment and self-
destruction? Does it always move so swiftly from delight to
torment? Beneath the battle of the sexes in this novel, there is
an underlying, almost morbid, concern with spiritual (at least)
castration; a stress on masculine virility which is dangerously
close to fear of impotence, and which can be attributed to personal as much as to cultural causes. What is curious, too, is that
all the officers in this epic novel of the American soldier are
viewed as false fathers. There is not a single decent or efficient
army man above the rank of sergeant that one can think of
offhand, except perhaps the final Jewish lieutenant Ross, who is
wise enough to accept the tutelage of Warden himself. The
dominant psychological concept in *From Here to Eternity* is that
of the Freudian son-horde, in ruthless revolt against the despotic,
but finally enfeebled king-father-officers. But the mother symbolism of women in love is also feared and denigrated. The central
notion of masculine virility is that of the Rebellious Orphan.

Yes, the class hatred of officers is overdone in *Eternity*. The
satiric descriptions of the American Way, as it appears to its
hired warriors, have certain ambiguous undertones. The historical
base of Jones's own radical anarchism ends apparently with the
collapse of the Wobblies in the western labor movement. There
is a strain of the superman mythology running through the book,
too. But within the purely military orbit of the thirty-year men,
all of these elements, social and psychological, are held in check
by the force and tension of the central narrative, are subordinate
to the major achievements of the book which I have tried to
suggest here. It was only with the arrival of Jones's second novel,
Some Came Running, in 1958, that the negative facets of his
literary temperament became, as the phrase goes, a clear and
present danger to his literary career.

The second novel was intended as a partial sequel to *Eternity,* as a novel of peacetime. A group of war veterans return to a southern Illinois town, where they become a group of "creative spirits" in the flat routines of business, domestic, and civilian life. The novel ranges from the underworld and Bohemian existence of Parkman, Illinois, and the rural patterns of the farm and hunting country (the "old America"), to the upper fringes of big business and politics. The novelist's attempt is to tell the whole truth about this area of our culture, and particularly the sexual truth—the secret life of the townspeople. There are echoes here of both Sherwood Anderson and Sinclair Lewis; while the scientific studies of Doctor Kinsey are a recurrent refrain, almost a chorus in the narrative. The period is the 1940's, and in the dawning epoch of conformity and complacency we see that the radical and rebellious novelist, Jones, is trying to tell the "real, real story" of the national life in the civilian area.

This is surely commendable, and far better in values and purposes than those novelists of the Wouk school who, sensing the same drift in the time spirit, used their talent to pamper, indulge, and flatter the Age of Euphoria. Yet the novel is much too long for what it says; the writing is poor. Compared with *Eternity*'s brilliant fusion of character, narrative, big scenes, complex emotions, and poetic language, *Some Came Running* is lacking in all these standard elements of the novel. The descriptions of hinterland life in Illinois are cast in the stereotypes of puritanism, middle-class respectability, and financial-political chicanery. The little band of angels, the "creative" group of war veterans who are opposed to these cultural taboos, are hardly more exhilarating. The one true artist of this group, David Hirsh, goes down in empty defeat. The influence here is from the "art" novels of the 1920's, which were probably a mistake to begin with.

The gambler 'Bama, who is Dave's patron, is a symbol of the creative outlaw; a faint echo of Milt Warden. But what is curious in the narrative is the almost stereotyped and recurrent pattern of oedipal symbolism. The artist-hero's mother, Mrs. Elvira Hirsh is a nagging, trivial, empty figure of middle-class ignorance and conformity. No wonder her husband has deserted her; but he is a drunken vagabond who is considered a disgrace to his family and the town. David, the son who repeats his father's course in the more fruitful path of creative Bohemianism, is in turn repudiated by his "respectable" brother Frank, whom he scorns for being a pillar of society. The novel is filled with the refrains and variations of "absentee parents," so to speak, and deep sibling hatreds. Gwen French, who is a mother symbol for the group, and is in love with Dave, rejects her feminine role out of puritanical fear. Ginnie Moorehead, the repulsive town whore whom Dave marries, in anger and despair, who offers him only sexual pleasure, turns out to be the most ambitious and proper female of them all.

The feminine portraits in *Eternity* were at least, if briefly, women, and women who could love, if disastrously, their men. Even 'Bama here, who is Dave's adopted spiritual father, has his own absentee family in the Illinois hinterland. The two hostile brothers, Raymond and Dewey, among the other members of the group, engage in a terrible fight over the question of war and peace. "All right," says Dewey, "I say *peacetime* is sad, *not* war." And this phrase summarizes the central view of American life in the novel—or in the novelist. For what *Some Came Running* really describes is the disintegration of that son-horde which in *Eternity* was held together and even inspired by the military authority and the military ethos. The subordinate theme of the Rebellious Orphan in the first novel is the dominant theme of the second. The hateful mother (whom David Hirsh never gets to visit until the very middle of this huge, sprawling work; whom he never sees again), the good-for-nothing father who abandons his children and is repudiated by them, the hostile brothers whose mutual hatred is their only bond: this outward picture of the Hirsh family is the true inner world, apparently, of the novelist himself. I should add that Frank Hirsh's daughter, Dawn, the only sister symbol in the family, has another disastrous love affair, with Wally French, and then (while possibly pregnant?) a hasty marriage with the socially desirable but personally odious young Shotridge male.

There is no love here either. Dawn is a Dos Passos-type bitch (or a Marjorie Morningstar in reverse) who is finally selected by *Weight: The Magazine of Opinion* as the typical young American girl of the year. And Frank Hirsh's adopted son, in the latter part of the novel, turns out to be a cynical and shrewd gnomelike orphan, who knows a good thing when he sees it. There is no love anywhere in this novel, to be precise. But can a novelist whose basic and primary symbols of human relationships (father, mother, son, daughter) are so odious and sterile, so lacking in affection or sympathy—can he really be capable of describing ordinary human relationships at all? No wonder that the central group of characters in *Some Came Running,* or the surviving members, turn back to the army life as a sanctuary, whose familiar evils are less to be feared than the horrors of civilian life. In the epilogue to the novel (and the best single bit of writing in it) we see Wally French, surrounded by the "antlike" hordes of Asiatics in the Korean War, dying a hero's death at least.

The colors are too black and white, the sources of the novelist's discontent are too obvious for serious fiction. The antlike vision of human life has occurred earlier in the book, too, and is applied not only to the Eastern peoples. The psychological orbit of *Some Came Running* is a post-Darwinian universe of dog eat dog, or brother eat brother at best; and the source of this is not so much in the patterns of American culture that Jones describes as in the writer's vision of life itself. (And here indeed, the superman strain in Jones's work emerges more sharply: that romantic contempt for "civilization," and for its modern products, which is ultimately a hatred of people.) Yet saying all this, I should return to the opening theme of this appraisal—that James Jones's second novel illustrates the dilemma of a whole group of young American war novelists in the Forties and Fifties. And that one is tempted to be more severe with it simply because we demand more, perhaps, from this writer than from some of his contemporaries.

This group as a whole has never had the mature experiences of civil life; their formative years were consumed in the caldron of war. Expecting too much from their society, perhaps, without knowing enough about it, or about life itself, they could very easily fall, as James Jones did, into an uneasy mixture of adolescent romanticism and cynical realism. They were both too young and too old for their age, as it were, and the link between childhood and maturity would have to be relearned, relived, if it could be. In its social milieu, *Some Came Running* shows this very clearly, while perhaps, in its psychological core, it is precisely the laborious, compulsive, repetitive, and tormented effort of the artist to discover the missing parents and siblings, the missing home and culture of his youth.

This theme, for whatever reasons, is particularly noticeable in other writers of the Forties and Fifties such as Saul Bellow and J. D. Salinger. Don't they record the identical search for roots and for one's true identity which is essential for the writer, and which the war experience may have cut off by that anonymous bond of the military son-horde that asks no questions and offers no future? In this sense, James Jones's second novel is a useful document just because it illustrates the meaning and necessity of a group problem so clearly. In another sense, we can put it down as a kind of spiritual documentary whose value or lack of value will have to be appraised in the light of the future.

Meanwhile, the writer who gave us the first great book of army life can hardly be omitted from the roll of contemporary American novelists, or, as I think, from the record of the national letters.

WILLIAM STYRON: THE END OF INNOCENCE

SHORTLY AFTER *Lie Down in Darkness* was published in 1951, I remember a party at Max Lerner's where I was being taken to task for a rhapsodical review of William Styron's first novel. "The best novel of the year," somebody said, quoting from the article, "and maybe the best novel since World War II." "Practically perfect!" said the host himself with a statistical gleam. "Come now, you don't really mean that."

I did indeed, but the trouble was that while I knew and felt the novel was unusual, I was not yet far enough away from living in and enjoying the story, however painfully, to be able to explain to this group of sociological scoffers just why this was so. The question of "feeling" in a work of fiction, which is the central source of its power, is also the most difficult thing for critical "explication." (And the New Criticism, from whose jargon I select this word, has resolved this problem by denying its existence.) During the intervening years, however, while Styron has never really had the popular recognition that he deserves, *Lie Down in Darkness* has found its own way.

It is indeed, along with *From Here to Eternity* and *The Devil Rides Outside,* among the three or four best novels of the decade. (And where, in fact, is the fourth?) Rereading it on the occasion of this essay, it seems quite as good as or even better than on first knowledge; and perhaps something of the novel's mysterious grace and power becomes a little clearer as we look back upon it with the perspective, the dimension of time, which also figures so sharply in the book.

At least the form, the beautiful technical virtuosity of the narrative, emerges more sharply. The "present" of *Lie Down in Darkness* is the period when we are waiting with Milton Loftis and Dolly Bonner and the Negro woman Ella Swann for the train which carries the body of Milton's daughter Peyton. During the long, long ride from Port Warwick to the cemetery, the hearse breaks down periodically (it is hot in the Virginia spring) and the mortician, Mr. Casper, gives us a very professional view of the "deceased." At every enforced stop, we are conscious of southern countryside itself, rich, almost exotic; of the appearance of the small city (Newport News); of the slum areas of "Niggertown," where the inhabitants, particularly the women, are preparing for the great revival meeting of Daddy Faith.

During this ride Dolly Bonner realizes that her affair with Milton is over. ("Say something." "Shut up.") And as we move from Dolly's mind to Milton's, to his wife Helen's, to her spiritual guide's the minister Cary Carr, to Peyton's husband, and then, just before the moment of her suicide, to Peyton's, we get the whole story in a single gossamer web of time, action, and character.

Is this narrative of a tragic marriage to some degree the history of all marriages? It is at any rate a remarkable document for a young writer who also derives from a contemporary literary tradition in which true studies of such domestic institutions have been rare. For Milton and Helen Loftis still love each other, or at least they still continue to try to love each other, as they have tried, disastrously, during the whole course of their relationship. The tension of their story is maintained by an alternation of hope and despair. Their bond is the memory of past happiness, and, yes, past suffering which has been shared; their bane is present calamity. They are continually drawn together by their dependence on each other; they are continually being thrust apart by their personal differences and antagonisms. They cannot bear to be separated, finally, from each other; but they can no longer really tolerate each other.

Perhaps it is their sexual differences which are at the bottom of everything. Their relationship has everything in it but pleasure. And yet the real causes of their mutual disintegration lie deeper, much deeper; this is a novel of cause upon cause. Helen has fixed all her motherly concern upon the defective daughter Maudie, who is indeed the perfect child. (Mother-dear! Papadaddy!) Milton has fixed all his obsessive fatherly affection upon the spoiled, wanton and willful daughter, Peyton. And in turn the two passions of these two parents both separate them more deeply and render them even more dependent upon each other. For Helen Loftis takes out her marital frustrations upon her daughter Peyton, whom she accuses of trying to destroy the little Maudie. And part of Milton's further dependence on Helen—and his underground hatred of her—is that even while he thinks she is destroying the daughter whom he loves, she alone, Helen, has the power to keep Peyton in the family circle, or to drive her out.

The description and narration of these tangled domestic relationships is brilliant in *Lie Down in Darkness*. This is the central tension behind the big scenes in the novel: the family birthdays, holidays, and reunions which always open with such high hopes and end in complete disaster. Helen Loftis is a remarkable portrait: this tragic, wounded, vain, and vicious woman, with her uncontrollable jealousy of both husband and daughter, her depressions and fears of insanity—"God help me please, I'm going crazy"—her return to religion, her moods of repentance and love, and then her final, desperate acts of frustration and hatred. She is powerful, sick, disordered, and she grows ugly—and Milton Loftis, feeling his share of guilt for her disintegration, drinking more heavily, begins to think his whole life is a hangover.

He needs his affair with Dolly more than ever, to sustain the illusion of youth and gaiety. His passion for Peyton, replacing his lost wife and home, becomes extravagant, obsessive, indecent. Their sexual games, a carry-over from childhood, have a deeper undercurrent now. Peyton is drinking a good deal. She moves from one to another of the young Virginia bloods, and Milton finds himself wondering if she—? Her pet name for Milton is "Bunny," and when Helen, accusing her of all sorts of wanton crimes, finally drives her from the family ring, Loftis follows her in despair. "Baby!" When Maudie is dying in Charlottesville ("By-by, Papadaddy."), Milton rallies to his wife's side once more; but then realizes that Peyton may be at the Halloween football game with the Cartright boy. Drinking steadily, he leaves the hospital, wanders into the KA house at noon, just to get a glimpse of her. ("Peyton!" someone cried. "The Body!") There is the marvelous drunken orgy scene, mad and hilarious, of the big game itself; and Milton, still drinking, still searching for the impossible pure dream of love he has created in his daughter (the real thing is Helen, is Dolly, is nothing), falls into a culvert, is rescued by a colored man, and staggers back to the fraternity house. "There's daddy," Peyton cries suddenly. "Oh, he's bleeding! He's hurt!"

The real thing, life, is a debacle, a nightmare—at least in these tormented, ironic, devastating sections of *Lie Down in Darkness*. When Peyton brings Milton back to the hospital to find Helen, it is too late. Maudie is dead, and Helen thinks they have been celebrating together. There is another savage mother-daughter scene, and another hangover for Milton. When Peyton is finally seduced by the respectable Dick Cartwright, who wants to marry her, she tells him to quit talking about such things. "And if you want to know why I'm like this it's because I don't love you and I never have. Not because of you or anything like that but just because I don't love and I can't love and isn't that too bad. Isn't that too bad, Dick? Because I'm sick isn't that too bad? That you'll never—" The sexual act is consummated nevertheless, and when twilight fell over their bodies "They were painted with fire, like those fallen children who live and breathe and soundlessly scream, and whose souls blaze forever."

On a deeper level there is no doubt that *Lie Down in Darkness* is the story of an illicit oedipal relationship of father and daughter. The Electra complex is here narrated with such brilliant and intuitive and natural Freudian insights as to be completely non-Freudian. As though Styron had simply lived this pattern through on an imaginative level of purely human events, and had never read a textbook, which I suspect he has not. In the ever widening circles of "guilt," in this novel of human behavior that carries no note of censure, this is surely the deepest and darkest source of Peyton's grief, which slowly emerges to her consciousness during that devastating final reverie in the book; which is present at the very moment she takes off her clothes and jumps, naked as a child, and perhaps now finally purged of her sins, from the loft building in Harlem. This is the guilt "past memory or dreaming" which impels her to the final act:

"I pray but my prayer climbs up like a broken wisp of smoke: *oh my Lord, I am dying,* is all I know, and *oh my father, oh my darling,* longingly, lonesomely, I fly into your arms! *Peyton you must be proper nice girls don't. Peyton.* Me? Myself all shattered, this lovely shell? Perhaps I shall rise at another time, though I lie down in

darkness and have my light in ashes. I turn in the room, see them
come across the tiles, dimly prancing, fluffing up their wings, I think:
my poor flightless birds, have you suffered without soaring on this
earth? Come then and fly. And they move on past me through the
darkening sands, awkward and gentle, rustling their feathers: come
then and fly. And so it happens: treading past to touch my boiling
skin—one whisper of feathers is all—and so I see them go—oh my
Christ!—one by one ascending my flightless birds through the
suffocating night toward paradise. I am dying, Bunny, dying. *But
you must be proper.* I say, oh pooh. . . ."

And so she jumps. The police who find her cannot identify her,
and she is buried in Potter's Field, where her husband Harry,
who has abandoned her as hopeless, still loving her, finds her
body and sends it back to her Bunny. But here the wingless birds,
who have pursued Peyton throughout the book, and who have
been symbols of her sexual guilt, are transformed into these
lonely souls who have suffered on this earth without soaring—
into the image of the falling girl herself, now flying at last into
her father's arms.

I must admit, incidentally, I was wrong about Peyton's reverie
in my original review of the novel. Once the story is fixed in our
minds, this reverie is much clearer, and is perhaps the best single
piece of writing in the book. Here, too, are the echoes of the
mother's nagging (and obscene) propriety: "You must be
proper," and Peyton's answer: "I say, oh pooh." But this is of
course the clue to the power and eloquence of the story. This is
Peyton Loftis' final response (and a good one) to the gnomes
and specters of conventional morality: and her last scornful baby
cry to the charges of oedipal guilt. If there are underground
precepts of Greek tragedy in this drama of a Southern household,
they are also couched in the lost and touching and tender accents
of childhood itself. The real point of *Lie Down in Darkness* is
that, dealing with the Electra complex itself, it has not only made
it human and domestic but has returned it, so to speak, to its
natural home of childhood feeling itself. We suddenly realize that
the true theme of the novel—all its tenderness and tragedy—lies
in the evocation of that childhood world of "illusion," where
all our feelings were direct and open and full and complete. Illusion indeed: when the later processes of maturity are, in one

sense, simply the repression and loss of this primitive rich stream
of human sensation and delight—from which comes the haunting
memory of the Lost Eden.

Thus when Loftis (the high one) realizes that his marriage,
his home, his mature life have all come to "Nothing! Nothing!"
and in a paroxysm of hatred attempts to choke his wife Helen,
it is with "a sudden, angry, almost childish gesture." In the
epilogue to the tale, when the Negroes are assembling for the
sermon across the water and the baptism of Daddy Faith, little
Stonewall has a sly question to ask of La Ruth. " 'Mama,' he
said, 'Christine say she want to frig wid me. Do dat mean—' La
Ruth gave him a crack on the head. 'You hush yo' nasty face,' she
said. 'You gonna need mo' dan baptism to save yo' dev'lish
soul.' " But here surely are just those accents of innocent childhood sexuality at the close of the narrative, which, at the start,
set the whole drama going. If the Negro figures throughout the
tale are viewed, perhaps, too deliberately as childlike, there is
still that final scene of the great revival meeting—its symbolism
extending from the dark ages of barbarism to the dawn of the
atomic age. Now the Negro women (in contrast to the whites)
refresh themselves, enjoy, accept, admire, wash away their sins,
and prepare themselves to believe, and to live.

Milton Loftis is no Daddy Faith. Just as he has pinned all his
stability, his desire, on an unreal vision of the love for his
daughter, so, too, even his alcoholism is an oral and infantile
regression, a desperate evasion of the unpleasant "facts" of life.
(When he turns to the familiar opiate of the bottle, his face is
described as being "like a frightened baby's, sucking on a nipple.") The wedding scene of Peyton and Harry in the novel is
soon transformed into another great nightmare scene, an inferno
of jealousy and hatred, at whose close Milton again turns on his
bitter and sick wife. "God help you, you monshter!" he cries, his
drunken tongue betraying him—or indeed revealing him. For this
is baby talk in the midst of his paroxysm of despair, and in
Milton Loftis' inner view of life, the world of childhood is followed only by a world of monsters. No wonder that he holds his
errant daughter to his breast, and "consoles" her with the familiar, sweet, soothing words: "That's all right, baby. That's all
right, child. That's all right, baby."

But no wonder too that Peyton Loftis, repeating this dominant parental pattern, must continually deceive and punish—in the psychological terms of infancy, she must "test"—the genuine love of her husband Harry. What has really corrupted her? In the final analysis, the incestuous level of the novel's action leads us to a still deeper cause of guilt and blame. "Let me in, Harry. I'll be a good girl," Peyton cries in that desperate last scene when she discovers that even a passion has its limits—that she can no longer remain a child and still be loved as a woman. But her irresponsible behavior, her extravagances, her drinking, her nymphomaniac adventures—the dirt under her bed which is symptomatic of the sin in her soul—have exhausted even the gentle Harry's patience. Her search to find "somewhere in the net of dreams a new father, a new home," is an impossible one. Her recurrent visions of drowning are, after all, only based on her endlessly flowing tears of self-pity. Beneath the lyrical and tender evocation of childhood emotions in *Lie Down in Darkness* there is also, in the central view of life, the hard moral of maturity. The final "sin" of Peyton Loftis is not indeed that she wants to sleep with her father—but that she is unable the leave the dense, smothering, protective orbit of infantile affection in which she has always been submerged.

"If he himself could love so much," Milton Loftis thinks, half aware of his folly, "only Helen could love so little." And yet too much love can be as fatal as too little. The enchantment of infancy, falsely maintained, too long sustained, can destroy all the true purposes of adult life. Perhaps it is the Greenwich Village aesthete in the novel, Albert Berger, who delivers the final moral with all the cynical wisdom of homosexuality. "You just stay as pretty as you are," he tells Peyton, "safe in your land where a whimpering Jesus gently leads Winnie-the-Pooh down a lane of arching plum blossoms." And yet we can still hear the haunting refrain of the novel: "Children . . . come back . . . come back . . . children," even while we see the tragic culmination of this childhood idyl. The final achievement of the narrative is that it presents both these levels of experience simultaneously: the idyl and the reality, and that we experience both and accept both. If *From Here to Eternity* is an epic book in the social area of the 1950's, surely *Lie Down in Darkness* is the key psychological work of the period, where the richness and variety of Styron's special inner world of feeling come to match the humor and vitality of Jones's panorama of the common soldier.

In a period of social conformity, too—where the atomic bomb promises a final quiescence—we may notice a recurrent literary stress on the return to childhood itself. As in J. D. Salinger's version of Zen Buddhism, and other forms of Eastern mysticism, this yearning for the experience of innocence may also be the attempt, neurotic or sentimental, to avoid facing the insuperable evils of the present. What Styron's work reminds us, finally, is that true childhood is both richer and more complex, more tormented and more rewarding than all this—and that we cannot afford to live there.

In Styron's first novel, as in James Jones's, moreover, there is evidence of so much life having been poured into the narrative, that we might have a legitimate apprehension after it, not as to the writer's talent, but as to his resilience and reserves. There has been, in fact, a long silence between novels from Styron's pen, during which *The Long March,* in 1952, was a partially reassuring sign.*

The second book was a long short story of army life, which was good, in one sense, simply because it was so different from the first novel. The narrator is a reserve officer in the Marines who has been called back for further training during the Korean crisis. He is no longer an eager kid from Quantico, he reflects, with a knife between his teeth. "He was almost thirty, he was old, and he was afraid." Are there echoes of Scott Fitzgerald in this age phobia of Styron's? But this is a very different world indeed from that of the earlier Orestes at the Ritz. The years after Okinawa have been happy ones for Lieutenant Culver. With a wife, a child, a home, he had put the thought of war out of his mind forever. And now back in these familiar and odious military barracks, he is haunted by a passage from Haydn.

* As of this writing, September, 1957, I am told that Styron is finally at work on the manuscript of a novel that will be published. But his "silence," or perhaps excessive self-criticism, should be measured against the opposite temptation on the part of any successful young writer (for example, the case of Norman Mailer's *Barbary Coast*) to publish another novel directly, no matter how poor.

It was one happy and ascending bar that he remembered, a dozen bright notes through which he passed in memory to an earlier, untroubled day at the end of childhood. There, like tumbling flowers against the sunny grass, their motions as nimble as the music itself, two lovely little girls played tennis, called to him voicelessly, as in a dream, and waved their arms.

It is the end of childhood, indeed, for this novelist, and for his country and his age. The hero of *The Long March* is the urban Jewish Captain Mannix, to be sure, the rebellious radio-store merchant from Brooklyn, who anticipates the worst of all the evil events that will follow. The villain of the tale is—who? In all Styron's work there is the unwillingness to censure aspiring, troubled, and weak humanity. Is it the athletic, dandyish, and movie-like Colonel Templeton, with his little pistol? Or the bootlicking Major Lawrence, or the "spirit" of the Marine Corps itself to which both give such fervent and blind worship? To Mannix this is the real danger.

He had a violent contempt for the gibberish, the boy-scout passwords which replaced ordinary conversation in the military world. To Mannix they were all parts of the secret language of a group of morons, morons who had been made irresponsibly and dangerously clever.

The Colonel thinks the Battalion is soft, and orders a "little walk" in the night of thirty-six miles. (He has been suspicious of Captain Mannix for voicing aloud the resentment of all these Reserve Officers at being called back to duty, and finding themselves unfit, both physically and psychologically, for any more wars.) "I don't want my marines doping off," says the Colonel. "They're going to *act* like marines. . . . If they meet an Aggressor enemy next week they might have to march a long, long way. And that's what I want this hike to teach them. *Comprend?*" But Mannix, already wounded in action, is through being a hero. "None of this Hemingway crap for me, Jack," he tells Culver, and he thinks that army life now is simply degrading. Loneliness, homesickness, and fright are their dominant emotions, while the Colonel has been lecturing them on their group destiny, "amphibiously integrated, from any force thrown against us by Aggressor enemy." As in *From Here to Eternity,* there is the

same conflict between the homely pleasures of the common man
and the lofty visions of their destiny which are voiced in this
abstract jargon. Only now the conflict is exactly within the officer
class itself, which James Jones could hardly tolerate from the
depths of the dark pit.

Yet the bitter, outspoken, and defiant Mannix will accept his
fate, too, so we are told. "Born into a generation of conformists,
even Mannix (so Culver sensed) was aware that his gestures were
not symbolic, but individual, therefore hopeless, maybe even
absurd, and that he was trapped like all of them in a predicament
which one personal insurrection could, if anything, only make
worse." This is close to the true state of mind of both Styron and
the whole group of his contemporaries after World War II.
Mannix's form of rebellion is indeed simply to outdo his fantastic
Colonel's wildest notions of a *Marine*. He is determined not only
to make the march himself but to bring in his entire company on
foot, regardless of the consequences to himself or to his men.
This is the central action of the story, and the course of the long
march is brilliantly described.

Mannix is the "Nix-man," now turned devout and fanatical
yea-sayer to the antics of the patriots. His mad subservience
hardly covers his scorn and hatred. The debonair Colonel pushes
ahead on the outrageous march "with the absolute mechanical
confidence of a wound-up, strutting tin soldier on a table top."
In the rear there is the voice of the Captain, brutal and furious,
lashing the men on—this "huge voice dominating the night,"
which is also, in its "affirmation," a continual protest and rebuke:
the tortured one torturing the torturers. "You people close it up
now! Dammit, Shea, keep those men closed up there. They fall
back they're gonna have to run to catch up! Goddammit, close
it up now, you hear me! I mean *you,* Thompson, goddammit you
aren't deaf! Close it up! *Close it up,* I said!" Even Templeton,
the impartial, stern "father," the correct soldier, the apostle of
the Marine Corps ideology, becomes uneasy. When a nail from
Mannix' shoe pierces the foot, and the ankle begins to swell, he
urges the Captain to get on the relief trucks. But this Colonel,
observes Culver, had too long been conditioned by the system "to
perform with grace a human act." The Captain refuses. The
Colonel thinks that he will regret his obstinacy. "Who cares what
you think?" says Mannix.

There is the refrain of the story that "they were as helpless as children," while another war, and years beyond reckoning, had violated their minds irrevocably. "For six years they had slept a cataleptic sleep, dreaming blissfully of peace," awakening in horror. The note of proud and willful submission in Mannix himself, of "rebellion in reverse" in this huge, heavy, hairy, proud, and defiant man, comes to the same futile end.

Amidst the mutinous murmurs of the men, Lieutenant Oliver persuades him to let them go, let them collapse and take to the trucks at last. In the final confrontation, the Captain accuses the Colonel himself of "crapping out," while the slavish Major Lawrence has paced the march. "Wait a minute, Captain, now—" says Templeton (the righteous but correct priest). "For your information—" "*Fuck* you and your information," says Mannix, while the Colonel's hand goes back to his pearl-handled .38, and he orders a court-martial for gross insubordination. But Mannix doesn't care any longer; he has made the impossible march. "Old Al," Culver thinks, where was he now: the "great unshatterable vessel of longing, lost in the night, astray at mid-century in the never-endingness of war?"

Very fine; and as in the final imagery of Mannix—"this old great soft scarred bear of a man"—what gives the tale its tenderness and lyrical quality, of course, is the minor melody from the lost world of infancy. There is the recurrent vision of the two little girls dancing and waving from across the rim of memory, amidst a shower of bright musical sounds. There is the last view of the Captain himself, trying to take a shower, dragging his crippled leg, dropping his towel, and then standing naked and helpless while one of the Negro maids watches him with compassion. "Oh my, you poor man. . . . What you been doin'? . . . Do it hurt? . . . Deed it does." And in this final juxtaposition of childhood vision and mature "reality" we can see the great temptation of the artist to cling to the past, to the tender dream, the bright vision of life. Or at least, as Styron has done, to compare the wide and full range of human affection with the bleak panorama of social "progress" at the middle of the twentieth century.

The Long March is also, to be sure, a little thematic and abstract. It is even something of a propaganda tale, embodying that "individual" protest which William Styron believes to be so hopeless today. (Though, is it?) The central action is somewhat narrow, the cast of characters limited, and the author's explicit "view of life" is used to replace the solid, rich, intense sense of life which comes to us so directly from the pages of *Lie Down in Darkness*. For life itself, we might almost say, has no ideas as such, but only desires, yearnings, fulfillments, disappointments. And an author's increasing preoccupation with "ideas" is almost always at the expense of the creative life which it is his first duty to express. In the prose of this tale, too, the imagery has become extended; there are literary echoes, perhaps of Stephen Crane, perhaps of Herman Melville's mad Ahab. The story is told, really, from the outside; and we are conscious of what the author *wants* us to believe.

Yet, saying all this, we can hardly quarrel with the intellectual purposes of *The Long March,* or its central human values, or on the whole its technique. It is a tour de force on the side of the angels, so to speak, and against the demons of industrial, scientific, and militaristic twentieth-century American life. "Do it hurt? Deed it does." Perhaps just because this writer is so conversant with the lingering accents of the nursery—and because he knows equally that childhood must have an end—he will yet become the most mature (as well as talented) member of the entire group of new writers in the 1950's. At least we may hope so.

JOHN HOWARD GRIFFIN: THE DEVIL
IN TEXAS

JOHN HOWARD GRIFFIN is the Texas novelist who lost his sight
in World War II, and who just recently regained it. The two
novels written during the period of his blindness are remarkable
and original documents. Nothing like them has been written in
American fiction of the modern period. For sheer talent, power,
and virtuosity of craft, Griffin ranks very high among the new
writers; but he has deeper powers still than these, and more
interesting facets in his temperament and work. It is another
ironic commentary on the literary quarterlies and popular press
of the present day that he is virtually unknown to many readers.

The Devil Rides Outside was first published by Smiths, Inc., in
Fort Worth, and perhaps because of this never achieved the
recognition which it deserved. But the novel is odd enough in its
own right to perplex the audience which might ordinarily welcome another story of Christian redemption. This is, to be frank,
a category of books to which I am ordinarily averse. What we
need now, in an epoch of underlying fear and hostility, is perhaps
a few less Christian converts and a little more Christian morality.
Part of the *Devil*'s distinction is that it embodies a true Christian
ethic, set against a background of pagan human nature—and it
is hard to say which element in the novel is more disturbing. (The
paper-back edition of this book by a devout Catholic writer was
banned in Detroit by Catholic censorship organizations, and its
validity as a work of art had to be guaranteed later by the United
States Supreme Court.)

But it *is* a work of art just because it is perplexing, disturbing,
eloquent, and entertaining. The hero-narrator is a young Ameri-

can, educated in France, who arrives at a Benedictine monastery in order to study the Gregorian chants. It is autumn, and he is appalled by the damp, the coldness, the dirt, the poverty, and what he feels to be the asceticism of a vestigal medieval order. There is the daily routine of the monastery which is intolerable, and wonderfully well described. The hero is filled with anger, disgust, and loneliness. He misses his girl in Paris, all the comforts and luxuries of city life—of modern life. He feels shut off, isolated, "out of all time." The animal-like eating of the monks, in a society cut off from all feminine grace, is repulsive.

There is the automatic "reader" at mealtime who recites the tortures of the Benedictine nuns at the hands of the Indians—until the monkish audience begins to giggle. There is the "malevolent crucifix" over his cot while he reads and studies to avoid the "nightmares of carnality." And then, slowly revealing itself in the narrative, there is the childlike manner, the great learning, and the great humanity of the individual Benedictine brothers. "Here you must develop a new standard of facial judgment, for these are men of great intelligence without appearing in any way intelligent, according to outside standards." This human understanding and companionship is the hero's only consolation for all his misery—it is indeed the spiritual state of mind which this misery is designed to create. "God makes suffer only those whom he loves." And still the hero yearns for Paris, life, and his girl— "to be happy and shallow!"—amidst the silence of Compline, the adoration of Vespers.

During a bout of illness, he reads and reflects upon Gide, the prophet of modern homosexuality, on Fabre and Valéry. He follows in his mind or on his radio the music of Kotzebue, Viardot, Stravinsky; and considers the nihilism of the Dada movement, of surrealism, cubism, and existentialism. "After all the intellectual searching one is offered only two obvious solutions: the *néant* of daily life on a level plane of mean juices, or the grace of mystical renunciation of the ego, opening floodgates of satisfaction in the denial of satisfaction." And yet, "No! To hell with the must and musk of sanctity!" the hero cries. He complains that even in his dreams a buxom country lass has refused him her favors. Winter has arrived at the monastery. It is bitter cold; the outside toilets do not work. Yet this confraternity of sacrificial ascetics consider the increase of their daily suffering as a further tribute to God, the body's pain exalting the spirit and the mind. In this regime of primitive communism a warm bath, a forbidden luxury except in case of special need, becomes a kind of subdued group orgy among several of the monks. The simple-minded hog-tender Brother Placide, who nurses the hero back to health with complete devotion, resists even this temptation. "He is nothing," the hero reflects, "but he is already in Heaven."

There are a series of brilliant and funny episodes with the village taxi-driver, Salesky, an avowed hedonist and accomplice in sensuality. "What's your favorite way of making love, M'sieu?" he says. Father Clément, the hero's confessor and spiritual guide in the history and meaning of the Benedictine order, is mildly disturbed by all this preoccupation with chastity, which is a pre-occupation with the flesh and lust, when, after all, there are so many other human failings. "My lechery is purer than my prayers, and more respectable," the hero says. And directly after this comes the encounter with the mysterious widow from Paris.

Can anything so natural and necessary, so friendly and ex-hilarating and comforting as making love, can it be really so evil? "Ah, that's pretty, for example," says the widow while she watches the hero relaxing in the bathtub. "You're suffocating me, my friend," she says drowsily after the act of her "seduction" has taken place. There is both an intensity of sexual emotion in this scene and a warm play of domestic comedy that may remind us, as it were, of D. H. Lawrence and of Jane Austen. Shocking thought! and this hero, too, returns to his monastic cell full of remorse for the communal life which he feels he has betrayed. "Stripped of its suggestive elegances, I have done nothing more than sleep with a woman. Nothing more than that. Only my guilt remains. In the chapel below, as I undress, many men pray. Men who have cared for me when I was sick. Men who share their food and goods with me. Men who are my brothers. . . . The pleasure of the many sacrificed for the pleasure of self. All that thrown away for the filthy little heats of holding a woman's naked buttocks in my hands."

This is rather hard on the charming widow; and these accents of disgust, self-laceration, and failure, are symptomatic in the

novel. The raggedness and turbulence of the outside world are
contrasted with the inner peace of the monastery, the devotion to
spiritual works, the consuming fire of total purity. The sexual act
is described recurrently as "hasty," "peremptory," "fumbling."
And yet it is so necessary, so desirable, so inevitable; chastity is
impossible! The novel's action swings out from the divine purity
of the monastic world, which the hero so yearns for and cannot
achieve, to the little French village nearby—and to the nether
regions of the flesh and the ego. Already the hero has met the
evidences of this lower "worldly morality" in the peasant family
of Chevissiers who have refused, out of ignorance and avarice, to
call a doctor for their dying child. Madame Renée, one of the
great ladies who run "the sordid affairs of the village," has con-
nived with them to get the dead girl a proper Catholic burial, and
then has blackmailed the parents in order to get money and food
for herself.

This provincial French village life, whose atmosphere is
rendered quite as brilliantly and vividly in *The Devil Rides Outside* as is that of the Benedictine monastery, may remind us in
turn of a Kafka nightmare with some Rabelaisian touches. In
this close, narrow, stifling little scene of scandal, intrigue, malice,
of petty power, jealousy, fear, and suspicion, Madame Renée is
the devil who rides outside of the monastery walls. She persecutes
the Paris visitor, Madame Vincent, for yielding to the hero. She
wants to drive out of the valley Salesky's mistress and the two
illegitimate children. She tries to destroy the impending marriage
of her unfortunate son, Michel, who is struggling to escape from
her imperious and avaricious dominion. She wants complete control of the hero himself, through feeding, nursing, and "protecting" him, and then by gradually offering her body to him under
the most "respectable," moralistic, and lascivious auspices. With
her devouring ego and vanity, her wiles, and then with her aging
and helpless passion for the young American stranger, she is a
remarkable literary portrait.

But this mother-son, mistress-lover relationship has some very
grotesque aspects. If Madame Renée is at once the hero's satanic
adversary and the cross he must bear, he allows himself to be
entrapped by her salacious advances of the flesh not altogether
unwillingly. Rage as he may at her infamy—"The remarkable

goodness of Christians!"—he is drawn back to her in a mixture
of attraction and repulsion.* It is only when he is on the verge
of actually yielding himself, indeed, that he escapes from this
odor of musk and rottenness, of moral evil and physical corruption at the highest peak of "village" society, and finds relief in
the company of the farm women. There is another bout of illness,
and he recovers from fever to find himself being nursed and
bathed by the aged Mother Nourire. Like the Paris widow, she
admires "the charming sight," and openly regrets the hero's
return to modesty. "Bye-bye, sweetness, bye-bye, young fatness,
bye-bye, nice thing, bye-bye, pinkness, bye-bye, prettiness, bye-
bye, fresh garden, bye-bye—" So she chants, and the shocked
hero is yet drawn to "this laughter, this pagan health." Just so, he
is openly drawn to the "devil odors" of the young Christianne at
an orgiastic village dance. And thus *The Devil Rides Outside*
really moves on three levels of human or historical development:
the primitive level of the senses, the medieval Christian level of
spiritual renunciation, the "modern" level of worldly society.

There is also the obvious fact that in this novel by a young
Texas writer there is hardly a reference to twentieth-century
American life. And the provincial French life of the narrative is
still essentially feudal and peasant. When the dark-hued Doctor
Castelar reproaches the hero for being, with all his wild outcries
of lust, an essentially pale and weak young man, restrained, inhibited, "good in a small little mean way," the Griffin narrator
agrees. "I think you're right, Doctor. . . . I'm the type who'd
make. An impeccable clerk. Or a good politician. I write a nice
neat hand. I can speak several languages. I'm soft. Where I
should be hard. I know this. And I loathe it. I'm the sort of
person. I can't tolerate. What do I do but take up space? Fill the

* Certain aspects of this relationship may remind us of Stephen Crane's
early novel, *George's Mother*. This is a direct mother-son story, where the
older woman uses the wiles and strategies of her very dependence, and
where the rebellious son threatens, bullies, repudiates her, and then
capitulates in much the same way as the present hero. But Crane's tale
dealt only with emotions, of course, while Griffin, by projecting this
oedipal love-hatred into foreign circumstances achieves a far greater
boldness of insight and intimacy of detail. It is the real thing, and is this
type of human entanglement really so unusual? It is common in our
fantasy life at least.

sewers? Vote like everyone else? Some day produce my share of children? Who'll be like me? Without understanding. Without ever understanding."

This is hardly a flattering view of either modern life or the modern protagonist. And does this haunting self-image account in some part for this hero's aversion to the narrow mediocrity— the "sordid affairs"—of even his little foreign village? Is this the impelling force behind his hatred of conformity and social compulsion in any form—legitimate and sharp as the satire is? Is it perhaps behind his wild carnal urges, and his recurrent and repentent moods of ego-renunciation, total purification of the flesh, and a purely ascetic exaltation? In the same remarkable scene with the demonic Doctor, where both protagonists become drunker and drunker as their discussion ranges more widely, Castelar finally admits that the search for God is the best of all the many narcotics. (Like his generation, the Griffin hero also believes that self-expression is no longer possible in the movements of social reform or social revolution.)

What is certain, at least, is that the cards are stacked here, as to both modern society and the values of common ordinary life.

The central dichotomy of utter purity (goodness) in the monastery and prevailing evil, or mediocrity, in the village surely represents an author's yearning rather than an established fact. (Yet Griffin's talent as a novelist can make both sides of this chasm equally interesting.) Even the village priest, Father Sauvac, is presented in a not altogether flattering light. In the battle with Madame Renée—"a woman literally eaten up with pride; a woman in love with herself"—the priest operates with worldly wisdom, rather than Christian humility. Outside the monastery, too, in the sway of Catholicism's temporal authority, we see the evidences of clerical superstition operating on the village people in terms that the Benedictines would hardly tolerate. ("Surely one little heathen smuggled into heaven can do no harm," the hero thinks in the struggle over the church burial of the Petite Chevissier.) Beneath the great abstractions of God and Art, all purely human motives and actions are bound to be imperfect. So, too, in the central thinking of the hero (and the author?), human morality is viewed as another absolute.

When a man can act "without the risk of another's judgment," we are told, then only is he real; and this is a commendable if a difficult standard of behavior. On the other hand, the tolerant and highly flexible moral judgments of the Benedictines proceed from the fact that in their orbit "there are no illusions to be destroyed—nothing that is forbidden." These saintly monks have indeed become brothers in "the search for the infinite"—but is there no brotherhood possible within the ordeals of the finite? It is the same Doctor Castelar (whose name suggests social caste as well as moral heights) who declares that "Man is basically an entity, complete unto himself, who has become dependent on society." And this striking statement may represent either the climax of spiritual aspiration or the deepest and darkest depths of man's primitive fear. The central psychological concept in *The Devil Rides Outside* is indeed that of the stranger, the exile, the solitary hero who struggles against not merely an imperfect but a hostile society. Beneath this chronicle of divine love, there are echoes of that somber and savage Darwinian cosmos of dog eat dog which for a while, earlier in the century, dominated American thought and art.

Yes, and maybe within the psyche of this estranged and gifted young American artist himself—conversant as he also is with Cocteau and Apollinaire, Huysmans and Mallarmé—there are still other ambiguous strains. The great charm of many of the sexual scenes in the novel is due to their direct infantile fantasy quality. The element of voyeurism is strong here, and how much washing and bathing, dressing and undressing, the forbidden (and delightful) fondling of child and nurse, and the incestuous physical contact of what is also, in effect, mother and son. This is beautifully done in the story, and is true at least to some of the deepest levels of the male psyche. But what is curious is the mixed tone of all the later, or more mature, sexual episodes. There is the enormous power of the sexual drive, and the immense revulsion either during or after the sexual act. Torn away from Christianne's alluring embraces, the hero reflects that after all, "with her needs and stinks," she is nauseating, impossible. After each episode with Madame Renée, in which the hero submits to her increasingly bold and lascivious advances, he despises himself more. "But in my mind I smell the unbearable reek . . . the stench of myself."

The final, most intimate moment of this terrible (and ridiculous) seduction is centered around "the detested goal"—the breast and nipple which Madame Renée exposes and offers to the hero. In a brilliant prose passage of mixed sexual desire and antipathy, the hero has visions of twisting bellies, "in a gigantic serpentine voluptuousness," of "strong legs, of distorted buttocks, of insatiable, slavering vaginas." Here, too, the novel expresses boldly some of the deepest and most discordant elements of the so-called "masculine revolt"—the modern fear of an insatiable, all-devouring feminine sexuality. (Though literature has many earlier examples of what is essentially a psychobiological rather than a chronological sexual attitude.) And what one notices also is that these powerful sexual drives, and equally powerful repulsions, are concerned always with lust and carnality, for good or for evil, rather than with mature sexual love. The hero's "passion" for Madame Vincent has only one direct sexual encounter in it, and then, burdened with guilt, relapses into a "pure" and a doomed friendship. The true sexual currents of the novel are divided between the phallic worship of the peasant women and the repressed, sinful, provocative puritanism of the aging Madame Renée.

For the literary temperament behind this novel, too, the monastic order must surely have an immediate appeal. Feudal and medieval in its thought, it is also close to the nursery world of childhood in its order and authority, in its spiritual serenity and "innocence"—where every "sin" is directly known even before the assuaging process of the confessional, or repentance and absolution. When Madame Renée leaves the village, spring returns once more to the Benedictines. "The air is mysterious, full of fragrant balm. . . . All France bows to the pre-Easter season with music." So the novel ends with the Christian theme of resurrection and rebirth (though the restless spirit within the monastery walls will not be content to stay there). And whatever the mysteries and enigmas which lie behind John Howard Griffin's tale, it is brilliantly told, and absorbing to read.

In a curious way, incidentally, this mystic and religious writer, so remote from his own time and place, is directly linked to the other leading talents of his day. If Griffin's touch is less subtle and tender than William Styron's, if it deals with bolder themes in broad and heavy colors, he is surely aware of that lost world of infantile sexuality which is here described in terms of both pagan laughter and Christian horror. And in one respect, what else is Griffin's Benedictine Brotherhood but a highly refined, intellectually and spiritually sublimated form of the military son-horde in which James Jones's restless anarchs also found their true home and refuge? And Griffin's second novel, *Nuni,* in 1956, was both completely different from his first one, and yet, psychologically and aesthetically, a revealing supplement to it.

The new hero is an English professor at a small Southern school whom a plane crash lands as the sole survivor on a south-sea island. We learn that as a placid-looking adolescent he has spent "the secret hours of the solitary night," reading the medical chronicles of Paré, the venerable sixteenth-century Flanders surgeon. In the separate life of this night-borne child, he remembers also the modern American Dr. Chase's *Receipt Book and Household Physician,* describing how young boys must train themselves with much exercise, hard beds, and cold baths for the ordeal of "vigorous manhood and virtuous marriage."

In a tiny room at Poitiers (where the author transports the personal retrospect of his shipwrecked or plane-wrecked hero during the first days of solitude on the island) he had felt the necessity to make:

. . . some sudden bold choice between the animal and the spiritual. His soul desires to enfold another in the ancient dream nurtured in him by Dr. Chase—the dream of health and homemade yeast bread, but his body drags the dream down into a swampy vision of a whore's belly, seen again and again in devastating reality of touch and sight. He smells the reek of humanity, seeing it only as frailty, and he hates it with all of his love, his body and soul distilled into a concentrated essence of loving.

Loving, indeed, or hating?—this reek of humanity within himself, this whore's belly which is opposed to the dream of health and yeast bread, in the hidden depths of this adolescent protagonist? "It is decency, mediocre decency and not love, decency that binds me and will not let me break way," this earlier hero had written in his journal, still divided between the hope of heaven and the desire for hell. Oddly enough, during the first few days of despair and solitude on his lonely island, he cannot bring himself to remember his wife, his home, and his children: the ecstasy which he has created in his mind from the "dullness of familiarity."

But this tantalizing glimpse into the origins of *The Devil Rides Outside* is all that we get in *Nuni*. Amidst the dazzling coral, the overpowering sun, the hallucinations of nourishment and water, the dreams and nightmares of tulips and giant purple grapes, Professor Harper is rescued by a curious and merry black child, and by an old black patriarch with a club. The tone of the narrative is reminiscent of Jack London's tales of the south-sea savages, along with something else. When the hero starts learning the primitive and gutteral tribal language: "Ta-eega. . . . Angua Kulangu . . . Kmai Kakosekani. . . . Au-goo-ah!"— these phrases which he repeats to himself in fear and panic are close to a sort of black Swiftian baby talk. And what Harper notices immediately is the contrast between the blank, inhuman eyes of the patriarch Tombani and the expressive young eyes of the child. "What has happened between childhood and age to glaze those of the old man?"

This is the real point of *Nuni* on its first level of import. The novel is a brilliant satire of a tribal culture whose whole aim is to suppress every human emotion. Tombani is a hostile old man whose eyes are indeed dead to affection, "eyes that speak only in degrees of contempt." Enforcing the tribal mores with his heavy club, this "black ball of whimsy and caprice" is without a trace of interest in his fellow human beings. And what mores! As the hero gradually learns the tribal language, he discovers the names for all parts of the body except the intimate parts, which are completely taboo. The normal functions of the body must never be witnessed under pain of death—though everybody is completely naked and completely sexless. Mating is "zagata"—no good—though it is necessary for the bearing of children. Sex is considered painful and unpleasant, to be consummated as a duty to society. Indeed, the sexual act means the loss of virility for the man who performs it.

"It is good to be with a woman," says the ignorant hero to the child Veedlie. "Ta-eega!" he screams. "It is bad, bad." *Nuni* is a world without love. The voices of the tribesmen are compounded of rage and anger. In the course of the hero's education, Tombani electrifies the air "with his thunderbolts of abuse and insults, telling me of my insignificance . . . of my worthlessness. This education is a form of brain-washing, and gradually Harper realizes that "no one here cares in the slightest for my existence." The village called Vanua is hidden in the jungle foliage near the bank of a swift-flowing silent river. The tribal huts are dark chambers of animal stench, the food is comprised of sour-tasting vegetable roots. The single recreation is the elaborate ceremony of betel-eating, which casts the men of the tribe into a drugged stupor for hours. But there is the freezing pool into which, at appointed intervals, the tribe plunges as a unit, to recover its "normalcy."

The faces of the people are "tattooed black masks, not human faces, masks with yaw sores around their eyes, stoic masks, cold and feelingless." The women, who are perhaps the saving element in all societies, are here "untouchable . . . disinterested, dulled by dusts of resignation." And Harper feels his own stability of character beginning to disintegrate under the tribal pressures. "We leave you in sunlight," says the witch Rauka to the corpse of Maigna, "and we go back and wait in shadows"— while the tribe howls in savage derision at a sudden mishap to one of the body-carriers. Nightmare imagery and a nightmare tale: at the mid point of the narrative *Nuni* is a novel which rouses all kinds of dark shadows in our mind. While Harper, giving up hope and pleasure, is lying in a desolate stupor, the little Ririkinger nestles into his chest and gives him the only affection he has met with in the tribe. He looks up to see the swinging genitals of Tombani over his face and the patriarchal club descending upon his head. It is taboo to touch a girl-child.

These children are not given names before the tribal tattooing because so many of them die during it. They are fastened to a stake before the ordeal in order to dull the pain of the cutting; the weaker ones do not survive. When Harper decides to prevent this from happening to Ririkinger, and becomes the direct adversary of Rauka, the tribal sorceress and lawgiver, the central drama of the novel begins. Rauka is hideous, aged, sexless, but cunning and wily—another symbol of odious maternal authority. No wonder that the hero yearns for and mourns over the lost world of childhood: "where all is guilelessness, all is innocence and gaiety," before the advent of maturity, of society, and of what appears always to be in Griffin's work an evil and scheming matriarchy! But just what are the further levels of meaning of a novel in which the stench of "betel-soured closeness" is almost the stench of humanity itself?

In Vanua "all that is right, all that is human, is taboo," the hero thinks. "If I move to counter it, I am clubbed." And there is the description of Tombani's "benign face" as he carries out the tribal "law"—making people into animals. On the surface *Nuni* is a grand vision of human evil which must be placed against the vision of divine good in *The Devil Rides Outside.* (And part of the attraction of this writer's talent lies just in its movement between these polar extremes.) In part, too, the angry satire of Griffin's second novel, the Swiftian tones of repudiation and disgust as well as the language, is certainly directed against the American social values and institutions which are carried to their ultimate point in Vanua. In the portrait of this hostile, angry, taboo-ridden, sexless, and loveless black tribe there are obvious references to the darker side of the national spirit.

Yes, and aspects of American life which other modern spokesmen, from the time of Mencken's bitter *Notes on Democracy,* and earlier, have commented on in similar terms. "A man can do anything but beg for that which must be freely given—some recognition that he exists and is known." This lament of the novel's hero, faced with tribal antipathy and indifference is a familiar refrain in modern literature—or of art, that is to say, in a social environment which has become increasingly scientific, industrial and abstract. The language in Vanua has no past tense, we are told (as Hawthorne and James remarked about the American scene). The tribal legends glorify only hostility, cruelty, and rapacity, and there are no words here for "reason, justice, kindness, charity." There is only the monotonous chant of derision which is the tribal form of "education."

In a larger sense, of course, *Nuni* is dealing with the tyranny of all societies: of Society. These are the constraints, repressions and taboos which are always put upon the innocent effusions of the human spirit that wishes to soar and to flower. Here Griffin is joining in a common chorus of the literary voices during the 1950's which beholds the warm and innocent life of childhood constrained into the mold of a civilization which is always repres-

sive and banal. (Ernst Schactel's thesis of "Childhood Amnesia"
—the loss between the original vision of childhood, the modes
of adult perception—is a key source for all these novels.) How
almost compulsively Griffin's novel describes these free, happy,
and nameless children, who are then trained in stoic renunciation,
who are crucified and cut in accordance with tribal mores, until
only the hardiest, most brutal survivors become the tribal "individuals"! There is the vivid image of the professorial hero
himself, so much like an indignant, outraged, ostracized child-
man, who stands apart from the odious mass of tribal humanity,
clutching his yellow buttercup as the single token of natural
harmony and grace. Not only in the more or less superficial view
of "social adjustment," but in the deeper, more personal psychobiological currents of *Nuni* there is a fundamental sense of
estrangement and alienation. Is the symbol of paternal authority
really that of the ignorant old savage with his heavy club—a
paternal authority, I mean, which is not that of the Lord himself?
On the distaff side, the witch-hag Rauka, though an "adversary
of stature," and in effect a more extreme version of Madame
Renée in *The Devil Rides Outside,* is hardly much better. And
are all the "children," for whom the professorial hero risks his
life in defiance of the tribal taboos, really so defenseless, crucified,
and cut?

Here indeed the earlier theme of the isolated stranger and the
hostile universe becomes dominant—a black, savage, and threatening world. All the submerged fears, hatreds, aggressions of the
first novel are channeled into a central hostility and alienation.
But this is a familiar phenomenon in literature. The major figures
of this "school" include such varied writers as Byron, Poe, or
Melville, as well as the archetypal Dean Swift himself, or the
nineteenth-century French decadents whom Griffin knows so
well. One notices the strain of incestuous affection in the present
writer's work too, as well as elements of both the superman and
the demonic spirit. Not all of this anger, rage, and cruelty must
be attributed to the hostile outer world. Some—how much?—
must reside in the hidden, fuming, sulphurous psyche of the artist
himself. If he seems to be a born, or indeed a hereditary outcast,
so was Lucifer, so was Satan. From another angle, the nightmare
visions of *Nuni* also project backward into the primitive childhood

of the race. (Are children, after all, so pure, innocent, and blameless?) And with this horrid dream of a "black birth" Griffin has allied himself, even more than in the earlier conflict of good and evil, with the "dark writers" of literature. The Devil also rides in Texas.

Perhaps, indeed, the intense struggle to reach God and the orbit of divine love—through the sanctity of monastic renunciation—derives its intensity just from its "diabolical" sources. (The possessed and "puritanical" Hawthorne, who was also conversant with witches, might see the attraction of this theme.) The voodoo world of Vanua is too well described, too vivid and intimately known, *too* familiar! But indeed, how many tantalizing levels of meaning are half revealed in the flickering midnight symbolism of *Nuni* which continually shifts between the personal, the social, the racial. If the primitive tribe of Vanua is meant to describe the worst aspects of white civilization, there may also be a latent content of the South's own deep and abiding fear of and guilt about the Negro race itself. How many other young artists from the nether world of Faulkner and Faubus have described so vividly their own terror and isolation among these savage black people?

Yet we must add that it is also the Griffin protagonist who sacrifices symbolically his own daughter in the hope of saving his adopted black child, Ririkinger. This is the final "message" of the tale, and the method through which the outsider regains his own sense of identity, of belonging and of love. In the end the professor tries to humanize both the tribe and himself through the black child who is indeed the missing "key" of the South's drama, as well as the novel's. On the rational and moral level, nothing could be better than this last gesture on the part of the outcast hero; and at the story's close, as in the Easter music of *The Devil Rides Outside,* there is the scent of flowers and "peace drifts to me on the lively twitterings of birds."

I have hardly had space to stress certain other aspects of Griffin's talent. (The element of broad sexual comedy and devastating social satire is again apparent in the section from his new novel, *Street of the Seven Angels,* published in *New World Writing: 12,* where Griffin's tone is close to Henry Miller's.) This writer is fertile and prolific, as well as bold and sweeping in emotional range, almost to the point of melodrama and farce. Still another novel is awaiting publication, and these works will doubtless sustain our interest in this original and, as I think, large-sized artist, who should be classified meanwhile in the upper bracket of contemporary writing.

AMERICAN CENTURY SERIES

ACW 48 *Benjamin Franklin* edited by Frank Luther Mott and Chester E. Jorgenson
AC 49 *Indian Tales* by Jaime de Angulo
AC 50 *A Time of Harvest* edited by Robert E. Spiller
AC 51 *The Limits of Language* edited by Walker Gibson
AC 52 *Sherwood Anderson: Short Stories* edited and with an Introduction by Maxwell Geismar
AC 53 *The World of Lincoln Steffens* edited by Ella Winter and Herbert Shapiro, with an Introduction by Barrows Dunham
AC 54 *Mark Twain on the Damned Human Race* edited and with an Introduction by Janet Smith
AC 55 *The Happy Critic and Other Essays* by Mark Van Doren
AC 56 *Man Against Myth* by Barrows Dunham
AC 57 *Something in Common and Other Stories* by Langston Hughes
AC 58 *Writers in Transition: Seven Americans* by H. Wayne Morgan
AC 59 *The Lincoln Nobody Knows* by Richard N. Current
AC 60 *The Disinherited* by Jack Conroy, with an Introduction by Daniel Aaron
AC 61 *Eisenhower As President* edited by Dean Albertson
AC 62 *Rebels and Ancestors* by Maxwell Geismar
AC 63 *Mount Allegro* by Jerre Mangione
AC 64 *Thoreau: People, Principles, and Politics* edited and with an Introduction by Milton Meltzer
AC 65 *The Big Sea* by Langston Hughes
AC 66 *The Golden Age of Homespun* by Jared van Wagenen, Jr.
AC 67 *The Senate Establishment* by Joseph S. Clark and Other Senators
AC 68 *I Wonder As I Wander* by Langston Hughes
AC 69 *Science in Nineteenth-Century America: A Documentary History* edited and with an Introduction by Nathan Reingold
AC 70 *The Course of the South to Secession: An Interpretation* by Ulrich Bonnell Phillips
AC 71 *American Negro Poetry* edited and with an Introduction by Arna Bontemps
AC 72 *Horace Greeley* by Glyndon G. Van Deusen
AC 73 *David Walker's Appeal* edited and with an Introduction by Charles M. Wiltse
AC 74 *The Sentimental Years* by E. Douglas Branch
AC 75 *Henry James and the Jacobites* by Maxwell Geismar
AC 76 *The Reins of Power* by Bernard Schwartz
AC 77 *American Writers in Rebellion* by H. Wayne Morgan
AC 78 *Policy and Power* by Ruhl Bartlett
AC 79 *Wendell Phillips on Civil Rights and Freedom* edited by Louis Filler
AC 80 *American Negro Short Stories* edited and with an Introduction by John Henrik Clarke
AC 81 *The Radical Novel in the United States: 1900–1954* by Walter B. Rideout
AC 82 *A History of Agriculture in the State of New York* by Ulysses Prentiss Hedrick
AC 101 *Fabric of Freedom: 1763–1800* by Esmond Wright
AC 102 *The New Nation: 1800–1845* by Charles M. Wiltse
AC 103 *The Stakes of Power: 1845–1877* by Roy F. Nichols
H 13   *Mark Twain and the Russians* by Charles Neider
H 26   *Citizen Toussaint* by Ralph Korngold
H 27   *Digging Up America* by Frank C. Hibben
H 33   *Free World Colossus* by David Horowitz